Puritanism
and Its Discontents

Puritanism
and Its Discontents

Edited by
Laura Lunger Knoppers

DELAWARE

Newark: University of Delaware Press
London: Associated University Presses

Associated University Presses
2010 Eastpark Boulevard
Cranbury, NJ 08512

Associated University Presses
16 Barter Street
London WC1A 2AH, England

Associated University Presses
P.O. Box 338, Port Credit
Mississauga, Ontario
Canada L5G 4L8

The paper used in this publication meets the requirements of the American National Standard for Permanence of Paper for Printed Library Materials Z39.48-1984.

Library of Congress Cataloging-in-Publication Data

Puritanism and its discontents / edited by Laura Lunger Knoppers.
    p. cm.
    Includes bibliographical references and index.
    ISBN 0-87413-817-5 (alk. paper)
    1. Puritans—England—History—17th century. 2. England—Church history—17th century. 3. Puritans—New England—History—17th century. 4. New England—Church history—17th century. I. Knoppers, Laura Lunger.
BX9334.3 P87   2003
285'.9—dc21   2002014507

PRINTED IN THE UNITED STATES OF AMERICA

Contents

Part IV: Puritanism and Community

Acknowledgments

THE PEW CHARITABLE TRUSTS CONTRIBUTED GENEROUSLY TO A SUMMER faculty seminar and subsequent conference at Calvin College in Grand Rapids, Michigan, from which selected papers for this volume have been drawn. I am grateful also for the kind encouragement and logistical support provided at various stages by Anna Mae Bush, C. Stephen Evans, Susan Felch, and Sandra van Kley. Richard Cunningham served ably as my research assistant for this project. It has been a pleasure to work with the contributors to this volume, who have been invariably courteous and gracious in sharing their knowledge of and enthusiasm for the rich and complex subject of Puritanism.

Introduction

Laura Lunger Knoppers

Dost thou think because thou art virtuous there shall be no more
cakes and ale?

—Shakespeare, *Twelfth Night*

In SHAKESPEARE'S *TWELFTH NIGHT*, SIR TOBY BELCH'S POINTED REBUFF
only begins the trouble for the meddling steward Malvolio, who, as
a "kind of puritan," a "time-pleaser," and an "affectioned ass," has
attempted to stop Sir Toby's late-night revelry.[1] Gulled by the
thwarted party-goers (and his own vanity) into believing that his
mistress is in love with him, Malvolio appears smiling, yellow-stock-
inged, and cross-gartered only to find himself imprisoned as a mad-
man. His apparent piety revealed as self-serving ambition, Malvolio
remains apart from the comic resolution of the play, vowing: "I'll be
reveng'd on the whole pack of you."[2]

Malvolio stands in a long line of literary and dramatic Puritans as
repressive killjoys and prurient meddlers, many of whom get their
comeuppance from their fictional counterparts or from the laughter
of the audience. From Ben Jonson's Tribulation Wholesome to Samuel Butler's Sir Hudibras to Thomas Morton's Captain Shrimp, literary Puritans variously spoil the party, "fight for religion as for
punk," brand sinners, and ax down maypoles; they in turn find
themselves cozened, cudgeled, and otherwise humiliated.[3] Puritans—like Freud's civilization—seem repressive and obsessed with
guilt, generating neuroses and discontents.[4]

Yet several decades of historical work have countered the literary
stereotype of the interfering Puritan, offering, rather, an image of
early modern Puritans as conservative, moderate, and apolitical,
negotiating a place within the mainstream of the English church
and society until pushed into reaction.[5] In his wide-ranging and
magisterial work on the Elizabethan church, Patrick Collinson
largely defines Puritanism as a movement for reform within the
Church of England.[6] Peter Lake distinguishes Puritans from their

9

less godly counterparts in terms of experience; Puritans were the hotter sort of "experiential" predestinationists within a broadly Calvinist church.[7] In important work congruent with Collinson and Lake that has greatly influenced revisionist historiography, Nicholas Tyacke has remade Puritans as responding to innovative Laudian Arminianism, reactive rather than radical.[8] Historians who differ from Tyacke on the impetus of Arminianism have largely pointed to other causes of increasing tension and breakdown leading up to civil war—the threat to Protestantism caused by the Thirty Years' War, problems within the three kingdoms—rather than reasserting the distinctiveness or impact of Puritanism.[9]

If Puritanism has lost some of its radical political and doctrinal edge in revisionist accounts, other historians have questioned a distinctively Puritan opposition to popular culture in early modern England. While some scholars attribute moral reform and attempts to abolish drunkenness and immorality as well as popular rural sports and pastimes to a Puritan impulse, others question the link between Puritanism and social control.[10] Alexandra Walsham shows how even such apparently notorious Puritans as Philip Stubbes shape a message for an audience in popular print.[11] Patrick Collinson has explored the extent to which fasts and sermon-gadding constitute a kind of alternative Puritan culture.[12] Kristen Poole has demonstrated that the stereotype of the grim, repressive Puritan was countered by an equally pervasive image of the Puritan as grotesque and carnivalesque, evinced in, for instance, Shakespeare's Falstaff.[13]

Similarly, recent scholarship depicts Puritanism in colonial America as more heterogeneous and less dominant than had been long assumed.[14] After decades dominated by Perry Miller's paradigm of New England Puritanism seen largely in intellectual terms and through the clergy, historians of early America have been increasingly attuned to the laity, to social and economic histories, to non-Puritan worlds within and outside of New England, and to the transatlantic context of early America.[15] While in 1965 Basil Hall complained that "from the time of Cotton Mather's *Magnalia Christi Americana* (1702), many American historians have suffered from what amounts to being an historical fixation on Puritanism," much more recently Charles Cohen describes a "post-Puritan" era, observing that the operative P-word for early American religious history is now pluralism, rather than Puritanism.[16]

How can we reconcile "moderate" and conservative Puritanism with historian William Hunt's comment that "a Puritan who minds his own business is a contradiction in terms"?[17] If revisionist historiography has provided a salutary corrective to teleological and overly determinative narratives, what has been left out or less well-accounted for? In the recent move to a "pluralistic" early America, has the force of Puritanism been too much discounted? Would a real-life Malvolio—far from denouncing late-night revelry as making "an alehouse of my lady's house" with "no respect of place, persons, nor time"—have simply joined the party?[18]

This volume reasserts the "discontents" of Puritanism, both the radical edge that fueled change and reform and the responses that Puritans evoked from discontented contemporaries. While acknowledging the difficulties of defining Puritanism in doctrinal, ecclesiastical, social, or economic terms, these essays nonetheless show that a distinctive "discontent"—with selves, others, community, church, and state—marked Puritans and Puritanism in seventeenth-century England and America. Dissent—and discontent—in these accounts is not simply outside of and opposed to Puritanism but part of Puritans' self-definition and evolution of identity.

Transatlantic in range and interdisciplinary in approach, this volume thus works to restore both a radical edge and a new specificity to the much-debated definitions of Puritans and Puritanism.[19] Although labeled and shaped by its "discontented" opponents, Puritanism was not simply reactive; rather, "discontent" with the self, community, church, state, and society fueled Puritan action. Seventeenth-century England and America provide a crucial point of reference for a study of Puritanism and its discontents, both because less attention has been given to the long seventeenth century than to questions of Elizabethan and early Stuart Puritanism and because the political, social, and religious changes of seventeenth-century England and America were an important crucible in which Puritanism was forged.[20] The various essays show how Puritanism evolved in context: faced with and shaped by opposition, but also incorporating discontent as a part of an ongoing impulse to purify and reform.

From Elizabethan times, when the godly were dissatisfied with the 1559 Acts of Uniformity and Supremacy, through the classical Presbyterian movement of the 1580s, the presentation of the Millenary Petition to James I in 1603, and the Hampton Court Conference of 1604, to agitation—or immigration to America—under Charles I, Puritans were marked by discontent with current practices and institutions. In the 1640s, these discontents, amplified by the explosion of print, spilled over into the actual conflict of civil war. But even when Puritans held power in church and state—in colonial New England and in England in the 1650s—relations among themselves and between themselves and others were marked by discontent, anxiety, and desire for reform.

"Discontents" tie together seemingly discrete definitions of Puritanism. Hence, Patrick Collinson's Elizabethan Puritans, advocating reform of the church from within the church, are motivated by discontent. Discontents also mark the distinctive style of the godly, including Peter Lake's experiential predestinationists. The edge of discontent distinguishes Puritan views—whether on doctrinal issues, companionate marriage, the Sabbath, or regulation of alehouses—from the otherwise similar views of their less godly contemporaries. Finally, discontents mark the discursive constructions that have garnered much recent scholarly interest, as Puritans were labeled and satirized on the page and stage and, in turn, defined themselves against and through perceived "Others."[21]

The lens of discontents also helps us realign English and American Puritanism, subjects still most often treated separately. Although Stephen Foster, David Cressy, Francis Bremer, and others have provided important transatlantic perspectives on early America, other studies still assume American exceptionalism, and scholars of English Puritanism tend to treat America as an afterthought, if at all.[22] Yet common themes and modes of operation make transatlantic comparison fruitful, even mandatory, for a full understanding of Puritanism. The essays in this volume show that Puritans—in England and America, separatist and nonseparatist—exhibit the same desire for reform: of the sinful self, of one's neighbors, of the broader community, of the nation, and even (in the case of America) of the Europe left behind.

A focus on discontents also enables a cross-disciplinary approach best able to define and describe the cultural forms and practices associated with Puritanism. Historians and literary scholars—exploring either English or American Puritanism—have tended to work discretely. Hence, literary scholars have not, for the most part, incorporated historiographical skepticism regarding Puritanism in their analyses; and historians tend to look at archival records and at doctrinal and political controversy rather than at literary representations. In this volume, historians and literary scholars together take up questions of literary form, polemical modes, and the role of print in shaping identity. The volume's focus on cultural history helps to demonstrate that there is no clear break between polemical constructions and perceived "reality" in the seventeenth century.

Although doctrinal issues have historically dominated scholarship on Puritanism, this study joins with other recent work in making clear that doctrine embodies only one—and perhaps not even the most important—aspect of Puritanism. Puritans strove to change not only the church but also institutions of state, not only the self but godly—and ungodly—communities. Under the rubrics of definitions, institutions, others, and community, the essays in this volume explore how discontents shape a complex and shifting Puritanism in seventeenth-century England and America. As such, these studies restore the anxiety-ridden, radical nature of Puritans, helping to account for the force of Puritanism in the seventeenth century and the popular and scholarly interest that it continues to evoke.

DEFINING PURITANISM

Writing *The Church History of Britain* for the year 1546, Thomas Fuller commented that "I wish that the word *puritan* were banished [from] common discourse, because so various in the acceptions thereof."[23] Anyone looking over the range of early modern usage—or the divergent scholarly accounts of Puritans—would agree. Striving to locate and define the nature of Puritan identity more precisely, the first three essays in this volume look at case studies: of particular persons and of uses of the term Puritan. Each essay shows how Puritans and Puritanism were defined through a core discontent and in situations of stress and conflict. In the opening essay of the volume, John Morrill looks at how three seemingly heterogeneous case studies share discontent with the local community, church, or state: all three find liberation as empowerment as they move through—and in one case beyond—Puritanism. In her newly discovered freedom from anxiety and fear, from the terror of hell and the search for signs and tokens, Sister Cornish, illiterate and penurious widow and mother, moves from the strictures of Puritanism to the inner light of the more radical Quakers. William Dowsing, East Anglian yeoman farmer-turned-iconoclast, is temporarily empowered by the words of the Puritan preachers to remove the monuments of idolatry and superstition in a church incompletely reformed. Morrill's last and most famous figure, Oliver Cromwell, finds a more enduring liberation as the words of Scripture lead him to discern the providence and necessity of regicide, an overturning of the structures of the state itself. Morrill's case studies approach shows a continuity of (various kinds) of discontent across class and gender, marking the relationship among the godly, and the attitude of the godly toward the material forms and practices of church and state.

The two essays that follow in part 1 show how the term "Puritan" functions as a tool of political, cultural, and theological conflict. In the context of scholarly debate over England in the 1630s, Dwight Brautigam finds that the polemical force of name-calling—and particularly of the weighted term "Puritan"—exacerbates existing tensions and leads to an erosion of civility, giving both Puritans and prelates a role in precipitating civil war. Brautigam's examination of the diaries and letters of William Laud and his circle, including Richard Montagu and John Cosin, shows how throughout the 1620s and 1630s these prelates used the term "Puritan" to stigmatize religious nonconformity as at the root of rebellion, disobedience, and schism in church and state. Such labeling evoked reactions in the Short and Long Parliaments, in which objections were raised to the labeling of godly men as Puritans. Laudian name-calling increased the discontent that spilled over into parliamentary debate and then into the battlefields of civil war.

Looking at the legacy of Puritanism, John Netland finds that in mid-nineteenth-century England, "Puritan" remained a term of opprobrium and a powerful cultural weapon in Matthew Arnold's campaign to replace Christianity with culture. Thomas Macaulay, Samuel Gardiner, and other Victorians rehabilitated the Puritans politically as the vanguard of liberty and democracy. Yet the religious heritage proved more contentious. Netland here shows how Matthew Arnold, in his *St. Paul and Protestantism*, resurrected the popular stereotype of the narrow-minded, meddling, and myopic Puritan to stigmatize the whole of traditional Christian doctrine as Puritan. By deploying a Puritan foil and drawing on the continuing negative connotations of the term, Arnold sought to redefine Christianity as ethical rather than doctrinal and to construct a post-theological national church.

PURITANISM AND INSTITUTIONS

If discontents are central to Puritans' own self-definition and the name-calling and discursive constructions of others, an analogous unrest and impetus for reform marks the relationship of Puritanism and institutions. Although the hoary divide of "Anglican mainstream" and "Puritan opposition" has now been much challenged and refined, nonetheless many Puritans were discontent with the practices and governance of institutions of church and state. Part 2 of this volume shows how institutions may be the launching pad, and yet ultimately insufficient for or even inimical to, the goals of the godly.

In the first essay of part 2, Margo Todd explores the complex relationship of individuals and institutions in the dramatic story of Isaac Dorislaus, the first history professor at Cambridge, in his inaugural lectures in 1627. From the position of lecturer in history, Dorislaus launches a veiled republican critique of monarchical tyranny: two admiring lectures on Tacitus, including an account of the deposition of Tarquinius Superbus by Junius Brutus and a discussion of the people's supreme power to hold kings accountable to law. Yet while the university provides Dorislaus with his forum, ideological rifts in pre–civil war Cambridge also ensure that the somewhat hapless Dorislaus becomes a lightning-rod for criticism and an example of punishment. In the case of Dorislaus, Todd finds a conjunction of radical Calvinism with republicanism, the implications of which reach out into the Commonwealth period, challenging the separation of political and religious ideologies.

In the following chapter, Steven R. Pointer's detailed account of the 1622 election at Emmanuel College provides a case history that reveals the tensions and constraints underlying what Peter Lake has explored as the institutional accommodations of "moderate Puritans." Pointer shows how the fellows of Emmanuel College react to their sense of "singularity," falling enrollments, and a difficult path to preferment within the University of Cambridge by replacing the aging master, Laurence Chaderton, with the well-connected John Preston. By such a change the fellows attempt to "bring ye college into reputation," yet they do not moderate their beliefs or practices.

The third essay in this section shows a more subtle form of "discontent" with the church as institution in the writings of Lady Mary Chudleigh. Turning to a layperson and a woman, Barbara Olive traces how the outwardly conformist Chudleigh rewrites an Anglican canticle in the service of toleration and reform. Asserting that many people who chose to conform during the Restoration nonetheless were shaped by or even continued to hold certain Puritan values, Olive explores how Chudleigh's *The Song of the Three Children Paraphras'd*, most likely composed in the late 1680s, draws on earlier Puritan ideals of more godly clergy and increased religious freedom for the laity, as well as evoking biblical texts on communities under persecution that were widely linked with nonconformity. While most scholars of Puritanism after the Restoration have focused on nonconformity, Olive looks to the established

church to trace how Lady Mary Chudleigh voices in religious poetry
her discontent with a church incompletely reformed.

PURITANISM AND ITS OTHERS

Part 3 of this volume foregrounds the construction of Puritan
identity vis-à-vis national, religious, or ethnic outsiders. Puritans
both defined themselves against "Others" and were themselves
made Other. Richard Pointer shows how Puritan views of Native
Americans, albeit ethnocentric, are more comprehensible from a
people whose collective identity is built on notions of imitation. In
an essay that spans New England history from 1629 to the 1660s,
Pointer traces the complexities and permutations of the Puritan
language of imitation, used in relation to the Indians. Puritan self-
identity was itself, Pointer argues, bound up in the notion of imitation, of a return to biblical simplicity and purity. Hence, the Puritans' injunction to the Massachusetts to imitate English (and
ultimately biblical) models; "praying Indians" in New England followed the godly English in Sabbath observance, conversion narratives, administration of the sacraments, and family prayer. Yet
Puritans feared that Indian imitation was only mimicry, even mockery, and the cultural transformation that they urged upon the Indians contradicted, rather than was consonant with, their own self-
identity as imitators, not innovators.

In the essay following, Glenn Sanders shows how Puritan traits
are exaggerated and stigmatized as Turkish in popular print during
the British civil wars and Interregnum. After the regicide, inflammatory use of the "Turks" coupled with printed epithets helped to
discredit Oliver Cromwell and the godly as threatening and alien to
a well-ordered state. In the early Restoration, satire on Cromwell
as a sultan and his army as janizaries reinterpreted the Protectorate as a time of tyranny and was an ideological means of naturaliz-
ing and accommodating the restored monarchy. If Puritans in
England and America defined themselves against the popish or the
American Indian Other, the orientalized, Turkish Other was also
used against them.

PURITANISM AND COMMUNITY

Scholars have long recognized that Puritan identities were
formed within and between communities—local, national, and inter-

national.[24] And others have shown how, as in the church, Puritans tended to cause friction with their less godly neighbors.[25] Yet division and discontent could also mark relations within the Puritan community.[26] Two essays in the final part, "Puritanism and Community," look at the formation of Puritan identity both inside and outside of godly communities in America. Looking at what was the greatest moment of crisis in Puritanism before the English civil wars, Timothy D. Hall shows how discontents from within the godly community both challenged and shaped Puritan doctrine and identity. Challenging accounts of Anne Hutchinson as protoliberal heroine against repressive Puritan hegemony, Hall contextualizes Hutchinson's story within negotiations over personal agency and responsibility opened for the redeemed self through the transforming experience of conversion. As John Cotton and John Wheelwright, the ministers influential on Hutchinson, argued that assurance comes by witness of the spirit prior to good works, that faith is wholly passive, and that one cannot look for evidence of election to salvation in good works, they more radically negated the self than did the New England ministers who opposed them. Rather than repressing the individual self, New England ministers made room for Calvinist individualism within the New England social order.

In the final essay in the volume, Stephen Woolsey broadens the traditional idea of "community" for Cotton Mather, whom he sees both as responding to a spate of negative representations of Puritans and as addressing not simply an American but an international audience. While Sacvan Bercovitch and others have examined the *Magnalia* as part of a uniquely American identity, Woolsey suggests instead a transatlantic context. The *Magnalia*, he argues, counters the stereotypical Puritan hypocrite of the stage and page with heroic and epic stories, but Mather, rather than eschewing the dramatic, uses the language of acting and drama to place his Puritans on the stage of a worldwide reformation. Mather's Puritans, according to Woolsey, live out exemplary lives with the moral force of classical tragedy: the life of John Winthrop provides one crucial chapter in the international drama of redemption.

Focused on the concept of "discontents," this volume thus offers a new understanding of Puritans and Puritanism in localized and particular contexts in England and America. Looking not only at the "discontented" reactions of others but at the anxiety and dissatisfaction within Puritan selves and communities, the essays restore a radical, reforming edge to Puritanism. Puritans once again appear close to the heart of religious and political controversy in seventeenth-century England and America, with an aftermath

stretching in popular, literary, and academic culture through the
nineteenth century to the present day.

This shifting, self-conscious Puritanism is far from being a repressive monolith in the image of Freud's civilization. Dissent and
difference, rather than being repressed on the outside, are a crucial
internal part of the evolution and definition of Puritanism. The essays in this volume explore the complex negotiations and evolution
of identity, tracing the discontents with self and others, with community and institutions of church and state, that shaped Puritanism
as a radical force for change and reform. To those stories we now
turn.

NOTES

1. William Shakespeare, *Twelfth Night*, in *The Riverside Shakespeare*, ed. G.
Blakemore Evans (Boston: Houghton Mifflin, 1974), II.iii.114–16, 147, 140.

2. Ibid., V.i.378.

3. Ben Jonson, *The Alchemist*, in vol. 3 of *The Complete Plays of Ben Jonson*,
ed. G. A. Wilkes (Oxford: Clarendon Press, 1981–82); Samuel Butler, *Hudibras*,
ed. John Wilders (Oxford: Clarendon Press, 1967); Thomas Morton, *New English
Canaan* (New York: Da Capo Press, 1969).

4. Sigmund Freud, *Civilization and Its Discontents*, trans. Joan Riviere (London: Hogarth Press, 1930).

5. This has been, in general, the effect of three decades of "revisionist" historiography, which has emphasized continuity and consensus over conflict and ideological difference. Revisionists have challenged views of the English civil wars as
the end point of a long process of difference—whether of class, religion, or ideology—and have focused, rather, on court faction and intrigue, patronage, personality, and short-term, even "accidental" causation. Along with long-term economic,
political, and social causes, "Puritanism" as a revolutionary ideology leading up
to civil war has been much discounted, although religion has taken a more central
role in recent accounts. See Conrad Russell, ed., *The Origins of the English Civil
War* (New York: Barnes and Noble, 1973); Anthony Fletcher, *The Outbreak of the
English Civil War* (New York: New York University Press, 1981); John Morrill,
*The Revolt of the Provinces: Conservatives and Radicals in the English Civil
War, 1630-1650* (London: Allen and Unwin, 1976), and his *The Nature of the English Revolution* (London and New York: Longman, 1993); and Kevin Sharpe, *The
Personal Rule of Charles I* (New Haven: Yale University Press, 1992). Important
critiques of revisionism are found in Richard Cust and Ann Hughes, eds., *Conflict
in Early Stuart England: Studies in Religion and Politics, 1603-1642* (London
and New York: Longman, 1989); Ann Hughes, *The Causes of the English Civil War*
(New York: St. Martin Press, 1991); and S. K. Baskerville, "Puritans, Revisionists,
and the English Revolution," *Huntington Library Quarterly* 61, no. 2 (2000),
151–71.

6. Patrick Collinson, *The Religion of Protestants: The Church in English Society, 1559-1625* (Oxford: Clarendon Press, 1982); *The Elizabethan Puritan
Movement* (Berkeley and Los Angeles: University of California Press, 1967); *The*

Birthpangs of Protestant England: Religious and Cultural Change in the Sixteenth and Seventeenth Centuries (New York: St. Martin's Press, 1988); and *Godly People: Essays on English Protestantism and Puritanism* (London: Hambledon Press, 1983).

7. Peter Lake, *Moderate Puritans and the Elizabethan Church* (Cambridge: Cambridge University Press, 1982), and his *Anglicans and Puritans? Presbyterianism and English Conformist Thought from Whitgift to Hooker* (London: Unwin Hyman, 1988).

8. Nicholas Tyacke, "Puritanism, Arminianism and Counter-Revolution," in *The Origins of the English Civil War*, ed. Conrad Russell (New York: Barnes and Noble, 1973), 119–43; and his *Anti-Calvinists:The Rise of English Arminianism, c. 1590-1640* (New York: Oxford University Press, 1987). More recently, Tyacke has stressed the continuities between the militant Presbyterianism of the 1580s and Puritan discontents in the early Caroline period in "The 'Rise of Puritanism' and the Legalizing of Dissent, 1571–1719," in *From Persecution to Toleration: The Glorious Revolution and Religion in England*, ed. Ole Peter Grell, Jonathan I. Israel, and Nicholas Tyacke (Oxford: Clarendon Press, 1991), 17–50, and *The Fortunes of English Puritanism, 1603-1640* (London: Dr. William's Library, 1990).

9. Peter White, "The Rise of Arminianism Reconsidered," *Past and Present* 101 (1983): 34–54, and his *Predestination, Policy and Polemic: Conflict and Consensus in the English Church from the Reformation to the Civil War* (Cambridge: Cambridge University Press, 1992). Among those historians usually thought of as "revisionist," Kevin Sharpe dissents in seeing Puritans as politically as well as doctrinally radical; see his *Politics and Ideas in Early Stuart England* (London and New York: Pinter, 1989), 28–31.

10. Variously linking Puritanism and reform, see David Underdown, *Revel, Riot, and Rebellion: Popular Politics and Culture in England, 1603-1660* (Oxford: Clarendon Press, 1985); William Hunt, *The Puritan Moment: The Coming of Revolution in an English County* (Cambridge: Harvard University Press, 1982); Ronald Hutton, *The Rise and Fall of Merry England: The Ritual Year, 1400-1700* (New York: Oxford University Press, 1994); and Anthony Fletcher, *Reform in the Provinces: The Government of Stuart England* (New Haven: Yale University Press, 1986). Margaret Spufford questions the distinctiveness of "Puritan" reform in "Puritanism and Social Control," in *Order and Disorder in Early Modern England*, ed. Anthony Fletcher and John Stevenson (Cambridge: Cambridge University Press, 1985), 41–57, as does Martin Ingram, *Church Courts, Sex, and Marriage in England, 1570-1640* (Cambridge: Cambridge University Press, 1987), and Kenneth Parker, *The English Sabbath: A Study of Doctrine and Discipline from the Reformation to the Civil War* (Cambridge: Cambridge University Press, 1988). Margo Todd shows that many presumed "Puritan" social attitudes are in fact part of a broader humanist tradition, in *Christian Humanism and the Puritan Social Order* (Cambridge: Cambridge University Press, 1987).

11. Alexandra Walsham, "'A glose of godliness': Philip Stubbes, Elizabethan Grub Street and the Invention of Puritanism," in *Belief and Practice in Reformation England*, ed. Caroline Litzenberger and Susan Wabuda (Aldershot, England: Ashgate, 1998), 177–206.

12. Patrick Collinson, "Elizabethan and Jacobean Puritanism as Forms of Popular Religious Culture," in *The Culture of English Puritanism, 1560-1700*, ed. Christopher Durston and Jacqueline Eales (Basingstoke: Macmillan, 1996), 32–57. Christopher Durston focuses more on the anticultural aspects of Puritanism in

"Puritan Rule and the Failure of Cultural Revolution, 1645–1660," in *The Culture of English Puritanism*, 210–33.

13. Kristen Poole, "Saints Alive! Falstaff, Martin Marprelate, and the Staging of Puritanism," *Shakespeare Quarterly* 46 (1995): 47–75, and chapter 1 in her book *Radical Religion from Shakespeare to Milton: Figures of Nonconformity in Early Modern England* (Cambridge: Cambridge University Press, 2000). On the stage making widely available the language and stereotypes of Puritanism, see Patrick Collinson, "Ben Jonson's *Bartholomew Fair*: The Theatre Constructs Puritanism," in *The Theatrical City: Culture, Theatre and Politics in London, 1576-1649*, ed. David L. Smith, Richard Strier, and David Bevington (Cambridge: Cambridge University Press, 1995), 157–69; and on the creation of the Puritan in satire, see Patrick Collinson, "Ecclesiastical Vitriol: Religious Satire in the 1590s and the Invention of Puritanism," in *The Reign of Elizabeth I: Court and Culture in the Last Decade*, ed. John Guy (Cambridge: Cambridge University Press, 1995), 150–70.

14. Historians on early America have shown, for instance, how popular culture intersected with and shaped Puritan doctrine; see David D. Hall, *Worlds of Wonder, Days of Judgment: Popular Religious Belief in Early New England* (New York: Knopf, 1989), and David Lovejoy, *Religious Enthusiasm in the New World: Heresy to Revolution* (Cambridge: Harvard University Press, 1985).

15. Miller's classic texts include *Orthodoxy in Massachusetts, 1630-1650* (Cambridge: Harvard University Press, 1933); *Errand into the Wilderness* (Cambridge: Harvard University Press, 1956); *The New England Mind: The Seventeenth Century*, 2d ed. (Cambridge: Harvard University Press, 1954); and *The New England Mind: From Colony to Province* (Cambridge: Harvard University Press, 1953). Responding to Miller, see Francis Butts, "The Myth of Perry Miller," *The American Historical Review* 87, no. 3 (1982): 665–94, and the overview by David D. Hall, "On Common Ground: The Coherence of American Puritan Studies," *William and Mary Quarterly* 3d ser. 44 (1988): 193–229. On lay influence, diversity of belief, and popular piety, see Hall, *Worlds of Wonder*; Philip F. Gura, *A Glimpse of Sion's Glory: Puritan Radicalism in New England, 1620-1660* (Middleton, Conn.: Wesleyan University Press, 1984); and Richard Godbeer, *The Devil's Dominion: Magic and Religion in Early New England* (Cambridge: Cambridge University Press, 1992). Examining transatlantic interconnections, see Jack P. Green, *Pursuits of Happiness: The Social Development of Early Modern British Colonies and the Formation of American Culture* (Chapel Hill, N.C.: University of North Carolina Press, 1988); Stephen Foster, *The Long Argument: English Puritanism and the Shaping of New England Culture, 1570-1700* (Chapel Hill, N.C.: University of North Carolina Press, 1991); and Ian K. Steele, "Exploding Colonial American History: Amerindian, Atlantic, and Global Perspectives," *Reviews in American History* 26, no. 1 (1998): 70–95.

16. Basil Hall, "Puritanism: the Problem of Definition," *Studies in Church History* 2 (1965): 286. Charles Cohen, "The Post-Puritan Paradigm of Early American Religious History," *William and Mary Quarterly* 3d ser. 54 (1997): 697. Also useful on the historiography of American Puritanism are Alden T. Vaughan's introduction to *The Puritan Tradition in America, 1620-1730*, rev. ed. (Hanover, N.H.: University Press of New England, 1997), and David D. Hall, "Narrating Puritanism," in *New Directions in American Religious History*, ed. Harry S. Stout and D. G. Hart (New York: Oxford University Press, 1997), 51–75.

17. Hunt, *The Puritan Moment*, 146.

18. Shakespeare, *Twelfth Night*, 2.3.89, 91–92.

19. See the useful definitions and overviews in Peter Lake, "Defining Puritanism—Again?" in *Puritanism: Transatlantic Perspectives on a Seventeenth-Century Anglo-American Faith*, ed. Francis J. Bremer (Boston: Massachusetts Historical Society, 1993), 3–29; Christopher Durston and Jacqueline Eales, "Introduction: The Puritan Ethos, 1560–1700," in *The Culture of English Puritanism, 1560-1700* (Basingstoke: Macmillan, 1996), 1–31; and John Spurr, introduction to *English Puritanism, 1603-1689* (New York: St. Martin's Press, 1998).

20. On the importance of linking pre- and post-1640 Puritanism, as well as England and America, see Jacqueline Eales, "A Road to Revolution: The Continuity of Puritanism, 1559–1642," in *The Culture of English Puritanism*, 184–209. Most recently, see Ann Hughes, "Anglo-American Puritanisms," *Journal of British Studies* 39, no. 1 (January 2000): 1–7.

21. On the stage making widely available the language and stereotypes of Puritanism, see Collinson, "Ben Jonson's *Bartholomew Fair*," in *The Theatrical City*, 157–69. On the creation of the Puritan in satire, see Collinson, "Ecclesiastical Vitriol," in *The Reign of Elizabeth I*; his *The Puritan Character: Polemics and Polarities in Early Seventeenth Century English Culture* (Los Angeles: William Andrews Clark Memorial Library, 1989); and his "A Comment: Concerning the Name Puritan," *Journal of Ecclesiastical History* 31 (1980): 483–88; Lake, "A Charitable Christian Hatred: The Godly and Their Enemies in the 1630s," in *The Culture of English Puritanism*, 145–83; and his "Anti-popery: The Structure of a Prejudice," in *Conflict in Early Stuart England*, 72–106.

22. Transatlantic links are treated extensively in Foster, *The Long Argument*; Green, *Pursuits of Happiness*; David Cressy, *Coming Over: Migration and Communication between England and New England in the Seventeenth Century* (Cambridge: Cambridge University Press, 1987); Francis J. Bremer, *Congregational Communion: Clerical Friendship in the Anglo-American Puritan Community, 1610-1692* (Boston: Northeastern University Press, 1994); and, most recently, Alison Games, *Migration and the Origins of the English Atlantic World* (Cambridge: Harvard University Press, 1999).

23. Thomas Fuller, *The Church History of Britain*, ed. J. S. Brewer (Oxford, 1845), 4: 327.

24. William Haller gives an early account of a "spiritual brotherhood" in *The Rise of Puritanism* (New York: Columbia University Press, 1938). Much more recently, Bremer, *Congregational Communion*, looks at the transatlantic clerical ties fostered through correspondence, publication projects, and fund-raising, and Thomas Webster explores "godly clergy" in East Anglia and the east midlands in *Godly Clergy in Early Stuart England: The Caroline Puritan Movement, c. 1620-1643* (Cambridge: Cambridge University Press, 1997).

25. Peter Lake concludes that "the whole thrust of the puritan conception of true religion and community was towards the division of existing communities and groups between the godly and the ungodly," "William Bradshaw, Antichrist and the Community of the Godly," *Journal of Ecclesiastical History* 36, no. 4 (1985): 589. See also Lake, "A Charitable Christian Hatred," in *The Culture of English Puritanism*, 145–83; and Patrick Collinson, "The Cohabitation of the Faithful with the Unfaithful," in *From Persecution to Toleration: The Glorious Revolution and Religion in England*, ed. Ole Peter Grell, Jonathan I. Israel, and Nicholas Tyacke (Oxford: Clarendon Press, 1991), 51–76.

26. Most recently, Peter Lake and David Como have written on the fragile balance in England until the 1640s in "'Orthodoxy and Its Discontents': Dispute Settlement and the Production of 'Consensus' in the London (Puritan) Underground,"

Journal of British Studies 39 (January 2000): 34–70; and Michael Winship describes the restoration of a precarious balance within the Puritan community after the Antinomian Controversy in " 'The Most Glorious Church in the World': The Unity of the Godly in Boston, Massachusetts in the 1630s," *Journal of British Studies* 39, no. 1 (2000): 71–98.

Puritanism
and Its Discontents

Part I
Defining Puritanism

A Liberation Theology?
Aspects of Puritanism in the English Revolution
John Morrill

WHATEVER THE ENGLISH REVOLUTION WAS, IT WAS A STRUGGLE FOR religious liberty, liberty for many from the obligation to drink in the dregs of popery with the cup of gospel ordinance, and for some the liberty from forms and prescribed public acts of worship and witness. By the 1650s it was a struggle about the extent of the liberty to be allowed to every individual to express her or his love of God in his or her own words and manner. There is thus a central irony that for the greater number it was a struggle to secure both liberty for themselves *and* the liberty to impose their own vision on others. It was a doomed struggle, and it ended in tears. And the process itself has recently been characterized as a claustrophobic, self-defeating one. We have returned to an essentially negative and gloomy account of the Puritan mind. I want to qualify that judgment.

I will—of course—need to begin my essay with a definition. I will take it from *The Persecutory Imagination,* a much and properly praised book by a literary scholar who died too young, John Stachniewski: "Puritans are people whose minds [were] captured by the questions whether or not they were members of the Elect, and how the life of the Elect (and of the elect community), in contradistinction to that of a reprobate community, should be ordered. In principle they took a literal view of the Bible and were either vociferous and vigorous in their attempts to purify the Church of England of perceived accretions to the practices of the primitive church or split off into sects which they thought conformed to those more closely."[1] This is a definition that touches on doctrinal matters, on ecclesiology, and on a distinctive biblocentrism, but that also focuses on Puritanism as a way of life, or (dare I say it?) as a self-fashioning, a psychological state. It reminds us that we are beyond seeing Puritanism as a commitment to particular ecclesial order; we are be-

27

yond seeing Puritanism as a particular pattern of soteriological preoccupation; we are closer to seeing it as a cultural *process*. It is a definition that helps us to recognize both a virus strain and the antibodies that the virus releases in the host body. Most of the sects of the English revolutionary period, including those labeled Ranters, Muggletonians, and above all Quakers, are not Puritans. They are men and women who define themselves by reacting against almost every clause in Stachniewski's definition: they were radical Arminians who rejected Puritan biblocentrism and Puritan regiment. They were the epiphenomena generated by Puritan preaching in a world of semianarchy. But they were the antibodies, not the virus. It is a point to which I will return.

Puritanism is a process more than an outcome, and like any cultural process, it represents a struggle to create a system of shared meanings, attitudes, and values and the symbolic forms in which they are expressed and embodied.[2] Such a process necessarily involves stress, the stress of seeking and never attaining, the stress of defining itself against the other. Peter Lake's recent work on antipopery, on the way godly identity was shaped by the dialectical interplay of opposing Puritan and anti-Puritan (or popish) images of the movement, is characteristic of this dimension. The resultant anxiety was all the greater in England because the struggle to erect stockades around the godly and against the Antichrist had to be accomplished within the structures of a national church. In Huguenot France or Protestant Ireland, the godly gathered on the Calvinist mottes and erected their ecclesiastical baileys; in Protestant England, the godly had to build their stockades inside a crowded city, their walls weaving through a suburban sprawl made up of complaisant and unregenerate Anglican conformists. In other words, English Puritanism by the second quarter of the seventeenth century defined itself by the rites and symbolic forms of semiseparatism. The 1640s are, at one level, an attempt to convert those semiseparatist attitudes and values into those of the state church. No wonder anxiety rather than joy was the hallmark of Puritans' daily lives.

The clergy had an easier time of it than the laity. Tom Webster's *Godly Clergy in Early Stuart England*[3] does not flinch before the trials and tribulations of the ministers, not least their internal divisions and conflicts; but he has brilliantly recovered the clerical sociability and collegiality by which they were able to affirm themselves in the face of a generally mild but mean-spirited persecution. For the laity, participation in conferences and collective acts of fellowship[4] was more partial and incomplete; their ability to separate out was much messier, and their ability to live out the life of the redeemed more difficult. The lives of Puritan laymen were generally even more anxiety-ridden and haunted by a sense of failure than were the lives of Puritan clergy. For that reason, and because less oceans of ink have been devoted to the lay Puritanism, I am going to offer three case studies of laymen and women. I want to explore the liberating effects of being Stachniewski-people at particular points in the lives of Oliver Cromwell, William Dowsing, and Sister Cornish, representing a high profile, a middling profile, and a very low profile case study. This will not deny the essential correctness of recent emphasis on the negative, anxiety-producing, repressed aspects of mid-seventeenth-century godlyism.

PURITANISM'S NEED FOR LIBERATION

Let us remind ourselves of the characteristics of this new emphasis on what Horace Walpole might well have called the "gloomth" of Puritanism. A striking example is Paul Seaver's study of Nehemiah Wallington, the London wood turner who for forty years was woken before the crack of dawn by dread and foreboding and who then dragged his aching limbs to the desk to add to one or more of his varied volumes of writing, each full of fastidious lists and scrupulous self-examination, amounting to more than twenty thousand tightly-packed pages by 1658, and notable for those spiritual circuit breakers that halted any surge of hopefulness. Typically addressing himself as the third party, he wrote: "Oh consider, all you who are civil honest, you that pay every man his own, you that hear the Word of God gladly, so did Herod; you that teach others, so did Judas; you that offer sacrifice, so did Cain. And oh, consider this, you [who] are kind to God's children and ministers . . . and not in love to God and aiming at God's glory. Oh then, woe, woe, woe unto you, when God shall awake your conscience, for, Oh, then it will terrify you to the quick." As Paul Seaver, commenting on this and similar passages, writes: "That was the problem, dilemma and paradox. The right action must be matched by the appropriate motive, but the very process of discovering and uncovering motive by self-examination inevitably produced an unwanted self-regard, a focus on oneself that seemed to vitiate the very love of God the good act should witness to."[5] The gambits for assuaging tortured consciences were the surges of hope that triggered the circuit breakers. Wallington found some peace at the very end of his life, but it was the peace of an ancient battlefield peopled mainly by ghosts.

Reviewing Seaver's book, Blair Worden drew a general lesson regarding contemporary difficulties in understanding Puritanism: "Our temptation is to soften the Puritan mentality and, as we suppose, to humanise it. . . . Possibly Wallington's literary gifts were unequal to the communication of those more cheerful and creative features of Puritan (and Calvinist) faith which our time has emphasised. Yet we err if we neglect the darknesses of Puritanism, at least in its 17th-century form. The volume of despair engendered by Puritan teaching on predestination is incalculable. . . . Puritanism roams the highway of our history, and before we could 'explain' it we would need to have the measure of the beast."[6] The diary of Robert Woodford, the town clerk of Northampton in the 1630s, offers a less extreme and perhaps more representative example of what I have elsewhere called the "coiled spring" of Puritan entrapment.[7] A self-made man without a powerful patron to protect him, Woodford was also in the public eye. When called upon to kneel to receive communion and to pay ship money, both of which he found offensive to his conscience, he thought of the pauperization of himself and his family if he defied orders and was dismissed from his position. But he then poured out his anger and dismay into a diary. Thus, when Bishop Dee succeeded in getting altar rails installed in the Northampton churches and when he ensured that communicants came to the rails and kneeled to receive, Woodford externalized his anger: "why should prophaneness be established or contenued by a law . . . why should the precepts of men be taught for doctrines, why should carnall ordinances and an earthly sanctuary still remayne, and the worship in spirit and in truth be yet refused?"[8] But he also *internalized* the contempt and blamed himself for his weakness and surrender to worldly calculation: "Oh my g[od], save me for the waters are come up to my soule . . . I sit in the dust, in mercye rayse me up, my feet sink fast in the dunghill, let your goodnesse . . . lift me out. The fiery injections and darts of Satan come thick uppon me."[9] Being amongst the elect brought him no sense of freedom in the 1630s. He was a claustrophobic man placed in a straitjacket.

The printed Fast Sermons delivered to the Long Parliament between 1640 and 1649 offer another case in point. There is indeed a brittle dynamism about them, at least until thick mists of uncertainty enveloped the preachers as Parliament won the war but lost its way in making the peace. But what strikes one more intensely is the transitory nature of the sense of accomplishment, the sheer difficulty of satisfying God's conditions for sustained victory over the Antichrist. God's gift of salvation to the elect was unmerited and could not be earned; but demonstrating the fruits of election called for both obedience to his will and a right discernment of the chain of providences that he provided for them to follow. And the pillars of fire were often hard to discern amongst the dust storms. A simple but not untypical example would be Edmund Calamy's sermon in December 1641, published under the title *England's Looking Glass*. It was based on Ezekiel 18:31 ("Cast away from you all your transgressions whereby ye have trangressed, and make you a new heart and a new spirit"), which might seem a liberating text: but not in Calamy's hands. At its core was a call to repentance rooted in two duties: humiliation and reformation, both essential, for "humiliation without reformation is a foundation without a building: Reformation without Humiliation proves often a building without a foundation." In calling for humiliation, Calamy identifies seven buckets to "draw the water of tears withal," the first two of which are the contemplation of personal sins and the second the consideration of national sins. Similarly, reformation had to be both personal and national, and the obstacles to such a reformation are presented as insurmountable. The tasks facing the godly were the tasks of Sisyphus, the rewards those of Tantalus.

As William Lamont put it in his review of the relationship of Puritanism and liberty: "the pursuit of freedom may have been an unintended consequence of the activities of the revolutionary Puritans; it was neither their cause nor their inspiration."[10] Similarly, J. C. Davis summed up his survey of writings on religious liberty in the mid-seventeenth century by concluding that "the handclasp of bigotry and liberty remains one of the enduring and distinguishing images" of the period, and that the only freedom that mattered to the Puritans was not the freedom of groups and of individuals, but the freedom of Almighty God.[11]

Gloomiest of all, however, is John Stachniewski. Not only does he show that almost all those—Protestant and Catholic—writers who speculated on the populating of heaven assumed that less than one in a thousand would be saved, but he also shows that they believed that many of those who came to believe themselves included in the decree of predestination would turn out to have been self-deluded. (Perhaps the most chilling column in the table of the causes of salvation and damnation in Perkins's *Golden Chain* is the one that proceeds from the decree of reprobation via "a calling not effectual" and "a yielding to God's calling" to damnation.)[12] Thus—Stachniewski asserts—"in the period when Puritanism was at its height, the new sense of the uniqueness of the individual was, above all, a source of anxiety."[13] In these circumstances, the pessimism even of the regenerate was, in Stachniewski's account, pretty unrelieved. Of all the vignettes he offers, none is more poignantly funny and sad than his account of the Monty Pythonesque exchanges of Henry Jessey and a fellow Baptist over the miserable state of their spiritual lives—an edifying contest in one-downsmanship as he puts it. His conclusion that "it is difficult to grasp the experiential actuality of Puritanism. Too much comment has simply refused to face Calvinist extremism, to inhabit imaginatively its assumptions about the world" is the most stern representation of a generation of scholarship.[14] My task is not to overturn this judgment but to ameliorate it.

LIBERTY FROM POPERY

Many Puritans did experience a liberation *from* popery and anti-Christian thraldom in the early 1640s. In 1641, Robert Woodford organized petitions against the bishops and the Prayer Book and for the remedial work of the Long Parliament, and he stopped keeping a diary. It was no longer necessary: the coiled spring had been released. There was a moment of intense liberation from oppression in 1641, similar to that which we witnessed when the Berlin Wall came down in 1989. Where in Eastern Europe is that spirit of liberation now and where in England was it by 1645? The rapid change of mood can be seen in the words of one of the diarists of the Long Parliament itself: "let my people go that they may serve you in the Desert." Between bondage in Egypt and the Promised Land lay the years of repining in the desert. Was this freedom?

There was also a moment of intellectual freedom, a freedom to think unthinkable thoughts and to publish them, because the regulatory mechanisms that restricted access to the presses had broken down or were less effectual. As the physical structures and certainties that had defined the world Englishmen inhabited, and that seemed its most fixed and enduring structures (the monarchy, the House of Lords, the Established Church) came tumbling down, so did the mental certainties.

It allowed men—and women—to ask questions that had been literally unthinkable a decade earlier. For those who accept Milton as a Puritan—Milton, who had no idea what a born-again experience was; Milton, who rejected almost every distinctive tenet of the godly; Milton, who would have assented to so little in the Stachniewski definition with which we started—then his courageous questioning of the sanctity of Christian marriage, of the nature of clerical authority, his fearful demand to consider whether the Councils of Chalcedon and Nicaea might not have got it wrong, was a process of liberation. But few rose to the challenge. As Gerrard Winstanley put it in 1649: "All men have stood for freedom; plenty of petitions and promises thereupon have been made for freedom; and now the common enemy is gone, you are all like men in a mist, seeking for freedom and know not where nor what it is; and those of the richer sort of you that see it are ashamed and afraid to own it, because it comes clothed in a clownish garment. . . . For freedom is the man that will turn the world upside down, therefore no wonder he hath enemies."[15] This passage inspired Christopher Hill's classic *The World Turned Upside Down,* but the brave, rash review of John Kenyon helps us to keep the ideas of that book in perspective: "this was not really a proletarian movement at all. It was an unexpected opportunity for failed shopkeepers, lazy artisans and eccentric academics to find their voice."[16] And it provoked a violent reaction that cost many their freedom as they languished in gaol or in internal exile or (as in the case of James Nayler) suffered physical tortures worse than anything meted out by Star Chamber. As Thomas Case told the House of Commons in 1647: "Liberty of Conscience (falsly so called) may in good time improve itself into liberty of estates, and liberty of houses, and liberty of wives, and in a word, liberty of perdition, of soules and bodies."[17]

Liberation for most Puritans, then, meant liberation *for themselves* rather than liberation for others; and all-too-often it meant liberation for themselves but not *from themselves*. It is this last that most historians have found the hardest to identify and that is the quest of the bulk of this essay. Our task then is to look at liberty as empowerment, at the ways in which a Puritan faith and Puritan practice made men and women not victims but movers and shakers, not those shoved around by events, but those who took control of their own lives and in some cases control of the lives of those around them. It is about those who rode the tiger of Revolution.

THE LIBERATION OF SISTER CORNISH

I will offer three case studies: Sister Cornish, William Dowsing, and Oliver Cromwell. I will begin with Sister Cornish, who only just fits into my theme. But since I discovered her in the papers of Colonel Robert Bennett in the Folger Library,[18] I have three times tried to incorporate her into papers. Twice before I have found that she does not quite fit and that I do not quite have space for her; and I will not deny her a third time. She was marginalized quite enough in her own lifetime

An illiterate woman living on the margins of society in Cornwall,

Sister Cornish has no ability to tell us her story. We have to hear it through the mediation of others. And yet it is, I think, a moving story of someone who finally took control of her own life and challenged others to take stock of their own most-cherished self-fashionings.

Sister Cornish lived in Hexworthy in the very center of Cornwall, just south of Launceston. The glimpse we have of her is in the spring of 1656, at which time she seems to have been a poor widow, perhaps with children. There are no parish records and she does not appear in any of the tax records of the period. It is clear that she was in receipt of alms. Her story is told in an exchange of letters between two lay elders in her local church, Colonel Robert Bennett and Abraham Cheare, letters concealed behind a false wall for more than two hundred years after the events they describe. In essence the story is a simple one. Bennett and Cheare discuss Sister Cornish's defection to the Quakers. How can such a thing happen, they ask one another, and how can they reclaim her? Each reports on his visit to see her and offers a detailed account of his conversations with her. When the correspondence ends, Sister Cornish is serene in her newly discovered freedom from anxiety and fear, and they are miserable and full of doubts.

The kernel of the story can be found in this account given by Bennett himself, recounting Sister Cornish's own words: "Her speech to me was to this purpose—that she had long wandred as a lost sheepe hither and thither, meaning from forme to forme that at last, meaning I thinke since the Quakers were with her, that shee had received such declarations from them and soe suitable to her owne experiences that she had found rest and had found Christ within, that ordinances and formes weare generally abused and that in such case god did remove them as shee instanced in the brazen serpent. She also made a regardful mention of the self-deniall & sufferings of the quakers & other matters to this effect." In the ensuing discussion, it becomes clear that Sister Cornish was a victim of Puritan preaching. For years, she had been told that God rescued a few men and women from the damnation that all merited, and that God gave those he called assurance of salvation. Specifically they had told her that the hallmarks of that call to salvation were a joyful and regular reading of the Scriptures, joyful participation in all the special events—the days of thanksgiving and humiliation, the funerals of saints, and so on—and joyful offering of charity to the needy and deserving. Such relentless advice made her desperate for she was illiterate; she was working every hour that God gave her to support her children, and far from offering alms, she was in receipt of them.

The Quaker message to Sister Cornish was that all that was needed was a willing heart able to open itself to the direct power of the spirit. The sweet talk of the preachers had turned her into a spiritual diabetic desperate for Quaker insulin. Without relentless Puritan preaching, there would have been none of the desperation that caused those on the margins of literacy and subsistence to turn to the biblopetism and soteriological universalism of the Quakers. As Cheare put it: "She declared herself established in the blood of Christ as the alone ground of justification & . . . refused that notion of absolute perfection of the saints heer in way of their attainments, yet spoke much in the way of comendation of the quakers zeale, holiness and activity for God, with a very full testimony against the formallity, want of love, pride, earthly-mindedness amongst the churches." So it was Sister Cornish who was empowered and invigorated. Her encounter with Puritanism was part of her journey in faith, but it was the rejection of everything in Stachniewski's definition that gave her a liberation into a new godliness.

Meanwhile, Bennett and Cheare were left to count the cost. They listed the heresies of the Quakers, but they frankly recognized that these errors had freed Sister Cornish from the terror of hell and the need to search for signs and tokens. They blame themselves for not protecting her from such heresies. But much more they blame themselves for their failure to live up to the gospel: "Doubtless as our own walking unworthy of God & our profession of him is the main advantage they have to make, [thus] their voluntarie & affective humility & holiness [are] admired by the simple, that are not able to see & judge of the principles they act upon, so the heavenly spotlesse demeanour of God's people would be the most prevailing weapon to smite their beguiling instruments out of their hands." As all three move back into the mists, it is Sister Cornish who strides out most purposefully.

THE LIBERATION OF WILLIAM DOWSING

Liberation can thus mean going *through* Puritanism and then *beyond* it. Nowadays we would probably call the Quaker religion a post-Puritan movement: not of it, but from it. The remaining two of my cloud of witnesses are straight Puritans, apparently perfect demonstrations of the Stachniewski definition.

William Dowsing was a Puritan working farmer from Suffolk in East Anglia. He lived from 1596 to 1668, and spent the last thirty years of his life in Stratford St Mary, just a mile across the river

Stour from Dedham, perhaps the most famous center of Elizabethan Puritanism. He was closely involved with the godly of that town throughout the years of revolution. It has long been known that for almost a year beginning in December 1643, he was active as a commissioner in charge of removing the monuments of idolatry and superstition from the churches of the Eastern Association, and that he kept a diary of his iconoclasm, covering the college chapels in Cambridge, 96 Cambridgeshire parish churches, and 147 Suffolk parish churches. Most of the remaining Suffolk churches were cleansed of monuments and images by deputies under his direct control.

In studying Dowsing's journal elsewhere, I have called him the bureaucratic Puritan. He moved with an orderly and purposeful self-righteousness and with a clear set of priorities: to remove all traces of altars as places of sacrifice and special veneration; to remove all inscriptions or images that encouraged the living to pray for the dead; and to remove all statues, carvings, and stained glass images of the persons of God or the host of heaven that were visible to those attending worship. Initially, he was also concerned with those images hidden from the view of the people but visible and therefore an affront to God; but as time and the scale of his task bore in on him, he became less obsessive about images in roofs, on holy water stoups, and so forth. And he stuck to the letter of the parliamentary ordinances: they did not mention the devil, so Satan's image remained wherever images of the Trinity were defaced or smashed.

Dowsing was unique. In no other part of England was anyone appointed systematically to carry out the work that the ordinances laid squarely on the shoulders of churchwardens. Indeed, the Earl of Manchester was acting *ultra vires* in appointing him. There was a legal basis for the removal of all the images that escaped the earlier iconoclasm of 1537–53, but not for iconoclasm by an itinerant commissioner escorted by a posse of troopers.

Why did Manchester, not himself the most zealous of Puritans, make this aberrant appointment, and why did he stand by Dowsing when he ran into opposition? In my previous study of Dowsing I offered a general explanation: Dowsing pestered Manchester and in the end he agreed. And why did Dowsing, of all the yeoman farmers of East Anglia, pester him? The answer seems to be in part because Dowsing was unusual, if not unique, in the breadth and depth of his reading. Although his library was dispersed after his death, his habit of writing his name on the flyleaves of his books, his extensive marginalia, and his habit of cross-referring to other books in his library allows us to identity about half of the 120 books he once owned. I have analyzed that library and its acquisition elsewhere: here we must just recall that it contained some of the most militant Puritan writing associated with the Pilgrim Fathers, as well as much biblical commentary, Roman history, three copies of Foxe's *Acts and Monuments*, and an almost complete set of the parliamentary Fast Sermons published between 1641 and 1645. It is only with the sermons that we can be concerned here. Dowsing added to each his name, the date on which he acquired it, and the date on which he read it. Then with the meticulous concentration of a commuter doing the crossword puzzle on the train journey to work, he supplied all the biblical references in the margins, making just enough errors to suggest that he was doing it from memory, and he used a sophisticated system of scoring in the margin, linked to indexing points of agreement on the front of the sermon and adversaria on the back page.

Just once, Dowsing departed from this practice and drafted a letter. By a providence, it is perhaps the letter of his we most wanted to survive. On 6 March 1643 Dowsing took a printed copy of Jeremiah Whitaker's *Christ the Settlement of Unsettled Times*, a Fast Sermon preached before the House of Commons the previous January, and he drafted a letter to the leading Puritan preacher and longtime Dedham and Colchester lecturer, Matthew Newcomen, onto the back of it. The opening must have made the recipient wince: "Syr my kind respect to you. This is to let you understand I canot but take it ille yt in 2 yeeres space you returne not my booke I lent you of Church Policy.[19] I have desired you to write to Mr Grimston[20] for it & tell him it was not your owne. You told mee you would writ I heare not of it yet. I pray with out more delay, write to him & let me begett the parties absolute answ[er] betwene this and march 25 & then if god permit me with life & helth I will come or send to you for it." The letter continues with some choice biblical reproofs. Dowsing then changes tack completely, and a thoroughly shaken Matthew Newcomen was given an opportunity to make amends: "Sir, if you have anie interest in parliament men, now we have an army at Cambridge it might be a fitt tyme to write to ye Vice Chancellor of Cambridge & Mayor to pull down all ther blasphemous crucifixes, all superstitious pictures and reliques of popery according to ye ordinances o' parliament. I only reffere you to yt famous story in Ed[ward VI's reign] how the English got the victory against the Scots in Museleborough field the same day & hower the reformation was wrought in London and images burnt—*A[cts] & M[onuments]*[21] edit[ion] last.[22] Ten days later Dowsing was called from the plough, though not to be iconoclast-general but to be provost martial general, in charge of managing the supplies to the army of the Eastern Association and its newly promoted general, the Earl of Manchester. What is the connection?

It is not wildly implausible to imagine that Newcomen, formerly the town lecturer at Colchester, shared Dowsing's letter with Harbottle Grimston, recorder and MP for Colchester and Newcomen's close ally in the past, who in turn shared it with his friend and mentor the Earl of Warwick, who had a word in the ear of his son-in-law, the Earl of Manchester. How else might this stolid yeoman have got the job?[23]

It is now possible to explain what made Dowsing write his letter on 6 March. On the same day on which he would have received his copy of the sermon on which he drafted the letter, he had on his desk a copy of the one preached on the morning of the same day in St Margaret's Westminster, John Arrowsmith's *The Covenant Avenging Sword Brandished*. Indeed in 1646, he had it bound into his collection immediately before the Whitaker sermon. On the final page of the Arrowsmith sermon—which he notes having read on 28 February, less than a week before he wrote to Newcomen—is printed the following: "Acts and Monuments. Mr Fox observes, that in King Edward the sixth time the English put to flight their enemies in Musselburgh field the self-same day and houre wherein the Reformation enjoined by Parliament was put in execution in London, by burning of idolatrous images. Such a dependence hath our increase upon our obedience."[24] These are almost exactly the words he uses in his letter to Newcomen a few days later.

For six months, Dowsing ensured that Manchester's army was fed and watered. Then in mid-December he made his way up to London to have his accounts cleared. They were signed by members of the relevant committee on 13 December. On 18 December he received his first commission to cleanse the churches of the six associated counties. Did anything happen in that third week of December 1643 to make that further change happen?[25]

Yes: on the 15th of December, when both Dowsing and Manchester were present in London, and when Manchester was acting as Speaker in the Lords, John Pym was buried in Westminster Abbey. Manchester certainly (and surely Dowsing too) attended and listened to Stephen Marshall's thunderous funeral oration entitled *Threnodia, or the Churches Lamentation for the Good Man his Losse*.[26] The central theme of this sermon was the need for iconoclasm. We are surrounded by idols, Marshall told the congregation, yet we are for ever making new ones: "We deal as the Israelites did in the wildernesse, turne our golden eare-rings into an idol, and thereby change our glory into our shame and misery, offering infinite injury unto God." To follow such a course would place all our endeavors on a par with "men that go to lotteries, with their heads full of hopes, and returne with their hearts full of blankes." We even turn our parliamentary heroes into idols, which is why "God doth often times take away the most useful men, when his church hath most need of them." There was a solution: "Let everyone whom God has fitted for any service, do what their hand findes to do with all their power. Lay not [then] thy talent in a napkin, thy master may suddenly call thee to an account for it."[27]

Is it not likely that there is a connection between those words, the eyes of Dowsing out on stalks as he heard them, and the commission he received on the third succeeding day to that one, which brought him to the chapels of Cambridge by what his adversaries persisted in calling Christmas Day? And if Dowsing truly believed that in 1547 iconoclasm in London permitted military victory in the Scottish borders, then is there any reason to doubt that he would believe that God gave victory to Sir Thomas Fairfax over the cavaliers on 19 January 1644 at Nantwich because he, William Dowsing, wrought destruction of images in the churches of Orford, Snape, and Saxmundham?

Dowsing was liberated by letting the words of Puritan preachers speak directly to his heart. He was empowered and released. It was not to last. By the middle of 1646 he could only see liberty running everywhere to license, a gangrene of heresy bringing a disabling agony to the church, and the rest of his life was one of doubt and guilt for a cause betrayed. But for a whole year this earnest farmer enjoyed the liberty of those who discerned and fell in with the will of God.

THE LIBERATION OF OLIVER CROMWELL

For Oliver Cromwell, that feeling was much more enduring, albeit spasmodically. But for him the empowerment that came from being the instrument of God's will came from a much more immediate interaction with the words of Scripture. Here was a man who never made reference to any book but the Bible, who learned something from the biblical hermeneutic of the preacher, but in the end found all his own messages in the Scriptures from his own prayerful confrontation with it. At all the great crises of his life he turned to the Scripture, and he explicitly explained to others how God's will had been revealed to him through the written Word. I shall begin with a brief overview of Cromwell's use of the Bible, followed by a briefer case study of how he came round to embrace regicide in 1648.

One telling passage gives an overall sense of Cromwell's use of the Bible. In October 1638 Cromwell wrote to his cousin, the wife of Oliver St John, and he gave her an account of his conversion experience several years earlier: *"In this I am confident.*[a] Truly then this I find: *That He giveth springs in a dry and barren wilderness where no water is.*[b] *I live* (you know where) *in Mesheck, which they say signifieth Prolonging; in Kedar which signifieth Blackness.*[c] Yet the Lord forsaketh me not. Though He do prolong, yet He will (I trust) bring me to His tabernacle, to His resting place. *My soul is with the congregation of the firstborn*[d], *my body rests in hope*[e]; and if here *I may honour my God either by doing or by suffering,*[f] I shall be most glad" (emphasis mine).[28] The letter as a whole is three times in length and contains three times as many biblical citations: Cromwell draws on eight psalms and five epistles. But the spine of the letter, the text around which it is based and to which the others are decorations, is Philippians chapter 4, in which Paul gives thanks for the support he has been given during his imprisonment and calls for the unity and perseverance of the faithful under persecution. The imprisoned Paul tells of the all-sufficiency of Christ in all circumstances.

Cromwell in 1638 was a born-again man, but a man who had lost his wealth, his health, and his social standing, and who had spent long years as a working farmer in the fen, where we get one glimpse of him in the records when a traveler noted him at church, suffering from chronic bronchitis and with a piece of red flannel across his chest and throat to keep out the fog and the damp. By October, the death of his childless uncle had brought him relief; he had inherited his uncle's job as land agent for the dean and chapter of Ely Cathedral, but the key sentence in the letter, italicized above, is from Philippians 4 and it reads: "if here I may honour my God by doing *or by suffering* I shall be most glad" (emphasis mine). Cromwell's years in the fen were his years in the desert, released from slavery to sin by God's free will, but not yet able to enjoy the fruits of his call. He was ready for that call and in 1640 he grabbed it with his whole being. Elected against all sense to the House of Commons, its poorest and meanest member, he had no doubt that the time of suffering was over and the time of doing was upon him. And he seized every opportunity to serve God by his reckless speaking against the bishops and popery in all its forms, by his reckless militarism even before civil war had broken out—such as in his seizure of the

Cambridge plate sent as a gift from the colleges to the king—and by his fearless leadership in war that saw him victorious on thirty-one battlefields and defeated on none. No wonder in 1648 he used that same phrase from Philippians in a letter to Fairfax. It was now the people of England who were called by God and who must honor him by their sufferings before they could serve him by their doing. They too must have their desert experience before they could enter the promised land, and this underlay the constant reference to himself throughout the Protectorate as the new Moses.[29]

In the years up to 1641, Cromwell's letters dwell on the Psalms and the Epistles, and they remain his most constant sources of inspiration. But by the late 1640s he is citing the early prophets much more, and from 1650 on the Pentateuch. Less than 2 percent of all his citations are to the Gospels and even fewer are to the apocalyptic books of the Old and New Testament. And just as Cromwell's letter to Mrs. St John has a core biblical text embroidered from other texts, so do many of his greatest letters and speeches of later years. Blair Worden has demonstrated how the story of Achan came to haunt Cromwell in 1657[30]—no liberation there—but his speech to the Nominated Assembly in July 1653 contains an extended meditation on what Cromwell termed "that famous Psalm, sixty-eighth psalm, which indeed is a glorious prophecy . . . of the gospel churches"—"Let God arise, let his enemies be scattered . . . Let the righteous be glad, let them rejoice before God, let them rejoice exceedingly."[31]

CROMWELL AND REGICIDE

I will conclude with a discussion of one crucial episode, Cromwell's conversion to the cruel necessity of regicide in 1648. At the Putney Debates in November 1647, Cromwell fiercely defended the monarchy against republican attack and he also dug in on the right of himself and his fellow senior officers to conduct a personal treaty with Charles I. Indeed, in another article, I maintain that it was a threat to the future of the monarchy that led to a news blackout at Putney as Cromwell and Ireton stormed out of a meeting on 5 November and ordered transcripts of that day's proceedings to be destroyed.[32] Yet a year later Cromwell was to prove the most resolute of all the military and political leaders in putting the king on trial for his life. What made it more possible for him than for so many others who had traveled with him in the wars of the 1640s to reach that decision?

Throughout his life Cromwell had a strong sense of God's providence. It was rooted in his reading of the Old Testament, which at one level is the story of God's personal appearances—in dreams, visions, burning bushes, pillars of fire—to challenge his chosen people and to give them stark choices: obedience and reward, disobedience and punishment; obedience and the rewards of Canaan, disobedience and slavery in Egypt or Babylon. Cromwell makes more references—especially in his writings to 1649—to the Psalms than to any other book of the Bible. And amongst the Psalms, he refers to those with the strongest sense of God's palpable presence and activity in the activities of mankind. This sense of God's visibility in Scripture and human events had no doubt been developed from his childhood by his teacher Thomas Beard, who was the author of one of the standard works on God's active presence in the world rewarding virtue and punishing vice: *The Theatre of God's Judgement*. But much more from the routine rhetorical device of godly preachers, he had learned that there was an actual and real parallel between the choices offered to the people of the Old Testament and the people of the present time. The particular dilemmas and choices of the people of England in 1648 were *precisely* the same as particular dilemmas and choices of the people of Israel. It was appropriate and necessary for men to identify the parallels in their own lives and to act on them.[33]

The sweep of Cromwell's writings throughout 1648 suggests a man who feels guided by God and clear of the end, though not quite of the means. The change can be traced back to Cromwell's histrionics in Parliament on the 3d of January 1648 when, gripping his sword handle, he asserted that the king had broken his trust and that this represented a fundamental change.[34] The Army had previously committed itself to monarchy "unless necessity enforce an alteration."[35] That word "necessity," as we shall see, is significant. Cromwell never again discussed the king except as someone who had put himself outside the protection of God's people. For the whole of 1648 Cromwell's concern was not whether to remove the king but when and how. A letter to Robert Hammond on 18 January about the Vote of No Addresses is already robust in its language about that.[36] Cromwell saw the second civil war as a sacrilegious act, as an affront to the sovereignty of God, and he called for condign punishment upon all its authors. And so after each major episode in the second civil war, unlike any of those in the first, the leaders were put on trial and some were executed in cold blood.[37] And the language of judgment on the authors of the war had to extend to the king himself. The questions were when and how, not whether. Cromwell spoke of providence throughout his life, but never with the persistence or confidence of 1648. Twelve letters speak of providence and eight of necessity.

By the time of Pride's Purge, Cromwell's encounter with the Bible had caused him to see in the choices God had presented to his chosen people in ancient Israel the same choices he was presenting to his new chosen people. The choices were strictly comparable, but they were false choices: to follow God's preferred route and enter the Promised Land or to ignore it and trek back to Egypt. My suggestion is that if we are to understand the confidence, drive, and certainty that allowed Oliver Cromwell to abandon his belief in the inevitability of Charles I and the necessity of monarchy, then these prayerful meditations on God's providence provide it.

By 6 December 1648, I do not believe that Cromwell doubted the need to put the king on trial. The only question was whether it was to be the culmination of the trials and investigations into the events of the previous year or an immediate act. Cromwell was aware of the desperately narrow basis of support for what was intended. If the trial of the king was the culmination of a sequence of trials revealing the depths of his duplicity, Cromwell could hope that the civilian Independents, at least, would come back to his side.[38] Similarly, Cromwell was behind the "Denbigh" mission to offer the king one more chance to negotiate. This was not, surely, the last hesitant, wavering act of a reluctant revolutionary, but the action of a man convinced that Charles Stuart was a man whose heart and mind God would harden so that the world would see how unregenerate he was. It was to be a final demonstration of his unfitness. Again, the aim was not to satisfy himself but others.[39]

But why was Cromwell so much in the lead, when so many comrades and close allies fell away, unable to steel themselves to regicide? In part, of course, it was the king's continuing duplicity that led on to the second civil war. It was this that led many junior officers and soldiers to demand in Cromwell's hearing at Windsor that Charles Stuart, as "a man of blood," should atone for his shedding of innocent blood in accordance with the requirements of the Book of Numbers (35:33): "Ye shall not defile the land wherein ye are: for blood it defileth the land; and the land cannot be cleansed of the blood that is shed therein, but by the blood of him that shed it."[40] The application of this text to that man of blood, Charles Stuart, sustained many in the months that followed. But Cromwell himself never endorsed it, nor did he ever cite from the Book of Numbers until 1656.

When I first planned this study, I thought I had a simple and powerful alternative. On four occasions in 1648 Cromwell makes reference to the story of Gideon, and I became convinced that he had come to see himself as Gideon. Indeed, his account of the battle of Preston, written the day after the battle and sent to Speaker Lenthall, reads less like other accounts of the battle of Preston than like the biblical account of Gideon's defeat of the Midianites at Ain Harod.[41]

Let us recall the story of Gideon.[42] He was called from the plough to lead the army of Israel. He winnowed that army, reducing it to a small, compact force made up of Israel's russet-coated captains, and he destroyed the Midianites and harried their fleeing army for two hundred miles, as Cromwell did after Preston. He then executed the kings of the Midianites, denying them quarter because they had shed innocent blood on Mount Tabor. Finally, he refused to take the crown himself and returned, loaded with honors, to his farm. It is not surprising that Cromwell found this a powerful story and suitable to his condition in 1648. And he drew powerfully on it, nowhere more than in an extraordinary outburst to Fairfax in the middle of a letter full of nitty-gritty military matters as he swept through South Wales in June 1648: "I pray God teach this nation . . . what the mind of God may be in all this, and what our duty is. Surely it is not that the poor godly people of this Kingdom should still be the objects of wrath and anger, nor that our God would have our necks under a yoke of bondage; for these things that have lately come to pass have been the wonderful works of God; breaking the rod of the oppressor, as in the day of Midian, not with garments much rolled in blood but by the terror of the Lord."[43]

This passage draws on Galatians, Acts, and 2 Corinthians, but the central image with its reference to the breaking of the Midianites is from Isaiah, and that might in the end be the more important point. For in fact Cromwell's allusions to Gideon are all passing ones; there is no sustained meditation on his story. On the other hand, he spends much time and space in several letters in extended meditation on Isaiah chapters 8 and 9. Indeed he wrote to Oliver St John on 1 September 1648, a week after the battle of Preston, telling him that "this scripture hath been of great stay with me, Isaiah eighth, 10. 11. 14. Read the whole chapter."[44] That chapter and the next are about how most of the people have missed out on righteousness and how those who follow the idolatrous leaders of Judah and Israel will be destroyed. Hence, the prophetic warning: "Associate yourselves, o ye people, and ye shall be broken in pieces. . . . gird yourselves and you shall be broken in pieces . . . But I will wait upon the Lord that hideth his face from the house of Israel, and I will look for him. Behold I and the children whom the Lord has given me are for signs and wonders in Israel."[45] Within days Cromwell was writing in wonder at how a godly minority had seized power in Scotland, expelled the corrupt majority from the Scottish Parliament, and set up godly rule: "Think of the example and of the consequences, and let others think of it too."[46] The connection between this wonderment and the subsequent purge of the English Parliament is palpable.

Cromwell was working out his own destiny in relation to God's plan, and God was no democrat. He had worked through a godly remnant in the days of Isaiah, and he could and would do so again. This is the essence of those remarkable letters that Cromwell wrote to Robert Hammond in the late autumn of 1648, pleading with him to discern God's providential hand in current affairs.[47] Nowhere was the clustering of biblical gobbets more dense. One paragraph alone in the letter of the 25th of November has twenty-four citations from eleven biblical books, with especial focus on the Epistle of James (1:2–6), with its exhortation to Christians "to ask in faith, nothing wavering. For he that wavereth is like a wave of the sea driven with the wind and tossed" (1:6) and from Romans 8, with its great cry that, freed from the law, the true Christian must look beyond present deprivations to the presence of the Holy Spirit. Life in such a situation, say both Paul and Cromwell, is life beyond hazard.

Cromwell's encounter with Scripture empowered him, and his only way of explaining and justifying himself in both his most intimate letters and his public statements was by taking his auditors through his own process of discovery and revelation. Time and again, he tells his critics that their arguments are intellectually strong—unanswerable indeed—but that they are not *necessary* arguments. And necessity for Cromwell meant the process of discernment and falling in with the will of God. Power, he told the Nominated Assembly in July 1653, "has come to you by way of necessity: by the wise providences of God."[48] In rejecting the offer of the crown in 1657, Cromwell begs those negotiating with him to show him the "necessary grounds," clearly meaning the God-given grounds. He could not rebut their arguments, he told them, they were "so strong and rational." They were arguments of convenience and "probability towards conclusiveness." But they were not rooted in necessity, for God had appeared providentially in striking down the person and office, and the only argument that could convince him was a providentialist one, that God had revealed his will to be the restoration of the title and office. That would be the "necessary ground."[49]

Thus when Cromwell says in 1648 that "providence and necessity" had cast him and his fellow officers upon regicide, he means not that they had fallen with political reality, but with the revealed will of God. As J. C. Davis put it: the concern for religious liberty in the English Revolution had "less to do than we care to think about with the preoccupation of groups and individuals, than with the freedom of God Almighty."[50] But the ability to discern and identify with God's freedom could be and was for men such as Oliver Cromwell utterly liberating and utterly empowering. Like all forms of belief in divine mandates, it troubles the modern secular mind. But when it comes to explaining the only true revolution in British history, it has an explanatory force whose depths we have yet to plumb.

NOTES

An earlier version of this paper was given at the Conference at St Mary's University College, Twickenham, on Religion, Culture, and Society in Early Modern Britain. I am grateful to all the discussants on that occasion for their comments, which greatly improved the paper before this version was produced.

1. John Stachniewski, *The Persecutory Imagination: English Puritanism and the Literature of Religious Despair* (Oxford: Clarendon Press, 1991), 11.

2. This draws on the definition of popular culture used by my colleague Peter Burke in *Popular Culture in Early Modern Europe* (London: T. Smith, 1978), preface, a definition already fruitfully applied to Puritanism by Christopher Durston and Jacqueline Eales in the introduction to their *The Culture of English Puritanism, 1560-1700* (Basingstoke: Macmillan,1996), 9.

3. Thomas Webster, *Godly Clergy in Early Stuart England: The Caroline Puritan Movement c. 1620-1643* (Cambridge: Cambridge University Press, 1997).

4. Tom Webster reminds us of the distinction that John Bossy has made about seventeenth- and twentieth-century meanings of "society." He writes: "I have taken society as the Northamptonshire divine Robert Cawdray defined it, as a fellowship rather than as a commonwealth" (*Godly Clergy*, 2), citing Bossy, "Some Elementary Forms of Durkheim," *Past and Present* 95 (1982): 3–18.

5. Paul Seaver, *Wallington's World: A Puritan Artisan in Seventeenth-Century London* (Stanford: Stanford University Press, 1985), 42–43.

6. Blair Worden, "Calvinisms," *London Review of Books*, 23 January to 6 February 1986, 16–17.

7. John Morrill, "William Dowsing, the Bureaucratic Puritan," in *Public Duty and Private Conscience in Seventeenth-Century England: Essays Presented to G. E. Aylmer*, ed. John Morrill, Paul Slack, and Daniel Woolf (Oxford: Clarendon Press, 1993), 201.

8. New College Oxford MS 9502, 337, cited in J. Fielding, "Opposition to the Personal Rule of Charles I: The Diary of Robert Woodford, 1637–1641," *Historical Journal* 31 (1988): 779.

9. New College Oxford, MS 9502, 298–99, cited in Fielding, "Opposition," 771.

10. William Lamont, "Pamphleteering, the Protestant Consensus and the English Revolution," in *Freedom and the English Revolution: Essays in History*

and Literature, ed. R. C. Richardson and G. M. Ridden (Manchester: Manchester University Press, 1986), 89.

11. J. C. Davis, "Religion and the Struggle for Liberty in the English Revolution," *Historical Journal* 35 (1992): 507–30.

12. William Perkins, *A Golden Chain*, in *The Workes of that Famous Minister of Christ in the University of Cambridge, Mister William Perkins*, vol. 1 (1612), between pages 10 and 11. There is an accessible modern realization of this diagram in *The Work of William Perkins*, ed. Ian Breward (London: Sutton Courtenay, 1969), and a rather shrunken reproduction in Stachniewski, *Persecutory Imagination*, 163–64.

13. Stachniewski, *Persecutory Imagination*, 78.

14. Ibid., 41–42.

15. R. C. Richardson and G. M. Ridden, *Freedom and the English Revolution* (Manchester: Manchester University Press, 1985), 5.

16. John Kenyon, "Christopher Hill's Radical Left," *The Spectator*, 8 July 1972, 55.

17. Thomas Case, *Spirituall Whordome Discovered in a Sermon Preach'd before the Honourable House of Commons* (London, 1647).

18. All the below is based on letters in the Bennett Papers in the Folger Library (MS X.d.483), fos.174–77, 202. There is an interesting short account of Robert Bennett in the *Dictionary of National Biography* (hereafter *DNB*) that tells us that he was a hard-line officer, a governor in turn of St Mawes and St Michael's Mount, a member of the Nominated Assembly in 1653 and of its Council of State, and no great friend of the Protectorate. He defended the trial and execution of the king in a charge to Truro Quarter Sessions (*DNB* wrongly states Assizes) in April 1649, and that charge was published under the title "King Charle's [*sic*] Trial Justified." He lived on in obscurity until 1683. I intend to spend more time tracking down the actors in this story.

19. Just possibly a reference to Hooker's *Of the Lawes of Ecclesiasticall Politie* (1593), but more likely a reference to T. Parker's *De Politeia Eccesiastica* (1620). I am grateful to Patrick Collinson for the suggestion.

20. Presumably Harbottle Grimston Jr., MP and Recorder of Colchester (where Matthew Newcomen had been born, and where his brother Thomas was a controversial Laudian minister). See *DNB*.

21. John Foxe's *Acts and Monuments* (or *Book of Martyrs*). The edition in question is that of 1610, and Dowsing's previous sentence is a close paraphrase of Foxe.

22. FS VI no. 3, verso of *imprimatur* (Jeremiah Whittaker, *Christ the Settlement of Unsettled Times*. London 1643).

23. Morrill, "William Dowsing," in *Public Duty and Private Conscience*, 187–88.

24. John Morrill, "William Dowsing and the Administration of Iconoclasm in the Puritan Revolution," in *The Journal of William Dowsing*, ed. T. Cooper (Woodbridge: Boydell and Brewer, 2001), 11. This is an extended and revised version of the essay listed in n. 23. I am grateful to John Blatchly for drawing this to my attention.

25. For this, see also S. L. Sadler, "Dowsing's Arguments with the Fellows of Pembroke," in *Journal*, 63–65.

26. Dowsing also owned a copy of this (FS II, no.12), but his annotations are light.

27. Marshall, *Threnodia, or the Churches Lamentation for the Good Man his Losse,* London, 1644, 12–14.

28. *The Letters and Speeches of Oliver Cromwell, with Elucidations by Thomas Carlyle*, ed. S. C. Lomas (London: Methuen and Co., 1904), 1:89–90 (henceforth *LSOC*). The biblical quotations are (a) Psalm 27:3; (b) Psalm 63:1; (c) Psalm 130:5 ff; (d) Hebrews 12:23; (e) Psalm 16:9; (f) a play in Philippians 4:11. Cromwell is writing from memory and is mingling the precise words of the Geneva and of the Authorized (or King James) versions.

29. *LSOC* 1:321.

30. Blair Worden, "Oliver Cromwell and the Sin of Achan," in *History, Society and the Churches: Essays in Honour of Owen Chadwick*, ed. Derek Beales and Geoffrey Best (Cambridge: Cambridge University Press, 1983), 125–45.

31. *LSOC* 2: 300.

32. For what follows, see John Morrill and Philip Baker, "Oliver Cromwell, the Regicide and the Sons of Zeruiah," in *The Trial and Execution of Charles I*, ed. J. Peacey (Basingstoke: Macmillan, 2001), 14–35.

33. For Beard, see John Morrill, "The Making of Oliver Cromwell," in *Oliver Cromwell and the English Revolution*, ed. John Morrill (London and New York: Longman, 1990), 26–33.

34. *LSOC* 1:290 n.

35. David Underdown, "The Parliamentary Diary of John Boys," *Bull.Inst.Hist. Res.* 39 (1966): 155–57.

36. *LSOC* 1:289–91.

37. Morrill, "Sons of Zeruiah," n. 53.

38. For this see Blair Worden, *The Rump Parliament* (Cambridge: Cambridge University Press, 1974), passim.

39. Morrill, "Sons of Zeruiah," part 6.

40. William Allen, "A faithful Memorial of that remarkable meeting of many Officers of the Army, at Windsor Castle in 1648," in *Somers Tracts* (London, 1811), 6:500–1.

41. *LSOC* 1:350.

42. See Judges chaps. 6–8.

43. *LSOC* 1:321.

44. *LSOC* 1:350

45. Isaiah 8:9.

46. *LSOC* 3:391–92.

47. *LSOC* 3:389–92 (6 November), *LSOC* 1:393–99.

48. *LSOC* 1:290.

49. *LSOC* 3: 54, 55, 59, 70–71.

50. Davis, "Religion and the Struggle for Liberty," 530.

Prelates and Politics:
Uses of "Puritan," 1625–40

Dwight Brautigam

By 1625, WHEN CHARLES I ASCENDED TO THE ENGLISH THRONE, THE TERM "Puritan" was already in wide use, though its users imparted a wide variety of meanings to it.[1] Yet during the first fifteen years of Charles's reign, the term became even more controversial. The primary reason for this change lay in Charles's decision to favor the "Arminian" element in administering the Church of England.[2] The most outstanding example of the Caroline elevation of Arminianism, was, of course, William Laud, who rose to become Archbishop of Canterbury and who enjoyed significant religious and political clout in the royal court. The use of the term "Puritan" by Laud and his circle gives an important window on political and theological tensions in the 1630s. How did Laud and his fellow prelates use the term? Did their hostile use of the term "Puritan" contribute to the breakdown of community and consensus, furthering the growth of Puritan discontent? Or was it of little consequence?

The term "Puritan" had been, as scholars have noted, largely one of opprobrium since its inception in the vestiarian controversy of the 1560s and uses in the Martin Marprelate tracts of the 1590s. Satirical literary constructions of the Puritan were well established by the end of the Jacobean period, with Ben Jonson's Zeal-of-the-Land Busy in *Bartholomew Fair* as one of many examples.[3] Lori Anne Ferrell has recently shown that the often-cited "Jacobean consensus" in ecclesiology nonetheless included the development of "a virulent polemic of denunciation of those who sought any further reform of the English Church."[4] It was in this environment that Laud and his allies rose through the ecclesiastical ranks of the Church of England, sharing assumptions about the dangers of Puritanism while honing their polemical skills.

With the accession of Charles I and his preference for their theological positions, Laudians were able to escalate anti-Puritan rhetoric in particular ways that provoked a heated response from their targets. Since Laud was powerfully positioned in the state, this meant that the Laudian circle's anti-Puritan language alienated more and more of the godly from the state itself, with reciprocating vitriolic language aimed, in turn, at church, state, and monarch. The Laudian use of "Puritan," then, served to widen the political fissures in early Stuart England.

Laud's own career is perhaps the best place to begin a closer analysis. By 1625 Laud had considerable influence both in the Church of England and at the Court. As a close associate of the Duke of Buckingham, Laud had risen quickly, holding a variety of church positions before becoming Archbishop of Canterbury in 1633. He also wielded considerable civil authority as a Privy Councillor, a position he held beginning in 1627, and as Chancellor of Oxford University, a position he acquired in 1629.[5] The Buckingham-Laud alliance paid significant attention to Puritanism.

Late in 1624 Laud prepared and gave to Buckingham "a little tract about Doctrinal Puritanism, in some ten heads, which his Grace had spoken to me that I would draw for him, that he might be acquainted with them."[6] Even more revealing is Laud's first recorded usage of the term "Puritan" in Charles I's reign. Not even two weeks after King James had died, Laud noted in his diary, "I exhibited a schedule, in which were wrote the names of many Churchmen, marked with the letters O. and P. The Duke of Buckingham had commanded to digest their names in that method; that (as himself said) he might deliver them to King Charles."[7] This note raises a number of suggestive questions. Why did Charles and Buckingham want the list in the first place? What did they intend to do with it? Did Laud know what it was for? Perhaps most intriguing, however, is the use of the term "Puritan" itself. Clearly if Laud was able to produce the list on what appears to be short demand, then he was also obviously familiar with the term. Moreover, he had to have familiarity with applying it to churchmen, which means that most likely for some time Laud and others had been counting and labeling heads in the Church of England. What is more, the new king and the duke must have known that Laud used the term "Puritan" in this way; perhaps they did so themselves. It is also likely that Charles and Buckingham knew quite well that Laud would not interpret those list members under "P." as allies. Laud himself had for years been marked by some as a closet Catholic, or at the very least not friendly to the predestinarian impulse that was part of mainstream theology.[8] Laud then, had enemies in the church for whom he was willing to use the "Puritan" label. Furthermore, someone thought those Puritans were significant or powerful enough to bear watching, or perhaps to prohibit from further advancement in the church. To the Court, the Puritans were no fringe group that simply could be ignored.

Additional confirmation of Laud's mistrust of Puritans appeared during the controversies over religion during the 1628–29 Parliament, when he produced a draft document for setting the king's policies on religion. Entitled "Considerations for the Better Settling of the Church-Government," the document had twelve points. These targeted such problems as absentee bishops, lecturers, and afternoon lectures. Laud's ninth point referred to Puritanism: "That Emmanuel and Sydney College[s] in Cambridge, which are the Nurseries of Puritanism; may from time to time be provided of grave and orthodox men for their governors."[9] This point is consistent with Laud's earlier cooperation with Buckingham in monitoring Puritans, but it also demonstrates an additional suspicion on his part that organized opposition was developing at Cambridge. While Laud was becoming more suspicious of Puritans, others in the Laudian circle were applying the term as well, and it is fairly certain that Laud was not only aware of such uses but also approved of them.[10]

Richard Montagu, part of Laud's circle and one of the most controversial figures of the Arminian controversy, was not at all shy about using the epithet "Puritan." In fact, even before Charles had become king, Montagu used it in reference to Laud's political clout. Writing to John Cosin, another of the Laudian circle, he asserted that Laud "must now and in such cases put for the Church with the Duke, and use his great credit, that we be not swallowed up with a Puritan Bishopriqry."[11] Montagu in these letters used "Puritan" quite often and in a consistent manner. He was using it as early as 1621 and continued to rely on it all throughout his correspondence with Cosin. By it he meant the radical fringe of English Protestantism, as exemplified in his letter of June 1624, when he wished for "some to stand in the gap against Puritanism and Popery, the Scilla and Charybdis of ancient piety."[12] Though Montagu did not always refer to "Popery" when using "Puritan," he did so often enough to make it clear that he saw Puritanism as an extremist strain, one dangerous to the true Church of England. For example, writing again to Cosin in May 1625, he notes that he has come to "understand at full the Puritan charity what it is, such as Arminius found amongst the brethren in the Netherlands. From their doctrine, discipline, and charity, Good Lord deliver me and all honest men."[13] There is no doubt that Montagu meant the term as an insult: "Let them come off roundly to my doctrine, I will eat my words of Puritans, etc. for personal quarrel have I none to any one of them. . . . If I have called conformitants, themselves I mean, Puritans, they have styled me, as conform I am sure, seditious and papist."[14] Later that same year he described the attacks on him in Parliament: "it is malice and puritanical zeal that nestleth."[15] He would stop name calling if and when his opponents did.

Though he depicted them as religious extremists, Montagu also saw Puritans as a political force. During the contentious Parliament of 1626 he was hoping for assistance from an ally as he exhorted Cosin to "have him put to his hand, and stand with us in the gap against noisy domestic enemies the Puritan faction, in my opinion as dangerous to Church and Monarchy as the now banished."[16] This sort of language depicts Puritans in political terms, perhaps understandably, given the attacks on Montagu by both the 1625 and 1626 Parliaments.[17] The 1626 Parliament in particular had taken aim at Montagu, and one of the charges leveled against him involved the name "Puritan." On 17 April 1626 John Pym reported to the House for the committee on religion, detailing the proposed charges against Montagu, the second of which was "sedition charged against him." As evidence of this sedition, the committee charged that, in his book *Appello Caesarem*, "Montagu does draw together in one collective name of Puritans the greatest part of the King's true subjects." He also describes "divers crimes laid to their charge, and endeavors to bring the King into jealousy with them." Further, he "by divers odious terms endeavors to bring them into hate and scorn with the rest of the people." And again, "to the bishops he extends that name of Puritans."[18] Though the Parliament never found time to carry out its prosecution of Montagu, the attention it paid him demonstrated that his use of "Puritan" was indeed offensive and divisive.

It is clear, then, that Montagu viewed Puritans as an organized group; he referred more than once to "the Puritan faction," and added the possibility that the "Puritans be like to prevail" in the summer of 1626.[19] What is more, Montagu thought he knew what his enemies' political goals were. "Shall I," he asked Cosin in a June 1626 letter, "make my peace with the Puritans and turn over a new leaf, and put the Bishops to some plunges another while?"[20] For him the Puritans were an organized political force arrayed against him and against the bishops of the Church of England.

Montagu and his circle saw Puritans as political enemies and predicted dire consequences. Writing to Cosin about the possibility of an English synod on the theological debate that his own publications had helped to fuel, Montagu asserts that if the "Bishops" want to allow that sort of discussion, "let them. You and I can answer it to God Almighty. We, I am sure, have less to lose then they have, by Puritans prevailing. I fear I shall live to see their rochets pulled over their ears."[21] This depiction of Puritans carries some weight, raising the possibility of their gaining control of the church as well as committing violence (perhaps) against the ecclesiastical authorities. One wonders which Montagu thought more likely, the Puritan victory or the disrespectful treatment of the bishops. One also wonders what sort of treatment he thought he and Cosin might receive, but that avenue Montagu did not explore.

What was Cosin's view of all this? We have one clue at least in the visitation articles he composed in 1627 when, as Archdeacon, he intended to visit the parishes of York's East Riding. Toward the end of the articles, Cosin posed a series of questions aimed at the "preaching, lecturing, and reading of homilies" in the churches. In the course of these questions comes this inquiry about ministers: "and yet, nevertheless, do they religiously and seriously labor to keep from the people as well the superstitious and gross errors of the Papist, as the profane and wild madness of the Anabaptist, whose offspring be the Puritans?"[22] So, to Cosin, the "Puritans" come with a destructive pedigree, dangerous to church and state. As Montagu put it in yet another letter to Cosin that same year, "malignant Puritans persecute you as well in the north as the south." Cosin himself, writing to Laud the following year, referred to William Prynne and Henry Burton as "barking libellers" who deserve "chastisement" from the government.[23] To both Montagu and Cosin, then, "Puritan" meant an enemy, both a theological enemy to the Church of England and a potentially dangerous political opponent.[24]

Both Montagu and Cosin consistently used "Puritan" as an insult, often a demeaning insult, as in the Anabaptist reference. While their using it in such a way is not surprising, the inclusion of political references is significant. Such usage suggests a grouping with a well-defined agenda for theological *and* political battle. The fact that Montagu and Cosin were using the term in this way early in Charles I's reign suggests that there would be little hope of congenial exchanges between the king's prelates and their opponents in the 1630s, when Laud rose to the see of Canterbury.

Montagu and Cosin were not Laud's only allies to attribute dangerous intent to Puritans. Samuel Brooke, master of Trinity College, Cambridge, wrote to Laud in late 1630 about his theological opponents: "I daresay: that their doctrine of predestination is the root of Puritanism, and Puritanism the root of all rebellions and disobedi-

ent intractableness in Parliament, etc. and of all schism and sauci-
ness in the country, nay in the Church itself . . . they, I say that hold
the same opinions, cry out now the Church of England, and will
have the Church of England to be theirs. I could justify this and
much more, but your Lordship knows these things to be so better
than I, etc."[25] These are strongly held opinions indeed. Brooke not
only lays both theological and political difficulties at the feet of the
Puritans, as Montagu and Cosin had also done by this time, but he
does so in more explicit terms. In addition to stirring up theological
disputes at Cambridge, Puritans also aim at control over the entire
church.

This is a significant point because it relates to one of the central
controversies of the 1625–40 period: who would exercise ultimate
control over the Church of England? The Laudians perceived Puritans as a threat because of their numbers, their apparent entrenched influence in some university colleges, and the expectation
that the godly aspired to gain control of the ecclesiastical structure.
This is readily apparent for Brooke: he sees those difficult Parliaments of the 1620s, including the last one that had produced the
Petition of Right and set Charles on the road to personal rule, as
troublesome precisely because of Puritanism. He has no qualms
about linking the theological and political difficulties facing the
king's government, seeing all those troubles as stemming from Puritanism. He also has no doubt that Laud agrees with this assess-
ment. Laud and his circle, then, were not only well acquainted with
the term "Puritan," but were assigning it significant meaning and
in particular using it as a label for people whom they viewed as dangerous political enemies.

Laud used "Puritan" in his diary again, in early 1633, not long
before he became Archbishop. Noting that the feoffees for impropri-
ation were "dissolved in the Chequer Chamber," he adds that "they
were the main instruments for the Puritan faction to undo the
Church."[26] This last is a striking sentence, for here Laud attributes
organized political activity to Puritans. They wish to "undo the
Church." The sentence also is notable for its repetition of Montagu's
phrase, the "Puritan faction." Just as Montagu had done years before, Laud uses the phrase in a context that definitely associates
that "faction" with a threatening role in the English body politic.

Laud apparently used another stock insult for Puritans during a
Privy Council meeting in November of that same year, just a few
months after becoming Archbishop. According to Prynne, Laud asserted that Sir Henry Martin, who had disagreed with Laud on the
placement of the Communion table, "was a schismaticall Puritan in

his bosome."[27] If Laud was comfortable with such language at the Council table, he must have known it would be appropriate there. If so, belittling enemies as "Puritans" was not a tactic confined to letters or diary entries. Later in the decade we find Laud returning to the "faction" insult, this time in a letter to the Vice-chancellor at Oxford in 1637. Laud expresses concern over both "the popish faction" and "the puritan."[28] Again he is suspicious of those who oppose him from both ends of the ecclesiastical spectrum, though he is not as explicit as was Montagu about the extremes being the "popish" and the "puritan." Also, his language reveals his assumption that these enemies are organized and, of course, up to no good.

Lest one doubt Laud's thinking in this vein, his diary provides additional evidence. Writing in April 1638, Laud alleges that "the tumults in Scotland, about the Service-Book offered to be brought in, began July 23, 1637, and continued increasing by fits, and hath now brought that kingdom in danger. No question, but there's a great concurrence between them and the Puritan party in England. A great aim there to destroy me in the King's opinion, etc."[29] One can scarcely imagine a more politicized use of the term "Puritan" at this particular time. Despite the arguments of some revisionist historians, Laud had no doubt that his enemies were in league, that the Scots in rebellion against the Prayer Book were colluding with that remarkable "Puritan party in England."

Further evidence of Laud's conviction appears in a letter he wrote to Joseph Hall, the Bishop of Exeter, in November 1639. In this missive, the purpose of which was to defend the Episcopal structure of the Church of England, Laud aligns "Prynne, Bastwick, and our Scottish masters" with those "of a milder and subtiller Alloy, both in the Genevan and the Roman faction," warning that "it will become the Church of England so to vindicate it, against the furious Puritans, as that we lay it not open to be wounded by either of the other two, more cunning and more learned adversaries."[30] What did these "furious Puritans" want? To bring down the Church of England and its Archbishop, quite naturally. At the same time, Laud could not resist a dig at the abilities of these opponents, even though he saw them as very threatening. In both of these passages there may be much of Laud's personally suspicious nature and tendency to see more than actually existed. But Laud's view of the "furious Puritans" is nonetheless important, as it undoubtedly affected his own decisions as well as the advice he gave to his sovereign. It is likely that Laud's views moved the already distrustful Charles to further intransigence when he eventually had to deal with his political opponents in the Long Parliament.

Other instances of Laud's using "Puritan" to describe his opponents show the term's wide-ranging polemical and political force. One of those instances is in Laud's annual Archbishop's report to the king for 1634, in which he states that the Bishop of Chichester, Montagu himself, reported "that some puritan justices of the peace have awed some of the clergy into like opinions with themselves, which yet of late have not broken out into any public inconformity." Five years later Laud reported an almost identical complaint from the same diocese (though Montagu was no longer bishop there): "that diocese is not so much troubled with puritan ministers, as with puritan justices of the peace, of which latter there are store."[31] This introduces an additional facet of the Laudian view of what Puritans were up to, since in this case local officials are seen as Puritans, though how being a Puritan might influence one's actions as a justice of the peace is not clear. Laud apparently believes that local officials are using their positions to influence clergy. One wonders why the clergy would not be more effective at conversions than the justices, but neither Laud nor Montagu offer us any help in that regard. Still, Puritans in any position of importance were a threat to the churchmen, in particular since they could not control the selection of local government officials. This is another example, then, of the Laudian perception that Puritans were seeking to gain influence through exercising political power.

An even more heated occasion when Laud used the term "Puritan" was his speech before the Star Chamber on 19 June 1637, concerning his longtime antagonists, John Bastwick, Henry Burton, and William Prynne. The speech has much in it of interest, but only twice does Laud actually use the term "Puritan." The first of these is in the course of defending the *jure divino* of the bishops as being "in as direct opposition to the Church of Rome, as to the Puritan humour."[32] The other use is later in the speech when, in defending the eastward placement of the altar table, Laud labels the source of opposition to this placement: "the Lincolnshire minister comes in to play the Puritan for that."[33] With these two quotes we get a clearer view of Laud's understanding of Puritanism. In the first it is a "humour," an insult to anyone who might dare claim the name. Puritanism is not just a contentious theological position; it is a dangerous sort of disease in the Church of England. The second phrase is likewise insulting, since "the Lincolnshire minister" is actually the Bishop of Lincoln, John Williams, also at one time Lord Keeper.[34] In this instance, then, Laud belittles a bishop of the church by referring to him dismissively as a mere "minister" as well as accusing him of Puritanism. When we put these two uses together with the admission by one of Laud's biographers that he had the capacity "to make enemies unnecessarily by the sharpness of his speech," we add to our understanding of why Laud became one of the targets of the Long Parliament.[35] He used "Puritan" as an insult, he meant it as an insult, and he was convinced that Puritanism was just as dangerous to England as "papism," a serious conviction indeed in the post–Gunpowder Plot world of early Stuart England.

But how did the opponents of Laudianism react to being labeled and stigmatized as "Puritans"? The reactions varied, depending on the context and the individuals involved, but it is clear by all accounts that the targets did not appreciate the spirit or the letter of the name calling; one might even say that they expressed considerable discontent. This discontent ranged from public expression in Parliament to privately voiced unhappiness with the epithet. In 1626 John Yates expressed a view that must have resonated with many of those who became Laud's targets, namely "that this offensive name of a Puritan, wandering at large, might have some Statute passe[d] upon it, both to define it, & punish it: for certainly Satan gains much by the free use of it."[36] Similarly, in a 1628 letter to Samuel Ward, Bishop Davenant questioned why orthodox beliefs were now stigmatized as "Puritan doctrine": "why [it should be] esteemed Puritan doctrine, which those held who have done our church the greatest service in beating down Puritanism, or why men should be restrained from teaching that doctrine hereafter, which hitherto has been generally and publicly maintained, wiser men perhaps may but I cannot understand."[37] Laud's aggressive, wide-ranging campaign against "Puritans" was both frustrating and inexplicable to stalwart church officials, then, producing more rather than less division in the Church of England.

Some of those whom the Laudians called Puritans did in fact embrace the label. For example, John Cosin found some significant opposition to his leadership in Durham, where Judge Yelverton, sitting on the assizes at Durham in 1629, asserted "that he had been always accounted a Puritan, and he thanked God for it; and that so he would die."[38] The next year some of Cosin's opponents brought charges against him and some of his fellow clerics, asserting in the process that "all Arminians in general are the cunningest, and most pernicious enemies, that the Church of England hath, or ever had: for, under pretense of defending the Book of Common Prayer, and oppugning Puritans, you undermine the Church, and overthrow the walls thereof."[39] These clerics, especially Cosin, in attacking Peter Smart, had "railed upon" him by calling him, among other things, "a Judas, a Puritan, a schismatic, and what not."[40]

But, in response to the epithet of "Puritan," others were not above some name calling of their own. Smart's response reveals the tensions that the Arminian-Puritan controversy had produced, at least in Durham, by 1630: "Nay, there is one good fellow, among our brain-sick Arminians of Durham, (come out, John Cosin, it is your own sweet self) which traitorously, schismatically, rebelliously, seditiously, will deprive his Sovereign Lord the King of his supremacy over the Church in ecclesiastical causes, and openly, in an ale-house, will maintain it stoutly, and dispute it with arguments, in the audience of a multitude, and pronounce it gloriously, standing upon his feet, that all round about might hear him, and see him, 'that the King is no more head of the Church, then the fellow that rubs his horse's heels, because he cannot excommunicate nor suspend.' "[41] It is clear from Smart's lengthy attack on Cosin and his fellows that he resented the way in which they used "Puritan" as an insult, as a name that indicated opposition to Christianity and the true Church of England. Yet one cannot imagine that Cosin enjoyed Smart's label of "brain-sick Arminian" very much either. Both sides in this case were willing to resort to such verbal attacks, in the process widening the gap between them and reducing the likelihood that the term "Puritan" would be used by anyone interested in compromise or in reducing ecclesiastical tensions in the church.

By 1640 the Laudian campaign, both in rhetoric and policies, had helped to provoke considerable opposition to the government of the Church of England. As events moved toward crisis, civil war, and eventual regicide, the government's opponents exhibited deep resentment at the way the Laudians had used the polemical epithet "Puritan." It had become one of the many grievances that strained the bonds holding together the body politic.

In April 1640, members of the Short Parliament focused on religious tensions as perhaps the most dangerous threat to the nation. Francis Rous, for example, asserted that "the roote of all our grievances I thinke to bee an intended union betwixt us and Rome," in the service of which goal "the word puritan is an Essentiall Engine . . . it is spoke to shame a man out of all Religion, if a man will bee ashamed to bee saved."[42] Francis Seymour, also speaking in the Short Parliament, espoused a similar view, noting that "Puritans (ye only true subjects of ye land, and servants of God) are now accounted rebels," and that Laudians "under the name of Puritanes condemne all, who truely professe religion . . . but to teach that a man can be too godly and too honest is a doctrine of divells."[43] Here is telling evidence of the weight "Puritan" carried for those oppos-

ing Laud. Rous and Seymour both saw it as a powerful weapon indeed, perhaps the most crucial weapon in the Laudian arsenal.

Another example of militantly divisive language at this time occurs in the writings of Laud's most famous opponent, William
Prynne. In his November 1640 pamphlet, provocatively titled *Lord
Bishops None of the Lord's Bishops*, Prynne called bishops "the
Seed of Antichrist, the Mystery of Iniquity."[44] Perhaps this is no sur-
prise since Prynne had published *A Looking-Glasse for all Lordly
Prelates* in 1636 and was by then wholly disenchanted with the entire idea of bishops, though he did not call for the elimination of the
episcopacy until 1641.[45] He did contrast the bishops with Puritans,
however, after calling for the removal of the prelates who were so
troublesome: "But it will be alleged that thy Reverend Prelates hate
a public fast, as being Puritanical, and consequently any such reformation, as aforesaid, as being all Puritanical: that their order is
most Christian, and consonant to civil government, and most agree-
able with the monarchy, and the like." Some wish to defend the
bishops under these circumstances: "If this be thy revolution, O England, then know this for a certainty that thou canst not long
stand."[46] The choice is clear for Prynne: either England accepts
bishops who condemn "Puritanical" religious behavior, or those
bishops themselves must go. Nonetheless, Prynne did not accept
Puritanism as a badge of honor; he only used it when describing
what his enemies were saying about those with whom he sympa-
thized. In fact, later in the decade when Prynne was building the
case against Laud, he listed as one of Laud's offenses: "What a
great favorite and Instrument he was to the Queen and Popish faction, and how grand an Enemy, a Persecuter of the zealous Protestant partie, under the name of Puritans."[47]

Prynne's cohort John Bastwick was less hesitant about the "Puritan" label, but just as certain about "prelates": "and for my own
particular, to speak now my Conscience, I had rather go the way of
the meanest Puritans, that live and die according to their profession, than of the greatest Prelates that ever lived upon the earth."[48]
The pattern is quite clear; if a dichotomy occurred, if there was no
middle ground, Puritanism was the choice for the Bastwicks and
Prynnes of the world. Prelates they could not endure.

Sir Benjamin Rudyerd stated similar thoughts in a speech before
the Long Parliament in November 1640. His summary captured the
frustrations of many as he described the attitude of the ecclesiastical hierarchy: "Whosoever squares his actions by any rule; either
Divine or Human, he is a Puritan. Whosoever would be governed by
the King's Laws, he is a Puritan. He that will not do whatsoever

other Men will have him do, he is a Puritan. Their Great work, their Masterpiece now is, To make all those of the Religion, to be the suspected party of the Kingdom."[49] Rudyerd could hardly be more clear; "Puritan" had become an all-purpose club with which the clerics were pounding their enemies, and he appreciated it no more than did the others.

Another Long Parliament speaker, Edward Dering, revealed a reaction to the Laudian use of "Puritan" when he came to the defense of a minister, Mr. Wilson, whom Laud had removed from his office for investigation of his ministerial duties. This Mr. Wilson, Dering said, was "now a sufferer (as all good men are) under the generall oblique of a Puritan," despite his being "conformable" and "orthodox." Dering had approached Laud about Wilson's case but could get little help from the archbishop. Though he had not succeeded, Dering said, "I hope (by the helpe of this House) before this yeare of threats be run out, his Grace will either have more Grace or no Grace at all."[50] Though not very subtle, clearly Dering had become so disgusted with Laud's tactics that he was willing to issue barely veiled threats against the Archbishop. Laud's expectation that Puritans were dangerous, accompanied as it was by hostile actions and words toward them, was becoming a self-fulfilling prophecy by 1640.

It is clear, then, that the Laudian circle had elevated the discontent of England's Puritans. From Montagu's aggressive use of the term to Laud's careful yet weighty references, we have seen how the high churchmen meant the term "Puritan" as a pointed insult, one that would stigmatize and discredit their opponents. Further, the term had broad meaning for them. It was not simply a theological term, nor was it only an ecclesiastical term. It was those things, and more. The Laudians had made "Puritan" into a political term as well, depicting deep disagreements in partisan ways using antagonistic language.

Henry Parker's 1641 *A Discourse Concerning Puritans* corroborates the point that at least some contemporaries believed that the name calling had serious negative consequences.[51] In Parker's view, Laudians were using the term Puritan indiscriminately to tar all enemies in religion *and* politics. Parker's categories of ecclesiastical, religious, political, and ethical Puritans served to illustrate that the bishops could find many ways to label someone a Puritan, since they used it so broadly and in such an ill-defined manner. Under his third category, Parker attributes the blame for the current political unrest, indeed the war with Scotland, to the bishops' use of a polemical epithet: "Our present civil, nay more than civil war with Scotland, and all the mischiefs thereon attending, the disaffection between the King and his Subjects, and all the mischiefs thereon attending the discontinuance of Parliaments, the proper remedies of all State maladies, and universal grievances, which is a mischief whereby all mischiefs become incurable, all are caused by the abusive mistaken and injurious misapplication of this word Puritan."[52]

In the inflamed atmosphere of polemical print, Parker is mincing no words, putting "Puritan" rhetoric at the root of a complex set of difficulties. Parker is convinced that things must change in England: "If the confused misapplication of this foul word Puritan be not reformed in England, and that with speed, we can expect nothing but a sudden universal downfall of all goodness whatsoever."[53] A strong conclusion indeed! But that conclusion allows us a fairly good insight into how Parker, whose views must have represented some significant segment of Englishmen, felt about how prelates were using "Puritan." Parker was frustrated and incensed at the state of affairs in his country, a state of affairs that he blamed in no small measure on those who insisted on such a label. He expressed his discontent forcefully, and in this, as we have seen, he was not alone.

As Parker's tract, and the various complaints regarding "Puritan" in the Short and Long Parliaments show, Laud and his circle had escalated anti-Puritan rhetoric in particular ways that eventually provoked a heated response from their targets. Laud's powerful position in the state meant that this anti-Puritan language had alienated many of the godly from the state itself. And the discontented reactions evoked by Laudian polemic began with, but soon moved beyond, reciprocating polemical language.

Additional questions arise about the Laudian circle's use of "Puritan" and the discontented reactions it evoked. How much significance *was* there in Puritanism as a political faction? Were the Laudians crying "wolf"? Or was there a growing awareness of a commonality of interests between the opponents of the king's fiscal policies and the opponents of his religious hierarchy? The members of the Long Parliament certainly linked those interests after 1640; we have little explanation otherwise for Laud's trial and execution. When would be too early to start looking for a political Puritanism? Montagu seemed to think that there was such a thing in the late 1620s or even earlier. Was he right? Or was he being paranoid? What about Laud's list of "P's" and "O's" in 1625? Why *would* such a list be necessary?

Clearly the Laudians made the term "Puritan" into primarily a political label, doing so with full knowledge of its provocative and antagonizing nature to describe people they viewed as formidable opponents. They may well have overestimated the strength of their

Puritan opposition, but they certainly always saw Puritans as opposition, and Laud and his compatriots used the term in ways that
virtually guaranteed ill will from its targets. By forcing the issue,
Laud may have helped to create a more powerful opposition than
he originally confronted, but one that fit more nearly his own expec-
tations of that opposition.[54]

By using "Puritan" as an inflammatory label, then, the Laudians
made an already bad situation worse. Their use of the term elevated
tensions in the Church of England, weakening an already divided
national institution. Further, these tensions culminated in deep suspicions of Laud himself, contributing first to attacks on bishops and
finally to Laud's own execution, when his fears of those "Puritans"
ultimately proved true.[55] Laud and his allies were no doubt responding to genuine tensions in the church and state. But their consistent
pejorative use of the "Puritan" label raised the level of discontent
among the godly. That discontent, combined with other forces, finally helped bring down not only the Laudian Church of England
but the monarchy that it had so closely supported.

NOTES

1. Anyone familiar with early Stuart politics and religion, or indeed with colonial New England studies, is aware of the thicket awaiting the scholar who seeks
to offer a satisfactory definition of the term "Puritan." For an excellent description
of the problem of understanding Puritanism in both the political and religious
world of early Stuart England, see Michael G. Finlayson, *Historians, Puritanism,
and the English Revolution: The Religious Factor in English Politics before
and after the Interregnum* (Toronto: University of Toronto Press, 1983), particularly chaps. 3 and 4. Two helpful introductory articles on the topic include Patrick
Collinson, "A Comment: Concerning the Name Puritan," *Journal of Ecclesiastical
History* 31 (1980): 483–88, and Peter Lake, "Defining Puritanism—Again?" in *Puritanism: Transatlantic Perspectives on a Seventeenth-Century Anglo-American Faith*, ed. Francis J. Bremer (Boston: Massachusetts Historical Society, 1993),
3–29.

2. I concur here with Nicholas Tyacke's definition of "Arminian." Despite the
controversy that has raged in recent years over who were the radicals and who
were defending the status quo, Tyacke's fundamental argument remains compelling. See Nicholas Tyacke, *Anti-Calvinists: The Rise of English Arminianism, c.
1590–1640* (New York: Oxford University Press, 1987), and his "Anglican Attitudes:
Some Recent Writings on English Religious History, from the Reformation to the
Civil War," *Journal of British Studies* 35, no. 2 (April 1996): 139–67, in which he
energetically responds to his critics. The most important of those include Julian
Davies, *The Caroline Captivity of the Church: Charles I and the Remoulding of
Anglicanism, 1625–1641* (Oxford: Clarendon Press, 1992); Peter White, *Predestination, Policy and Polemic: Conflict and Consensus in the English Church
from the Reformation to the Civil War* (Cambridge: Cambridge University Press,

1992), and Anthony Milton, *Catholic and Reformed: The Roman and Protestant Churches in English Protestant Thought, 1600-1640* (Cambridge: Cambridge University Press, 1995).

3. For an excellent recent discussion stressing the stereotype of the "grotesque" Puritan, see Kristen Poole, *Radical Religion from Shakespeare to Milton: Figures of Nonconformity in Early Modern England* (Cambridge: Cambridge University Press, 2000).

4. See Lori Anne Ferrell, *Government by Polemic: James I, the King's Preachers, and the Rhetorics of Conformity, 1603-1625* (Stanford, Calif.: Stanford University Press, 1998), 9. For additional insights into how significant words were to Puritans, see Peter Lake and David Como, "'Orthodoxy and Its Discontents': Dispute Settlement and the Production of 'Consensus' in the London (Puritan) Underground," *Journal of British Studies* 39 (January 2000): 34–70, particularly the introductory paragraph.

5. *Dictionary of National Biography*, hereafter *DNB*, s.v. "William Laud." Throughout this paper I have kept dates old style, but with the year beginning on 1 January.

6. William Laud, *The Works of the Most Reverend Father in God, William Laud, Sometime Lord Archbishop of Canterbury* (Oxford, 1847), 3:155–56. William Prynne also quotes this excerpt, seeing it as evidence of Laud's desire "that so the Arminian might be imbraced, as Orthodox." See his *Canterburies Doome* (London, 1646), 156.

7. Laud, *Works*, 3:159. While Laud does not actually say what the letters stood for, William Prynne asserts that they meant "Orthodox" and "Puritan" in his *A Breviate of the Life of William Laud* (London, 1644). I have found no historian who disagrees with that interpretation, including Laud's biographers, and perhaps most important his chaplain Peter Heylyn, who makes no argument about the point in his biography and defense of Laud, *Cyprianus Anglicus* (London, 1668). Prynne also asserted that the list had been put into use; he named Montagu and others as examples of "unorthodox Clergymen" who received positions, while "all Puritans as they termed them" were "kept from preferment" (*Canterburies Doome*, 367).

8. Numerous historians place Laud in the Arminian camp, including H. R. Trevor-Roper, *Archbishop Laud, 1573-1645* (Hamden, Conn.: Archon Books, 1962), and his "Laudianism and Political Power," in *Catholics, Anglicans and Puritans: Seventeenth-Century Essays* (Chicago: University of Chicago Press, 1988), 40–119. Tyacke certainly concurs in *Anti-Calvinists* (see appendix 2, 266–70, for documentation). See also Tyacke's "Archbishop Laud," in *The Early Stuart Church, 1603-1642*, ed. Kenneth Fincham (London: Macmillan, 1993), 51–70.

9. Prynne, *Canterburies Doome*, 368–69. When Charles issued the revised document as instructions for Archbishop Abbott to send to all the bishops, this clause had disappeared (*Canterburies Doome*, 370–71). Laud, however, had certainly thought it important.

10. In November 1629 John Donne used the term in a sermon preached at Paul's Cross, a sermon that Laud would have approved in his role as Bishop of London at that time; Tyacke, *Anti-Calvinists*, 182. I should note that I have not attempted to include all the instances in which Laudians used "Puritan" or some derivative; rather, I have selected some examples that appear to be typical for the Laudians. I have tried to include most of Laud's own uses of the term since his actions and the words accompanying them are so crucial to our understanding of the period.

11. Montagu's correspondence with Cosin is found in printed form in *The Corre-*

spondence of John Cosin, D.D., The Publications of the Surtees Society, vol. 52 (London, 1869), primarily 9–138 and spanning 1621 to 1627. This particular reference is in part 1 of that correspondence, 22.

12. Cosin, *Correspondence*, 21.

13. Ibid., 69.

14. Ibid., 72.

15. Ibid., 86.

16. Ibid., 93.

17. For this and additional context on the parliamentary ramifications of the religious debate in the 1620s, see Conrad Russell, *Parliaments and English Politics, 1621–1629* (Oxford: Clarendon Press, 1979), 231–33 for the 1625 Parliament, and 298 for the 1626 Parliament. While I do not always agree with Russell's conclusions, his work is essential for those studying politics and religion in the 1620s. For a fuller discussion of Montagu's stormy interactions with the Parliaments of the 1620s, see Tyacke, *Anti-Calvinists*, chap. 6.

18. *Proceedings in Parliament 1626,* Vol. 3: *House of Commons*, ed. William B. Bidwell and Maija Jansson (New Haven: Yale University Press, 1992), 7. The footnotes there also offer some examples of Montagu's uses of "Puritan" in his *Appello Caesarem: A just appeale from two unjust informers* (1625). They are quite similar to those in his letters to Cosin. For the rest of that day's activities concerning Montagu in the House of Commons, see *Proceedings*, 7–11. Montagu was never prosecuted by the House, though another investigation of him did occur in the 1628–29 Parliament; see the *DNB* entry on him for additional background information.

19. Cosin, *Correspondence*, 100, 98. "Puritan faction" was a popular phrase with the Laudians. Another Laudian, Peter Heylyn, uses both "Puritan faction" and "Puritan party" in *Cyprianus Anglicus*, e.g., 129, 209, 261, 356, and 406.

20. Ibid., 96. "Plunges" means "straits" or "difficulties," according to the footnote in the Cosin collection, which cites a 1629 usage by Laud in his diary as an illustrative example.

21. Ibid., 75.

22. Ibid., 123.

23. Ibid., 137, 139. Laud's interaction with Prynne and Burton (and John Bastwick) in the 1630s, when he was Archbishop of Canterbury, is justly famous. It is treated below.

24. Tyacke effectively makes the case for Montagu's use of "Puritan" as a theological cudgel; see *Anti-Calvinists*, 140–41.

25. As quoted in Prynne, *Canterburies Doome*, 167.

26. Laud, *Works*, 3:217. Prynne sets forth a much stronger picture of Laud's actions in this case, citing witnesses who testified that Laud had said of the feoffees "that they were the bane of the Church . . . I was the man that did set myself against them and I thank God I have destroyed this work." Prynne asserts that Laud "uttered these words in a vaunting manner" while "clapping his hand upon his breast" just prior to the "I thank God" line. *Canterburies Doome*, 388. See Prynne's background material and explanation of Laud's role in doing away with the feoffees, 385–88.

27. Prynne, *Canterburies Doome*, 88. The phrase "schismaticall Puritan" was not unique to Laud; Samuel Clerke also used it when writing to Sir John Lambe about parishioners who were resisting the Laudian ceremonial innovations in Northampton in 1638; see *Canterburies Doome*, 92–93.

28. Laud, *Works*, 5:182.

29. Ibid., 3:230.

30. Prynne, *Canterburies Doome*, 234.

31. Laud, *Works*, 5:330, 369–70.

32. Ibid., 6:43.

33. Ibid., 6:62.

34. This citation is fascinating in light of the fact that soon after Laud became Archbishop of Canterbury, Williams, seeking Laud's favor, exchanged several letters with him. In the first he professed to "renounce" anyone who favored "Puritans or Sectaries," and later he claimed "that I never favoured, but cordially hated and abhorred all schismatics and puritans." See Laud, *Works*, 6:313 and 336, along with the other letters of those last months of 1633. Of course Williams would never have used such language if he did not already know what Laud thought of "Puritans." For additional background on the Laud-Williams dispute, see Tyacke, *Anti-Calvinists*, 209–10.

35. Trevor-Roper, *Archbishop Laud, 1573-1645*, 141–42. Tom Webster reinforces this point by noting that "Clarendon, no friend to Puritans, attributed to Laud 'a hasty, sharp way of expressing himself' "; Tom Webster, *Godly Clergy in Early Stuart England: The Caroline Puritan Movement, c. 1620-1643* (Cambridge: Cambridge University Press, 1997), 195.

36. John Yates, *Ibis ad Caesarem, or A Submissive Appearance before Caesar* (London, 1626), 40.

37. Quoted in Tyacke, *Anti-Calvinists*, 138. Henry Burton reacted to Montagu in 1626 by defending himself against the label, calling himself "conformable"; see Tyacke, *Anti-Calvinists*, 187. Tyacke also recounts evidence of others who rejected Montagu's Puritan label for them, asserting their loyalty to the Church of England; see 155–56.

38. Cosin, *Correspondence*, 156.

39. Ibid., 162.

40. Ibid., 172. For additional background on the controversy between Smart and the Arminian prebendaries of Durham Cathedral, see Tyacke, *Anti-Calvinists*, 116–19.

41. Cosin, *Correspondence*, 189.

42. *Proceedings of the Short Parliament of 1640*, ed. Esther Cope and Willson H. Coates (London: Royal Historical Society, 1977), 146–47.

43. Ibid., 233–34, 253.

44. William Prynne, *Lord Bishops None of the Lord's Bishops* (London, 1640).

45. Tyacke, *Anti-Calvinists*, 226.

46. Prynne, *Lord Bishops*, n.p. Tyacke asserts in *Anti-Calvinists* that Prynne did not advocate the elimination of episcopacy until 1641 (see previous note), but he came very close to it in this little pamphlet.

47. Prynne, *A Breviate*, 34.

48. John Bastwick, *The Confession* (London, 1641), 3.

49. Benjamin Rudyerd, *The Speeches* (London, 1641), 3.

50. Edward Dering, *Four Speeches Made by Sir Edward Dering in the High Court of Parliament* (London, 1641), 3–4.

51. For a comprehensive analysis of Parker, see Michael Mendle, *Henry Parker and the English Civil War* (Cambridge: Cambridge University Press, 1995); chapter 3 examines *A Discourse Concerning Puritans*.

52. Ibid., 41–42; Parker is responding here, and in much of his treatise, to a 1638 speech delivered by Bishop Henry Leslie during a visitation of Downe and Connor. In this address Leslie referred to "the present rebellion of the Puritans" as the key

to the uproar in Scotland. While he did not use "Puritan" again in the speech, he strongly attacked the ideas and practices of the Scots, whom he had already associated with "Puritans." See Henry Leslie, *A Full Confutation of the Covenant Lately Sworne and Subscribed by Many in Scotland; Delivered in a Speech at the Visitation of Downe and Conner* (London, 1639). Parker, as his response indicates, was outraged by this speech and the policies it represented.

53. Ibid., 57.

54. Stephen Foster forcefully argues this point in *Notes from the Caroline Underground: Alexander Leighton, the Puritan Triumvirate, and the Laudian Reaction to Nonconformity* (Hamden, Conn: Archon Books, 1978).

55. For a recent fuller examination of this dynamic, see Darren Oldridge, *Religion and Society in Early Stuart England* (Aldershot: Ashgate, 1998), particularly chapters 3 and 4. I concur with Oldridge's view that while divisions already existed in the Church of England prior to 1625, Laud's policies provoked significant fear among those he labeled as "Puritans" and enemies. As this essay argues, the inflammatory use of "Puritan" coupled with these policies produced the strong reaction that became part of the chaotic 1640s and its civil wars.

Of Philistines and Puritans:
Matthew Arnold's Construction of Puritanism

John Netland

> To be either a Puritan, a prig or a preacher is a bad thing. To be
> all three at once reminds one of the worst excesses of the
> French Revolution.
>
> —Oscar Wilde

AN EARLY SCENE IN GEORGE ELIOT'S NOVEL FELIX HOLT EXPOSES A PECULIAR
Victorian anxiety. In the course of her conversation with the Baptist
minister, Rev. Lyon, Mrs. Holt apologizes for her son's lack of deco-
rum: " 'he said you was a fine old fellow, and an old-fashioned Puritan—he uses dreadful language, Mr. Lyon; but I saw he didn't mean
you ill, for all that.' "[1] That Mrs. Holt should feel such consternation
over the epithet "Puritan" is curious, given that by the 1860s, when
Felix Holt was written, the Whig-Liberal coalition was regularly
"playing the Puritan card" on behalf of the political reforms that
would welcome Puritan progeny such as the Rev. Lyon and Felix
Holt into fuller participation in British society.[2] Mrs. Holt's apology
for her son's "dreadful" utterance of "Puritan" suggests that while
the Victorians might well have vindicated the parliamentarian
cause, "Puritan" remained an ambiguous linguistic sign. One might
admire the Puritans of old; one might invoke the name of Puritanism on behalf of political reforms; one might even confess to being
a descendant (either genealogical or ideological) of Puritans. Nevertheless, few self-respecting Victorians actually claimed to *be* Puritans, for the epithet appears to have retained the stigma it had
generated since it was first used derisively against "hot Protestants" in the sixteenth and seventeenth centuries.[3]

That the accusation of Puritanism could shame Victorians during
the 1860s and 1870s is ironic, for it is commonly accepted that nineteenth-century historiography had rehabilitated the hitherto disrep-
utable Puritans.[4] Eighteenth-century historians such as David
Hume had denounced the "Puritan" Interregnum as a threat to the

constitutional balance between monarch and Parliament,[5] while Edmund Burke had warned of dangerous parallels between Puritan extremism and Jacobin excess, seeing in both ideologies a penchant toward rebellion and regicide.[6] In less than a century, however, the Puritan cause had been largely vindicated. From the Romantic recovery of John Milton[7] and John Bunyan[8] to Thomas Carlyle's midcentury tribute to Oliver Cromwell,[9] the spirit of Romantic historiography found courage and principle in what the Augustan historians had dismissed as fanaticism. Furthermore, the changing demographics of Victorian society demonstrated that the dissenting heirs of the Puritans had become a political force to be reckoned with.[10] Whether as cause or effect of the Puritan reclamation, mid-century Victorian politics were shaped by increasingly favorable assessments of the parliamentarian cause. Popular historians such as Thomas Macaulay appealed to Puritan nonconformity to justify nineteenth-century liberalism and its disestablishment politics,[11] while Samuel Gardiner's magisterial history of England would by century's end sanction Puritanism not only as the political harbinger of liberal democracy, but also as "a great moral force."[12]

Raphael Samuel suggests that along with the political and social reclamation of the Puritan cause, the word itself underwent "a vast metaphorical inflation. . . . It reentered the field of religious and political controversy, providing a newly-awakened and increasingly militant nonconformity both with a symbolic inheritance and a source of borrowed prestige."[13] My contention is that the cultural signification of "Puritan" in Victorian England was considerably more complex and double-sided than Samuel's phrase suggests. Its frequent invocation in the cultural criticism of Matthew Arnold suggests that as much as the term signified the accumulated moral capital of a newly valorized past, it also continued to bear a social stigma.

One could argue that the honorific signification of "Puritan" was inversely proportionate to the proximity of its referent. For instance, we see an historical admiration for Puritanism in Charles Kingsley's reflections on his ancestors. He honors his Puritan forebears for their fortitude but quickly dissociates himself from too close an identification with their beliefs: "My forefathers were Independents, and fought by Cromwell's side at Naseby and Marston Moor; and what is more, lost broad acres for their Puritanism. The younger brother of an ancestor of mine was one of the original Pilgrim Fathers, so I am full of old Puritan blood, though I have utterly—indeed, our family have for generations—thrown off their Calvinism: yet I glory in the morale, the God-fearing valour and earnestness of the old heroes, and trust I should have believed with them had I lived in their day, for want of any better belief. But it will not do now, as you have found already. The bed is too short and the cloak too narrow."[14] A similar distanced respect permeates Leslie Stephen's history of *English Thought in the Eighteenth Century*, which bestows more favor on the "old Protestantism" than on what he calls the "new Puritanism" of his own day.[15] Stephen's rhetorical precision is revealing. He never refers to the historical Puritans by that name, instead speaking in vaguely honorific terms of the "old Protestantism." It is Victorian nonconformity that he dismissively characterizes as the "new Puritanism."

The Victorian construction of the "Puritan" thus created an equivocal term, both an emblem of national pride and a mark of shame. This double referentiality helps to explain the frequency with which Arnold invoked the dread specter of the "Puritan" in his ongoing polemic against middle-class culture. Arnold was convinced that the enduring legacy of the Puritan cause had less to do with advancing political freedom than with hastening cultural decline. Hence, the economic and political strength of Puritanism's latter-day heirs made them, in his view, a significant threat to British culture and an adversary to contend with. Ironically, his best rhetorical weapon against a seemingly triumphant Puritanism was the term itself, an epithet that functioned as both accusation and evidence of cultural transgression.

It is in *Culture and Anarchy* (1869) and *St. Paul and Protestantism* (1870) that we find Arnold's most sustained use of "Puritan" and its twin epithet, "Philistine." Arnold's Puritan construct resurrects some of the familiar stereotypes of intellectual narrowness, Calvinistic mean-spiritedness, and unctuous religiosity that date back to the first uses of the term, but he departs from the traditional Puritan caricatures in one important respect. Through Arnold's pen, the Puritan becomes what its historical antecedents had often claimed but were seldom acknowledged to be: the representative type of the Reformation. Thus, Arnold's playful Puritan-baiting rhetoric allowed him to transfer the stigma still latent in the term onto a much broader cross-section of Victorian Protestant Christians, a strategy that reveals a serious theological agenda: to reconstruct a post-theological Church of England.

Arnold's complex and paradoxical vision of a redefined Church of England was shaped by a set of competing religious influences. His ecclesiastical ideal reflected both an antiquarian nostalgia for a pre-Reformation church establishment and a progressive adherence to the demythologizing creed of the higher critical hermeneutic. If the former might seem to place him among the High Church Tractarians, the latter would situate him within the latitudinarian wing of the Broad Church. These two factions, as demonstrated by his father's notorious opposition to the Tractarians, would seem to be incompatible with each other, but the Puritan foil demonstrates how Matthew Arnold could synthesize the Tractarian and Broad Church influences of his religious upbringing on behalf of a radically redefined Church of England.

It is to the early Tractarian Movement that we must turn to uncover the biographical origins of Matthew Arnold's distaste for Puritans. Galvanized by the Rev. John Keble's 1833 Assize Sermon, the Tractarians protested against the declining authority of the nineteenth-century church. They decried Parliament's jurisdiction over diocesan affairs; they affirmed the liturgical use of vestments, ritual, and high ceremony; they argued for a high view of the sacraments, and some advocated a restoration of the sacraments abandoned during the Reformation; they asserted church authority and claimed apostolic succession as the basis of that authority; and they appealed to church tradition—especially the Elizabethan and Stuart churches—in their understanding of the Thirty-nine Articles. Although the immediate objects of their disaffection were the evangelicals and latitudinarians, their high Anglo-Catholicism implied an animus against the Reformation itself, of which they saw Puritanism as the purest expression. Hence, they decried the historical Puritans as the nemeses of true religion, as despoilers of beauty, and as unprincipled regicides.

Matthew Arnold did not follow the Tractarians on their sacramental pilgrimage toward Rome, nor did he share the virulent dislike of his father, Thomas Arnold, for these Oxford reformers. Still, Matthew did learn two important lessons from his father's scathing attack on the "Oxford Malignants": he inherited not only his father's rhetorical gamesmanship, but also his belief in a strong national church. Offended by the Tractarian opposition to the appointment of Dr. Hampden to the Regius Professorship of Divinity at Oxford, the elder Arnold had vilified the Tractarians as "formalist Judaizing fanatics . . . who have ever been the peculiar disgrace of the Church of England."[16] He dismissed their scruples as "the fanaticism of mere foolery. A dress, a ritual, a name, a ceremony;—a technical phraseology;—the superstition of a priesthood, without its power;—the form of Episcopal government, without the substance." Interestingly, he contrasted this sacerdotal fanaticism with Puritans, who could at least claim the slight merit of being "fanatics for freedom, and for what they deemed the due authority of God's own word."[17] But if Puritan fanaticism was mitigated by its noble principles—"entire freedom towards man, and entire devotion towards God"—it remained a dangerous form of extremism that Thomas Arnold would no more tolerate than he would the Tractarian precisionists.[18] The reason lay, ironically, in what Arnold shared with his High Church adversaries: a belief in a strong national church, an issue on which they were reluctant allies against Puritan and dissenting nonconformity.[19] Although this ecclesiastical ideal would eventually succumb to the disestablishment politics of Whig liberalism, it would decisively shape Matthew Arnold's ecclesiastical sympathies.

The godson of Tractarianism's purported initiator (Keble) and the son of its most strident critic, Matthew Arnold matriculated at Oxford University in 1841, just when tensions were reaching their peak. In 1841, John Henry Newman's infamous *Tract Ninety* had outraged his opponents with the claim that the Thirty-nine Articles should be interpreted " 'not according to the meaning of the writers, but . . . according to the sense of the Catholic Church.' "[20] In the inflamed atmosphere of Balliol College, one could hardly avoid the ecclesiastical factionalism. The topic of the Newdigate Prize competition of 1843, for instance, was deliberately chosen to check Tractarian influence. Park Honan explains that "Professor Garbett, who perhaps won election to Oxford's poetry chair for the 'purpose of excluding a follower of Newman and Pusey,' had selected Oliver Cromwell as Newdigate Prize topic—thus aiming a timely blow at Oxford's Puseyite cult of King Charles the Martyr."[21] Although a few years before both Macauley's and Carlyle's historical rehabilitation of the Lord Protector, the topic was certainly intended to elicit sympathetic treatments of the Puritan leader. Matthew Arnold's prize-winning poem, however, was hardly the polemic that Garbett had intended, for it generated sympathy for Cromwell less as the historical leader of the Puritan movement than as a generic protagonist of a contemporary bildungsroman. The historical references to Cromwell's life are perfunctory and hardly anti-Tractarian. Honan describes "Cromwell's enemies [as] utterly benign and forlorn, particularly the 'friendless' King Charles who awaits decapitation."[22] The poem offers little support to the Puritan cause, except in the most unobjectionable affirmations of individual liberty.

Arnold's refusal to join in the Whig reclamation of Cromwell as Puritan not only demonstrates his aversion to factionalism and to theological controversy, but it also suggests that he had absorbed a cultural and ecclesiastical ethos from Newman and Oxford. Honan observes that "there isn't a leading conception of Matthew Arnold's about culture, the nature of criticism, philistinism and liberalism, or the relation between poetry and religion that fails to reveal a Newmanic tincture."[23] J. Dover Wilson attributes this ethos more generally to "the spirit of the Oxford Movement . . . [and to] the traditions and beauty of the city itself, 'spreading her gardens to the moonlight and whispering from her towers the last enchantments of the middle ages.'"[24] In addition to this religious aesthetic, Arnold also absorbed from Newman a critical view of Liberalism as subversive to the enduring virtues of culture.

But Arnold was hardly the typical High Church Anglo-Catholic Newman devotee, for he had been raised on far more malleable theological fare than Newman's Catholic orthodoxy. He was, in his own words, "a Liberal," albeit one "tempered by experience, reflection, and renouncement, and . . . above all, a believer in culture."[25] Arnold's Liberalism was primarily theological rather than political. He inhabited what Hans Frei has called a postcritical theological milieu,[26] rendered evocatively in "Stanzas from the Grande Chartreuse" in the image of one "wandering between two worlds, one dead and the other powerless to be born."[27] For Arnold, the old world of Christian orthodoxy had died under the scrutiny of modern scientific analysis. "Rigorous teachers," he wrote,

> seized my youth,
> And purged its faith, and trimmed its fire,
> Showed me the high, white star of Truth,
> There bade me gaze, and there aspire.
> ("Stanzas from the Grande Chartreuse," ll. 67–70)

Ruth apRoberts has documented Arnold's firsthand familiarity with the historical-critical study of the Bible, which to him undermined traditional understandings of the Bible and hence of Christian belief itself.[28] Yet Arnold did not abandon religion entirely in the face of the new biblical criticism. Indeed, he was severely critical of biblical scholars whose work undermined the foundations of faith and offered nothing to replace the loss.[29] For Arnold, religion could not be dismissed that easily, but it needed to be reconstructed. Bernard Reardon summarizes Arnold's dilemma: "Supernatural Christianity, he was convinced, would have to be discarded. . . . In his own essays on religious philosophy . . . he set out to present the public with a revised Christianity from which the incredible and the irrelevant, supernatural miracles and abstruse dogma, had been pruned away; a Christianity preserving the essential values but acceptable to the modern mind, impatient as that now was both of miraculous portents and of metaphysical puzzles."[30] Unwilling to grant the referential reality of historical Christian theology, Arnold sought to reconstruct Christian faith almost exclusively as a project of ethical and cultural formation.

Arnold's critique of Puritanism emerged in his cultural criticism of the 1860s and 1870s. Both *Culture and Anarchy* (1869) and *St. Paul and Protestantism* (1870) berated middle-class culture, which Arnold defined as the legacy of Puritanism. What started out primarily as a cultural endeavor soon evolved into an ecclesiastical and theological mission as well. In calling for a transformation of British society, Arnold advocated a theologically inclusive though culturally prescriptive church that would shape the cultural and spiritual ethos of the nation.[31]

Arnold's mission of cultural formation shifted profoundly following the 1866 Hyde Park riots, which he watched directly from his apartment balcony.[32] Already a well-respected literary critic who sought to cultivate *"the disinterested endeavour to learn and propagate the best that is known and thought in the world,"* Arnold saw that his cultural mission needed to be taken out of the esoteric confines of literary criticism and disseminated throughout a middle-class society, which he believed to be culturally bankrupt.[33] Although it was not the middle classes who inspired the rioting mobs, he believed that such anarchy was inevitable in a society that glorified individualism and economic self-interest.

Arnold was equally offended by what he saw as the individualism, vulgarity, intellectual myopia, and separatism within nonconformity. He identified the center of the dissenting impulse as the principle of "Doing as one Pleases," and he lamented its permutations into laissez-faire economics, politics, and popular culture. Like Newman, Arnold attributed this dissenting individualism to the spirit of Liberalism. Its expressions included "the Reform Bill of 1832, and local self-government, in politics; in the social sphere, free-trade, unrestricted competition, and the making of large industrial fortunes; in the religious sphere, the Dissidence of Dissent and the Protestantism of the Protestant religion."[34] For Arnold, the problem with a do-it-yourself culture was that self-determination alone could not provide sufficient safeguards against the anarchy he saw in the Hyde Park riots. A transcendent cultural ideal was needed to raise humanity above self-interest, to keep one from catering to the baser instincts of humanity.

Arnold understood culture to represent the best that had been thought and said in the world, and this excellence he characterized as a synthesis of moral, aesthetic, and intellectual virtues. The latter two he referred to by the phrase "sweetness and light," and it was primarily to classical Greece that he turned for this sweetness and light. Complementing Hellenism in the formation of culture was Hebraism, that is, the strict moral conscience given supreme expression in the Judeo-Christian Scriptures. Believing that culture needed both the aesthetic—intellectual and the moral to flourish, Arnold nevertheless felt that English society had since the Reformation overcompensated on its Hebraism and desperately needed the corrective graces of the sweetness and light that emanated from Hellenism. Hebraism, which he associated with the Reformation in general and with Puritans in particular, he saw as a surrender of intellectual and aesthetic liberality to the strictures of moral discipline. The result was an undue narrowness of mind that made even the moral virtues of Hebraism intolerable. Arnold claimed that "Puritans, ancient and modern, have not enough added to their care for walking staunchly by the best light they have, a care that that light be not darkness; [rather,] they have developed one side of their humanity at the expense of all others, and have become incomplete and mutilated men in consequence."[35]

Arnold's case against these offending middle classes was hardly novel, for he invoked a long-standing cultural tension between the pragmatic John Bull and the cultural brokers of British civilization. Arnold renewed this cultural antagonism by resurrecting one pejorative epithet (Puritan) and coining another (Philistine), applying them with equal relish to nineteenth-century dissent.[36] Not only do these two complementary terms unite the economic and social opprobrium implicit in "Philistine" with the theological and cultural disdain signified by "Puritan," they also parody the biblicism of dissent. After all, the reproach of "Philistine" can sting only one who is familiar with the Old Testament narratives that make Philistine virtually synonymous with antagonism toward God's chosen people.

Arnold's nineteenth-century Philistines are characterized by a single-minded obsession with economic well-being: "The people who believe most that our greatness and welfare are proved by our being very rich, and who most give their lives and thoughts to becoming rich, are just the very people whom we call Philistines."[37] Lest his biblically literate audience fail to appreciate the reproach implied by "Philistine," Arnold kindly elucidates his meaning: "For *Philistine* gives the notion of something particularly stiff-necked and perverse in the resistance to light and its children; and therein it specially suits our middle class, who not only do not pursue sweetness and light, but who even prefer to them that sort of machinery of business, chapels, tea meetings, and addresses from Mr.

Murphy and the Rev. W. Cattle, which makes up the dismal and illiberal life on which I have so often touched."[38] Valentine Cunningham notes that this reference to tea-meetings often served as a dismissive cultural shorthand for dissent: "A sort of diluted version of the Methodist Love-Feast, [tea meetings] came to characterize Dissent in [the age]: 'tea and experience,' the Dissenting formula. The grocers had tea before attending Sunday evening chapel, while smarter Anglicans stayed at home for dinner. Wine was superior, tea merely vulgar. How otherwise should Arnold sneer at a 'life . . . [of] tea meetings'?"[39]

Arnold's readers certainly recognized the class condescension. The Rev. Henry Allon, a Congregationalist minister writing in the *British Quarterly Review*, responded to Arnold with acerbic politeness, questioning his tendency "to reprobate as Philistinism all forms of intellectual life that have not upon them the mint-mark of the national universities."[40] And in a pointed jab at the Oxford-educated gentleman who was offended by dissenting vulgarity, Allon reminded Arnold that few nonconformist ministers were "younger sons of noble or wealthy houses; nor, whatever their comparative scholarship, have many of them received that last exquisite touch of gentlemanliness which is supposed to distinguish Oxford and Cambridge."[41]

Others likewise pointed out the unfairness whereby the church establishment not only excluded nonconformity from its cultural institutions but then proceeded to abuse this subculture for its vulgarity. Robert Vaughan lamented the social rancor inspired by the Established Church: "Our social relations are everywhere embittered by the airs which are thus assumed in the one quarter, and the resentments manifested in the other. . . . The language in which our clergy and their admirers indulge toward nonconformists is often the most offensive that can be imagined. We know that there are exceptions to this rule; but we know what the rule is, and we know what the effect of it is."[42] Even a High Churchman such as the Dean of St. Paul's, the Rev. R. W. Church, found Arnold's rhetoric distasteful. He noted that Arnold had frequently been criticized for "amusing himself with his own ingenuity and caprices of taste and prepossession." He understood why readers took exception to Arnold's terminology and why they might "resent being ticketed as Barbarians or Philistines by the preacher of culture."[43]

Beyond the vulgarity of Philistinism, Arnold disliked the singularity of dissent, calling the nonconformist one "who has worshipped his fetish of separatism so long that he is likely to wish still to remain, like Ephraim, 'a wild ass alone by himself.'"[44] The slogan adorning the masthead of the *Nonconformist* particularly drew his scorn: " 'The Dissidence of Dissent and the Protestantism of the Protestant religion.' There is sweetness and light, and an ideal of complete harmonious human perfection!"[45] As his dismissive tone reveals, Arnold saw dissent as a negative impulse and this slogan as an endorsement of willful perversity. Of course, Arnold was hardly alone in characterizing nonconformity in such terms, but his stigmatizing of dissenters for the separation that most of them believed to have been forced on their ancestors rankled many of his readers.[46]

In *Culture and Anarchy* Arnold excoriated "Philistine" dissenting classes for reducing human culture to economic well-being and for creating a virtue out of obstinacy. In the three ecclesiastical essays that comprise *St. Paul and Protestantism*, Arnold turned to a theological critique of dissent, this time resurrecting the Puritan as his foil. These essays reveal an ambitious agenda, nothing less than a reconstruction of the Church of England on a nontheological foundation. To accomplish this feat, Arnold resorted to some loose theological and historical revisionism, constructing an ahistorical, anachronistic Puritanism. The first, and title, essay purported to rescue St. Paul from his Puritan interpreters. The second, "Puritanism and the Church of England," sought to welcome dissenters back into the church by demonstrating that the Anglican Church never did insist upon doctrinal precision and could therefore accommodate Puritan dissenters and latitudinarians alike.[47] Both of these essays gain their polemic force as much from the invective power of the term "Puritan" as from their theological argumentation.

In a letter to his mother, Arnold described his pleasure at having confounded the Puritans and demonstrated that their confident reading of Pauline theology was "baseless, made them narrow and intolerant, and prevented all progress."[48] In an expansive definition that might have surprised the Elizabethan and Stuart critics of Puritanism, Arnold claimed that the heart of Puritanism lay in the concepts of "original sin, free election, effectual calling, justification through imputed righteousness."[49] This list suggested that it was not just the obvious points of Calvinistic contention (such as total depravity or election) that defined Puritan theology; it was the entire panoply of redemption, of mediated justification through the sacrificial death of Jesus Christ, that Arnold attributed to Puritanism and that he claimed to be a misreading of St. Paul. Certainly, Arnold was not the only Victorian to question the forensic interpretation of the Atonement. Writing in the Broad Church *Contemporary Review*, R. H. Hutton was willing to relinquish the forensic interpretation of the Atonement, but not—as Arnold did—to dispense with the theology of redemption altogether.[50] Arnold's argument was both larger and more subversive than a debate about a particular tenet of theology, for he was calling into question theology itself. This agenda becomes clear when we consider the eclecticism of his constructed Puritan. Arnold referred to both Calvinist and Arminian Puritans, suggesting that while they put a different face on election and justification, each theological system insists that humans stand in need of Christ's imputed righteousness in order to be delivered from their sinful condition.[51] Arnold found the winsomeness of Wesleyan Arminianism more appealing than the stern logic of Calvinism, but he insisted that both infer a theological system from the Pauline epistles that was never intended. In a sense, Arnold paid Puritanism the compliment that its Elizabethan and Stuart antagonists refused to concede. He granted that Puritan theology was not only well within the mainstream of Protestant Christian theology, but also that it represented the entire Reformation. The only problem, according to Arnold, was that this theological system of redemption was not what St. Paul had in mind.

Arnold's attempt to rescue St. Paul from Puritan misreadings involves a deliberate subversion of Reformation hermeneutics and soteriology. Even beyond tweaking the Reformation slogan, *sola Scriptura*, through his oft-repeated maxim that "no man, who knows nothing else, knows even his Bible," Arnold advanced a complex rereading of Pauline discourse.[52] First he claimed that St. Paul had been misread by Christian theologians who did not understand his "Orientalizing" rhetoric and thus literalized his meanings in ways that he did not intend. Arnold defined "Orientalizing" as a type of nonreferential, figurative discourse: "the vivid and figured way in which St. Paul within the sphere of religious emotion uses words without carrying them outside it."[53] Thus, Arnold concluded that "in St. Paul's essential ideas this popular notion of a substitution, and appeasement, and imputation of alien merit, has no place. Paul knows nothing of a sacrificial atonement."[54] For Arnold, the notion of a substitutionary atonement represented a legal metaphor superimposed onto Pauline language; the real import of the crucifixion, for Arnold, was that it represented a dying to sin that the believer was to emulate in imitation of Christ. The real meaning of St. Paul was to cultivate righteousness.

But, as readers of Paul might suspect, that argument alone did not completely satisfy Arnold, for he offered a supplementary explanation as well. Sometimes Paul did make soteriological claims, but those were an unfortunate reflection of what Arnold called "Judaizing" discourse: "A Jew himself, he uses the Jewish Scriptures in a Jew's arbitrary and uncritical fashion, as if they had a talismanic character; as if for a doctrine, however true in itself, their confirmation was still necessary, and as if this confirmation was to be got from their mere words alone, however detached from the sense of their context, and however violently allegorised or otherwise wrested."[55] There is something circular to Arnold's argument: theologians have misunderstood St. Paul by literalizing his figures of speech, but when his statements are too self-evident to permit non-literal fluidity, we must conclude that St. Paul himself was blinded by his "Jewish" perspective. In effect, St. Paul must be rescued from his own zeitgeist: "To get, therefore, at what Paul really thought and meant to say, it is necessary for us modern and Western people to translate him. And not as Puritanism, which has merely taken his letter and re-set it in the formal propositions of a modern scientific treatise; but his letter itself must be recast before it can be properly conveyed by such propositions."[56] This task involves differentiating between primary and secondary themes in the Pauline epistles. Conceding that "St. Paul undoubtedly falls into" Calvinism, Arnold insisted that "this Calvinism, which with the Calvinist is primary, is with Paul secondary, or even less than secondary."[57] Arnold claimed that Pauline theology was concerned primarily with a practical religious ethic, the pursuit of righteousness, rather than with soteriology.

Having argued that the doctrines of justification and the atonement are derived from misreadings of Paul, Arnold turned his attention in his next essay to argue that a rigid adherence to such doctrines has never been required of Anglican communicants or clergy—nor ought it be. In the same letter to his mother, Arnold claimed that "the Church, though holding certain doctrines like justification in common with Puritanism, has gained by not pinning itself to those doctrines and nothing else, but by resting on Catholic antiquity, historic Christianity, development, and so on, which open to it an escape from all single doctrines as they are outgrown."[58] Arnold supported such doctrinal malleability, seeing it as proof of the church's theological diversity and tolerance and its receptiveness to historical development.[59]

Perhaps we can only speculate why Arnold created this Puritan foil for his theological project. While the Victorians had plenty to say about the historical Puritans, no other Victorians made the term "Puritan" bear as much polemical weight as did Arnold. To be sure, late Victorian wits such as Oscar Wilde or Algernon Swinburne made passing quips about their puritanical contemporaries. But none of these tangential uses of Puritan as an epithet resembled Arnold's systematic construction of a Puritan foil. In seeking to redefine Christian faith as ethical rather than doctrinal, Arnold made the objectionable doctrines bear the weight of their presumed guilt by association with Puritanism. His reasons for doing so suggest both the radical nature of his revisionist religion and the continued stigma of being called a Puritan. Although there were plenty of Broad Church as well as agnostic critics of doctrines such as redemption, Arnold's notion of a nontheological church was unlikely to command widespread assent in 1870. What made Arnold's project even more problematic than that of other Victorian critics of orthodoxy was that his theological deconstruction was accompanied by the paradoxical reconstruction of a strong national church, an institution that would retain full ecclesiastical and cultural authority while abandoning its doctrinal foundations. The relentless barrage of critical reviews of *St. Paul and Protestantism* suggests that few Victorians found that combination appealing.

This context suggests why Arnold needed to resurrect the popular stereotype of the Puritan. His narrow-minded, theologically smug, culturally myopic, anti-intellectual Puritan Philistine retains much of the satirical capital stored up in a long tradition of anti-Puritan satires, ranging from the anti-Marprelate tracts to the stage Puritan of the Elizabethan and Stuart theater and even to the caricatures of dissent in the nineteenth-century novel. Moreover, there was something of an anti-Semitic overtone to this anti-Puritan invective. Terms such as "Hebraism," "Orientalizing," and "Judaizing" not only link the Puritan with the Old Testament but also play on anti-Semitic cultural associations to marginalize the Puritan. Such stigmatizing of the Other may well have been necessary to argue a claim that most Anglican churchmen were simply not prepared to accept: that a national church could generate sweetness and light long after its theological heart stopped beating. Only by his caricaturing traditional Protestant soteriology as Puritan extremism could Arnold's own model of a national church assume the reasonable moderation of the center.

As for what Arnold's use of Puritan tells us about Victorian attitudes, it does suggest a complex cultural situation. Even though political reforms had largely vindicated the Puritan-cum-Whig agenda, Puritan discontents remained throughout Victorian society. Arnold's exploitation of the shame still associated with Puritanism coupled with the heated responses to these essays demonstrate that the social and ideological wounds inflicted during the civil wars and their aftermath festered on well into the Victorian era.

NOTES

1. George Eliot, vol. 3 of *Felix Holt, The Novels of George Eliot* (New York: Harper and Brothers, 1866), 67.

2. The phrase "playing the Puritan card" comes from Raphael Samuel's illuminating essay "The Discovery of Puritanism, 1820–1914: A Preliminary Sketch," in *Revival and Religion since 1700: Essays for John Walsh*, ed. Jane Garnett and Colin Matthew (London: Hambledon, 1993), 220.

3. See Dwight Brautigam's "Prelates and Politics: Uses of 'Puritan,' 1625–40," and Glenn Sanders's "'A plain Turkish Tyranny': Images of the Turk in Anti-Puritan Polemic" in this collection for analyses of the polemical use of the term "Puritan" in the seventeenth century.

4. I am indebted to the following studies of Victorian historiography: Rosemary Jann's *The Art and Science of Victorian History* (Columbus, Ohio: Ohio State University Press, 1985); John Kenyon's *The History Men: The Historical Profession in England since the Renaissance* (London: Weidenfeld and Nicolson, 1983); Timothy Lang's *The Victorians and the Stuart Heritage: Interpretations of a Discordant Past* (Cambridge: Cambridge University Press, 1995); and Samuel's "The Discovery of Puritanism."

5. Lang, *The Victorians and the Stuart Heritage*, 4–13.

6. Ibid., 38.

7. For the influence of *Paradise Lost* on the Romantic imagination, see Lucy Newlyn's *"Paradise Lost" and the Romantic Reader* (Oxford: Clarendon Press, 1993). Milton's relationship to Puritanism is, of course, problematic, and many scholars are reluctant to call Milton a Puritan. Whether the association was an act of historical recovery or a constructed identity, Raphael Samuel points out that "it was the nineteenth century which turned Milton back into a Puritan" ("The Discovery of Puritanism," 204).

8. Both Robert Southey and Samuel Taylor Coleridge wrote sympathetic accounts of Bunyan. Southey published *The Pilgrim's Progress, with a Life of John Bunyan* in 1830 (London: John Murray), while Coleridge's marginal notes on Southey's *Bunyan* were published for an early Victorian audience in his posthumous *Literary Remains*, ed. H. N. Coleridge (London: William Pickering, 1838).

9. Oliver Cromwell, *Letters and Speeches of Oliver Cromwell, with Elucidations by Thomas Carlyle*. Ed. S. C. Lomas. 3 vols. (London: Methuen and Co., 1904); Thomas Carlyle, *On Heroes and Hero-Worship* (1841; reprint, London: Chapman and Hall, 1897).

10. For a useful genealogy of the transformation of seventeenth-century nonconformist Puritans into the varieties of nineteenth-century dissent, see John Spurr, "From Puritanism to Dissent, 1660–1700," in *The Culture of English Puritanism, 1560–1700*, ed. Christopher Durston and Jacqueline Eales (Basingstoke: Macmillan, 1996), 234–65.

11. Thomas Macaulay, *The History of England from the Accession of James II*, 5 vols. (London: Longman, Brown, Green, and Longmans, 1849–61).

12. Lang, *The Victorians and the Stuart Heritage*, 20.

13. Samuel, "The Discovery of Puritanism," 206.

14. Charles Kingsley, *Charles Kingsley: His Letters and Memories of His Life*, ed. [F. Kingsley] (London: Macmillan, 1894) 2:52. My thanks to J. M. I. Klaver for alerting me to this excerpt via the Victorian listserv discussion group.

15. Leslie Stephens, *English Thought of the Eighteenth Century*, 3d ed. (New York: Peter Smith, 1949), 2:433.

16. Thomas Arnold, "The Oxford Malignants and Dr. Hampden," *Edinburgh Review* 63 (April 1836): 235.

17. Ibid.

18. Ibid.

19. Although Thomas Arnold and the Tractarian reformers shared a belief in a strong established church, they differed significantly in their understanding of the relationship between church and state. Arnold's Erastianism assumed the consonance of church and state; it was precisely against such diminishment of ecclesiastical power to statecraft that Keble's Assize Sermon was directed.

20. John Henry Newman to Mr. Bowden, 15 March 1841, quoted in Newman, *Apologia Pro Vita Sua*, ed. David J. DeLaura (1865; reprint, New York: Norton, 1968), 113.

21. Park Honan, *Matthew Arnold: A Life* (Cambridge: Harvard University Press, 1983), 69.

22. Ibid.

23. Ibid., 61.

24. J. Dover Wilson, introduction to *Culture and Anarchy*, by Matthew Arnold, ed. J. Dover Wilson (Cambridge: Cambridge University Press, 1969), xiii.

25. Arnold, *Culture and Anarchy*, 41.

26. Hans Frei, *The Eclipse of Biblical Narrative: A Study in Eighteenth and Nineteenth Century Hermeneutics* (New Haven: Yale University Press, 1974).

27. Matthew Arnold, *The Poetry and Criticism of Matthew Arnold*, ed. A. Dwight Culler (Boston: Houghton Mifflin, 1961), ll. 84–85.

28. Ruth apRoberts, *Arnold and God* (Berkeley and Los Angeles: University of California Press, 1983), 22–79.

29. Arnold, "The Bishop and the Philosopher," in *Lectures and Essays in Criticism*, vol. 3 of *The Complete Prose Works of Matthew Arnold*, ed. R. H. Super (Ann Arbor, Mich.: University of Michigan Press, 1962), 40–55; *God and the Bible*, vol. 8 of *The Complete Prose Works of Matthew Arnold*, ed. R. H. Super (Ann Arbor, Mich.: University of Michigan Press, 1970), 147.

30. Bernard M. G. Reardon, *Religious Thought in the Victorian Age: A Survey from Coleridge to Gore* (1971; reprint, London: Longman, 1980), 383.

31. This notion of the cultural mission of an established church owes something to Samuel Taylor Coleridge's idea of a "clerisy." See Ben Knights, *The Idea of the Clerisy in the Nineteenth Century* (London: Cambridge University Press, 1978), as well as apRoberts, *Arnold and God*, 80–103.

32. Honan, *Matthew Arnold*, 341.

33. Matthew Arnold, "The Function of Criticism at the Present Time," *National Review* (November, 1864); reprinted in *Poetry and Criticism of Matthew Arnold*, 257.

34. Arnold, *Culture and Anarchy*, 62.

35. Ibid., 11.

36. Long before Arnold coined the term, as Donald Davie notes, the established church had "disseminated the *canard* that Dissent is of its nature philistine." Davie adds wryly that nineteenth-century dissent "cooperated by becoming as philistine as the church had always said it was. In this, English dissent betrayed its own tradition" (*A Gathered Church: The Literature of the English Dissenting Interest, 1700-1930* [New York: Oxford University Press, 1978], 56–57).

37. Arnold, *Culture and Anarchy*, 52.

38. Ibid., 101–2.

39. Valentine Cunningham, *Everywhere Spoken Against: Dissent in the Victorian Novel* (Oxford: Clarendon, 1975), 13.

40. [Henry Allon], unsigned review of "St. Paul and Protestantism," *British Quarterly Review* 52 (July 1870): 170–99; reprinted in *Matthew Arnold, Prose Writings: The Critical Heritage*, ed. Carl Dawson and John Pfordresher (London: Routledge and Kegan Paul, 1979), 262. The *Wellesley Index* identifies the author as the Rev. Henry Allon.

41. Ibid., 265.

42. Robert Vaughan, "The Act of Uniformity: Its Antecedents and Effects," *British Quarterly Review* 35 (April 1862): 320–23.

43. R. W. Church, "The Church and Nonconformity," *Quarterly Review* 103 (April 1871): 423–61; reprinted in *Matthew Arnold, Prose Writings*, 274.

44. Arnold, *Culture and Anarchy*, 34.

45. Ibid., 56.

46. For example, R. W. Dale reminded Arnold that as a result of the 1662 Act of Uniformity, "the 'Two Thousand' did not secede from the National Establishment; they were 'ejected' from it," in "Mr. Arnold and the Nonconformists," *The Contemporary Review* 14 (July 1879): 543.

47. Arnold was not alone in his gracious invitation to the dissenters. In the Bampton Lectures of 1871, George Herbert Curteis did the same, graciously extending the hand of tolerance, which simultaneously insists that the dissenter abandon his deepest convictions. Curteis, *Dissent, in its Relation to the Church of England*, the 1871 Bampton Lectures (London and New York: Macmillan, 1872).

48. Matthew Arnold to Mrs. Mary Arnold, 13 November 1869, *Letters of Matthew Arnold, 1848-88*, ed. George W. E. Russell (New York: Macmillan, 1896), 2:24.

49. Matthew Arnold, *St. Paul and Protestantism*, in *Matthew Arnold: Dissent and Dogma*, ed. R. H. Super (1870; reprint, Ann Arbor, Mich.: University of Michigan Press, 1968), 13.

50. R. H. Hutton, "Mr. Arnold on St. Paul and His Creed," *The Contemporary Review* 14 (June 1870): 333.

51. Arnold, *St. Paul and Protestantism*, 15–18.

52. Ibid., 7.

53. Ibid., 21.

54. Ibid., 62.

55. Ibid., 22.

56. Ibid., 23.

57. Ibid., 60–61.

58. Matthew Arnold to Mrs. Mary Arnold, 13 November 1869, *Letters*, 2:24.

59. Undoubtedly Arnold has Newman's notion of development in mind, but with a crucial alteration. Newman's view of development was intended to explain how the church continues to develop dogma inferentially from, though not at odds with, Scripture and tradition. For Arnold development implies much greater deference to the zeitgeist, suggesting that dogma must be accommodated to the modern scientific temperament. One reviewer, Edith Simcox, was unimpressed with Arnold's use of the term, arguing that calling his revisionist theology "development" was simply a euphemistic way to avoid the harsher sound of skepticism. Simcox, "Pseudonymous Review," *Academy* 13, no. 1 (August, 1870): 282–83; repr. in *Matthew Arnold, Prose Writings*, 269.

Part II
Puritanism and Institutions

Anti-Calvinists and the Republican Threat in Early Stuart Cambridge

Margo Todd

IN CASTING ABOUT FOR THE ORIGINS OF THE CIVIL WARS, THOMAS HOBBES NO-
toriously judged that "the core of rebellion" lay in the universities,
and especially in "reading of the books of policy and histories of
the ancient Greeks and Romans." Classical history had in his view
furnished the rebels of the 1640s "with arguments for liberty out of
the . . . histories of Rome and Greece, for their disputation against
the necessary power of kings." John Aubrey agreed, explaining that
John Milton's "being so conversant in Livy and the Roman authors,
and the greatness he saw done by the Roman commonwealth, and
the virtue of their great commanders" had "induced him to write
against monarchy."[1] Hobbes and Aubrey were right—as far as they
went. But, of course, there's more to the story. In the seventeenth
century, historiography and political theory intersected at every
point with religion. An event that occurred in the 1620s in Cambridge University—Milton's Cambridge—rather neatly encapsu-
lates that intersection and illumines the interplay between religion
and political thought, and more specifically between Calvinism and
republicanism.

In Michaelmas term of 1627, a new history professor arrived at
Cambridge University. Isaac Dorislaus was, in fact, the university's
very first history professor, appointed to the chair newly founded by
the Puritan Lord Brooke.[2] He was Dutch, staunchly Calvinist, tightly
connected with the Cambridge Puritan community, and a republican. The combination would prove fatal. Dorislaus delivered only
two lectures (on Roman history) before he was ousted from tenure
of his chair, and at length from the university.

The charge against him was maligning monarchy and advocating
popular resistance to constituted authority. It was brought to the
University Vice-chancellor's court by the evidently irate master of
Peterhouse, Matthew Wren. The ensuing lines of division in the consistory court (comprised of the heads of the sixteen colleges) sug-

gest that differences in political theory paralleled and may have been exacerbated by religious differences. Without exception, Wren's supporters in the case against Dorislaus were Laudians— Arminian in theology and defenders of ceremonies in worship. On the other side, Dorislaus's defenders, led by his good friend and master of Sidney Sussex College, Samuel Ward, were zealous Calvinists and opponents of Laud's "innovations" in religious practice. Whether Wren was in reality offended more by Dorislaus's Calvinism than by his admiration for the Roman republic is uncertain, but it is suggestive that Laudians would in the coming decades regularly associate Calvinism with the twin specters of regicide and republicanism. Dorislaus's later involvement in the trial of Charles I would naturally confirm their perception. Wren never identified Ward or other Cambridge Calvinists as republicans (nor could he), but he clearly thought that they had been deceived by their common theological ground with the Dutchman and failed to see the political danger inherent in his lectures, and perhaps in Calvinism. Wren took it upon himself to point out the danger.

Dorislaus delivered his first Cambridge lecture in the Old Schools on 7 December 1627. Following the instructions of his patron, he read on the *Annals* of Cornelius Tacitus.[3] The mandate itself was not particularly radical: Tacitus and other classical republicans had found their place in Oxbridge tutorial studies at least a century earlier, and with the publication in 1581 of Lipsius's commentary on Tacitus, the place of the Roman historian in Western curricula was established.[4] Of course, there were dangers inherent in Tacitus's political discourse: his discussions of republican government, of civil liberty, and of resistance to tyranny had inspired Renaissance republican and resistance theorists from Bruni and Machiavelli to Lipsius and Buchanan.[5] It was *not* usual, however, for formal teaching on Tacitus to commend either republican government or resistance to monarchy in any historical context.

At Cambridge, however, Dorislaus departed from the norm. He focused his first lecture on the origins of regal authority in ancient Rome, delineating two categories of legitimate monarchy. Both, he said, are founded on the voluntary transfer of a natural sovereignty from the people to be ruled to the ruler. Sometimes the people transfers its power and rule to a monarch, "nulla juris parte sibi retentā" [no part of this right being kept for itself].[6] Dorislaus noted that the Dutch had thus offered rule to Queen Elizabeth, who, presumably out of respect for the traditional rights (*jus*) of the people, had rejected this "παμβασιλεία," or absolute sovereignty.[7] In the second and more usual category, a more complicated but clearly preferable "σϰέμμα πολιτιϰόν" [political theory], the people elect to reserve particular rights for themselves while bestowing strictly limited powers upon a king.[8] The distinction, and indeed the whole lecture, might have been construed as merely descriptive—if only Dorislaus had not added a concluding phrase to his second category: "sic ut alteri in alteris Jus involare nefas sit" [so that it is a crime for one forcibly to take possession of another's rights]. This caveat may seem innocuous enough, but remember the context: this judgment was here rendered by a Dutch republican in the presence of ardent monarchists sensitive to increasing parliamentary complaint about unjust taxation and enforcement of objectionable religious policy by Charles I and his bishops. Dorislaus did have the good sense to praise the English form of monarchy; however, the only specific example he gave of the goodness of English monarchy was Elizabeth, whose posthumous popularity had been won at the expense of her Stuart successors.[9] He continued the lecture, moreover, presumptuously to advise monarchs to moderate passion with reason and above all to beware provoking their subjects by haughty disdain and scornful treatment: "Qui populos imperio regunt, affectus suos ratione moderantur, et super omnia caveant, ne contumeliā fortes viros provocent" [those who rule the people with supreme authority should moderate their passions with reason, and take particular care not to provoke brave men by maltreatment]. As if this were not enough, he followed his advice with what might be construed as an implied threat, first by quoting Homer's praise for the best men, the ἄριστος, who judge it most virtuous to fight in defense of their country, and then by immediately introducing Brutus's expulsion of Tarquin from his throne and country.[10] The best, bravest men act to expel tyrants. All of this drove Matthew Wren to complain to the heads of colleges. The lecture "contented not me," he told them privately, because "however he highly preferred a monarchy before all other forms, and ours above all, yet he seemed to acknowledge no right of kingdoms, but whereof the people's voluntary submission had been the *principium constitutionum.*"[11]

The second lecture, given five days later, was even more alarming to the master of Peterhouse. Here Dorislaus continued his story by recounting at greater length the illegal actions of the ancient tyrant, Tarquinius Superbus, and his resultant deposition and the replacement of monarchy with consular government by Junius Brutus—a deed that brought Brutus "the applause of gods and men"—the language of Dorislaus, not Tacitus.[12] Apparently unaware of the vigorous opposition in the audience, Dorislaus effectively treated this incident as a case study in legitimate deposition of monarchs who violated established law. As Ward recounted it, "His author mentioning the conversion of the state of Rome from government by kings to government by consuls, by the suggestion of Junius Brutus, he took occasion to discourse of the power of the people under the kings and afterward."[13] Tarquin's overthrow, the lecturer had explained, was the result of his "excesses" and "his infringing of the liberties of the people."[14] The worst of such infringements was one that in fact the people of England were to suffer in the next decade: rather than consulting the Senate as custom dictated, the tyrant administered his realm and made war and peace on his own or at most with the advice of his friends, rather than by the consent of the people and their representatives.[15] While the eleven years of Personal Rule was still a bit in the future, Charles's last Parliament had ended unsatisfactorily enough, and sufficient petitions remained unmet, to make Dorislaus's more sensitive auditors wonder at the implications of his lecture.

The heroes of Dorislaus's account were as unwilling as their English counterparts would be to allow rule without Parliament. They did not act precipitately, but only when their patience had been exhausted by the misdeeds of the prince.[16] Then, however, the people of the Roman republic, strong and mature in their political understanding and appreciating the "bonam frugem libertatis" [good fruit of liberty], responded by seizing upon their right to overthrow a sovereign who had disregarded the law: "Omnibus destinatum erat, quaevis è libertate incommoda potius perpeti quam Regali superbiae obnoxiis more mancipiorum vivere" [It had been agreed upon by all, rather to live with the inconveniences of liberty than to live as slaves subject to the offensive pride of kings].[17] Popular consent (omnibus destinatum erat) he conjoined with liberty; the offensive pride of kings (regali superbiae obnoxiis) he conjoined with slavery (mancipiorum).

John Milton, likely one of Dorislaus's auditors in 1627, would later echo the lecturer's next bold assertion, that the Roman people, from whom the kings had derived their power in the first place, had supreme power and could hold kings accountable to law, just as the kings had held individual citizens accountable.[18] Supreme right of rule clearly resides in the people ("summū imperiū in populo remanserit"), who may for just cause legitimately seek to repossess the rights they had once given the king. If necessary, they might even resort to arms in order to recover their liberty, since one who holds part of the supreme authority cannot also have the right of defending this same part. Only in a παμβασιλεία, or absolutist government, is armed resistance not permissible, but Dorislaus had suggested in his first lecture that such absolute power had been rejected for England by Elizabeth, and in any case no Englishman would prefer such a government, in which "indigna digna habenda sunt, rex quae facit" [unworthy things that a king does must be considered worthy].[19]

In Dorislaus's account, the *right* of a good citizen to rebel against a monarch who has violently encroached on the customary rights of a senate shades into *obligation*: "jus" [rights] is transmuted into "boni civis officium" [the duty of a good citizen]. That obligation had been taken on in ancient Rome by Junius Brutus, whom Dorislaus depicted in both lectures as the liberator of the people and the defender of law in its pristine state, before the extortion of power by kings or emperors. "Libertatem et consulatum Lucius Brutus instituit" [Lucius Brutus established freedom and the consulship], Tacitus had said in the first sentence of the *Annals*; Dorislaus made it as clear as had the subject of his lecture that the combination of freedom and consular government was the glory of ancient Rome.[20] Then, lest the contemporary implications of this political doctrine be lost on his audience, Dorislaus compared the virtuous action of ancient republicans to his own countrymen's resort to arms in defense of liberty against the tyranny of the king of Spain.[21] He did warn that one must take care in making the judgment to take up arms against a king, noting that in the previous century, wicked powers had sent the Jesuits, "evil monsters from Hell, . . . [to] free subjects from allegiance" to *legitimate* kings, and their example was hardly to be followed.[22] Despite this caveat, however, the conclusion of the lecture was its most radical statement. Even when the free republic of Rome was overthrown by princes who usurped power from the people, the ultimate authority of the people to confer *imperium* was not abrogated in law. By implication, neither was their right to repossess *imperium* from a tyrant.[23]

Hearing these sentiments expressed in the Old Schools, before an audience of impressionable undergraduates, was too much for Matthew Wren. He protested on the spot: "The second lecture, December 12, was stored with such dangerous passages (as they might be taken) and so appliable to the exasperations of these villanous times, that I could not abstain before the heads there present to take much offense, that such a subject should be handled here, and such lessons published, and at these times, and *e cathedrā theologicā* [from the seat of theology] before all the University."[24] When he failed to get any sympathy from the heads who heard his complaint, Wren proceeded to demand action against Dorislaus from the Vice-chancellor and master of Christ's College, Thomas

Bainbridge. Unfortunately, the Vice-chancellor had been absent from the lecture, but Wren so vehemently insisted on the danger and "required him to look to it" that Bainbridge agreed to call two senior doctors who had been present to render their judgment of the lecture.[25]

Now Bainbridge was a Calvinist and had already had numerous clashes with the Arminian Wren over theological issues on the Vice-chancellor's court.[26] He was careful, therefore, to choose a fellow Calvinist, Samuel Ward, as one of the senior doctors. Ward and his unnamed colleague did not share Wren's alarm. As Ward reported to Archbishop Ussher, Dorislaus "was conceived of by some to speak too much for the defence of the liberties of the people"; however, Ward thought that "he spake with great moderation." More important, the master of Sidney pointed out in defense of the man who was by now his houseguest that Dorislaus had clearly indicated in his lecture that the English situation was not parallel to that in ancient Rome. He had spoken "with an exception of such monarchies as ours, where the people has surrendered their right to the king, as that in truth there could be no just exception taken against him."[27] In any case, Ward carefully added, King Charles was obviously not guilty of the misdeeds caused by royal arrogance (*regali superbiae obnoxiis*) from which the subjects of Tarquin had suffered.[28]

But Wren was not satisfied. With the assistance of Thomas Eden, the Laudian master of Trinity Hall, he persuaded the Vice-chancellor to initiate proceedings against Dorislaus in consistory by calling for copies of the offending lectures.[29] To be on the safe side, he also copied the most offensive passages from his notes and sent them to Laud. Furthermore, as he told the bishop in his cover letter, he also enlisted the aid of "my Lord elect of Winton," none other than Richard Neile of St. John's College, to whom Laud was of course heavily indebted for his own advancement.[30]

There is no surviving indication that actual prosecution in the Vice-chancellor's court ensued, but in any case Wren found other mechanisms to inhibit Dorislaus's influence.[31] On the day following the second lecture, he was able to prevent the Dutch scholar's incorporation as a doctor of Cambridge University: he reported to Laud, "A congregation had been called before, against the next day, of purpose to incorporate him here a doctor with us. But that being in my power this year, as I am *De Capite Senatus pro facultate theologiae* [head of the university's theology faculty], I made stay of that."[32] Dorislaus promptly came to Wren for an explanation of this unprecedented affront to a visiting professor, only to be told in no uncertain terms that his "two lectures have been heard by most of the University, not without much distaste and exception, especially against the latter."[33] Wren did make it clear in his correspondence to Laud that his animosity toward Dorislaus was not personal but ideological: "The gentleman (coming to me about it) gave me as much satisfaction, as in such a case could be. Surely he has good learning, and seems to be very ingenuous, and not to have spoken anything maliciously, but partly out of some wrong grounds of history and politics (as I shewed him) and chiefly out of inexperience of our state. He thought that what they hear with applause in their own country might as freely be spoken anywhere, for which he is now very sorry, that he was so foully mistaken."[34]

Unfortunately, neither ingenuousness nor contrition could win Wren over. Ward soon got word that complaint had been made to the king, and in an attempt to forestall royal interference, he arranged for Dorislaus to "come and clear himself before the heads." Appearing in consistory on the appointed day, Dorislaus "carried himself so ingenuously that he gave satisfaction to all [except, presumably, Wren], whereupon letters were written to his patron, to the bishop of Durham, and others, to signify so much."[35] Wren, however, was still unhappy and opted to continue pursuit of the matter at the highest levels. He wrote both to Laud and to Buckingham, requesting that his name not be mentioned lest he thereby incur "the reproach of being a delator," but insisting that it was "incompatible of any member tho but seeminge to trench upon our soveraigne right, whose Royal hart standing so much for Doe my prophets no harme, we hope shall fynde every affection in his universitye as much for Touch not myne anoynted."[36] His concern for the safety of royal sovereignty of course guaranteed the king's attention to the matter.

Meanwhile, Dorislaus, having apparently cleared himself with the heads, hastened to his patron with the exonerating letters from consistory in hand. Brooke suppressed the copies of these letters that had apparently been made for "the Duke [Buckingham], the Bishop [Laud], etc. [?]," judging it foolish to defend oneself before any charge had been brought. He assured Dorislaus that should he be further assailed, he [Brooke] would be equal to the task of defense, "so that all the smoke would disappear."[37] Dorislaus came away from the meeting optimistic, writing to Ward on 4 January 1628 that he hoped soon to return to Cambridge.[38] In the same letter, he expressed special gratitude to Ward and to another Calvinist on the consistory, Henry Mansell of Queens' College, for his "fierce defense" of his innocence.[39]

Dorislaus's hopes were short-lived, for the challenge to Wren proved to be mistimed: Wren's letters had already been sent and had done their work. Ward reported, "After[ward], word came from the bishop of Winchester [Neile], then Durham [Cosin, Wren's successor both at Durham and as master of Peterhouse], in His Majesty's name, to prohibit the history reader to read."[40] The royal gag order was not to be resisted. The situation was, in Dorislaus's words, "malo, imo pessimo."[41]

Dorislaus again appealed to his patron, but Lord Brooke was apparently no longer inclined to defend his lecturer. Whether it was because he disagreed with Dorislaus's republican views or simply because he recognized his own political insecurity with the ascendancy of the opposing Buckingham-Neile-Laud faction at court, he advised his lecturer to lie low.[42] Dorislaus sent a futile appeal to Ward to intervene with Brooke and to call on other friends and supporters in Cambridge for their help; however, he soon discovered that he had overestimated the extent of Ward's influence.[43] Ward apparently did try to help, but two weeks after Dorislaus's appeal to him, another letter informed him that his efforts had been to no avail, and that Brooke's initial confident reassurances to Dorislaus had been replaced by morose resignation and even anger toward the unfortunate scholar.[44] Dorislaus remained in London with Brooke, fatiguing both his patron and himself with his importunity to resume his lectureship. By 7 March, Brooke finally decided that he could no longer endure the man's constant petitions. Failing to convince him to return to the Netherlands, he decided to ship his lecturer off to the country until the controversy should blow over. Dorislaus declared to Ward his intention to "remain here [in Brooke's country house] in hiding some weeks and, when spring is further advanced, to flee to you, either to recover the office that was given to me or . . . to give my final lecture." (He was sufficiently confident in this plan that he also asked Ward to store his "meager possessions" in his home.)[45] Dorislaus moved to Yorkshire, where he lived "sunk in [my] provincial solitude" and continued to collect his stipend, but was still forbidden his Cambridge lectern. Brooke rekindled his hope in May by recalling him to London and resubmitting his lectures to the Cambridge consistory, but apparently to no avail. There is no record of the consistory's recommendation, but Dorislaus continued to send complaints and petitions to Ward for advice and intercession.[46] This state of affairs was made permanent when Brooke was assassinated in September: a codicil added to his will shortly before his death made Dorislaus's tenure of the lectureship lifelong and guaranteed his annuity, but it could not recover his right actually to lecture.[47]

Dorislaus did return after Brooke's death to Cambridge, where he apparently recommenced his fast friendship with Samuel Ward. References to that friendship and to Mrs. Ward's hospitality to Dorislaus during this difficult time abound in letters that survive. Ward provided a sounding board for his friend's wrath and indignation, sheltered and apparently fed him well in the Sidney Master's Lodge, and kept him busy responding to his own and others' scholarship.[48]

There is some evidence that their conversations at this time included discussions of political theory. Ward was also at this time corresponding with another Dutch Calvinist, Jan de Laet, about the latter's work on the treachery of princes—although, as de Laet commented, the subject lay "outside the limits of either of our professions, since it is political and not theological."[49] References to such matters are understandably infrequent and cryptic in the extant letters, however: Ward was not unaware of the danger of his papers falling into the wrong hands. But Dorislaus's assertion in one brief note in the context of comment on the third book of Aristotle's *Politics* that "he will not drive away this liberty in speech when there is many a voice so free" may well refer to more than the author's own situation.[50]

In the end, Dorislaus was persuaded by Ward to set his anger aside and take advantage of the terms of his lectureship. He traveled extensively during the following decade, enabled thus to live in some tranquility during a time of increasing religious turmoil in Cambridge.[51] The only threat to his security was an unsuccessful attempt in 1630 to replace him with Vossius (Brooke's first choice for the lectureship, and also a friend and frequent correspondent of Ward).[52] After some continental travel, Dorislaus returned to England, settling with his family in Essex. He wrote thence to Ward in January of 1634 with news of the war and the need for English assistance for the Protestants abroad, suggesting either recent travel abroad or his own inclusion in an international news network. He also reported that his three sons had died, and that his wife was wasting away from the same disease that had taken them.[53] He made no reference to the lectureship; he seems to have resigned himself to his loss of the position. Indeed, the lectureship itself seems to have turned into a sinecure after his patron's death.[54] Lord Brooke's foundation was effectively destroyed before it had fairly begun: the teaching of history had proved too great a threat to monarchy for it to be sanctioned by the upholders of the early Stuart establishment.

It may be that to modern practitioners of the historian's art, the Wren-Eden faction at Cambridge represented the worst results of early modern political paranoia: the bigoted persecution of intellectual speculation in defense of tradition and vested interest. Certainly, the effective demise of the first history chair at Cambridge was a setback for seventeenth-century scholarship that should not be downplayed. But in fact, the Laudian cohort in the university and at court had some reason for their harassment of the history lecturer. Read in the context of other events in early Stuart Cambridge, and of subsequent events in the lives of the primary actors in the affair, the Dorislaus incident is comprehensible. Indeed, it sheds a good deal of light on the nature and development of political theorizing in the period, and on the association of Laudianism in religion with extreme royalism.

The events of 1627–28 were not the first perceived threat to monarchy in early Stuart Cambridge. For at least a decade before, the heads of colleges in consistory had been obliged to keep a close watch on the contents of Cambridge booksellers' inventories, given the apparent popularity of the works of both British and continental resistance theorists. In May of 1622, booksellers were examined in consistory concerning purchases of several Calvinist works of political resistance theory: the *Vindiciae contra Tyrannos*, Bucanus's *Loci communes*, and David Pareus's *Ad Romanos*.[55] The upshot of the investigation was the burning in Regent Walk of the works of the Heidelberg radical Pareus in view of the political threat they embodied.[56] Even so, they continued to appear in the booklists of Cambridge scholars during the next decade and more.[57] That Pareus was a Calvinist of some note doubtless reassured and perhaps recruited much of his English readership, but the combination of Calvinism and political radicalism was duly noted by the Arminian Vice-chancellor Leonard Mawe. Wren's predecessor at Peterhouse, Mawe was not only a fervent supporter of Bishop Laud and his ceremonies, but also something of a courtier—he would accompany Prince Charles to Madrid in 1623—and his support for monarchy and *jure divino* episcopacy was beyond question.[58] He was also the inveterate enemy of Calvinist members of the consistory—the "adverse faction," as Wren labeled them.[59]

The alarm over Pareus in the 1620s was occasioned in part by the 1618 case of the Calvinist Ralph Brownrigg, later master of the very Puritan St. Catherine's College (1631–45) and Vice-chancellor of the university during the Civil War (1642–45). Brownrigg, it seems, had openly questioned the defense of monarchy offered by David Owen's *Herod and Pilate Reconciled. Or, The Concord of Papist and Puritan . . . for the Coercion, Deposition, and Killing of Kings*.[60] Owen's anti-Puritan treatise attributed to the hotter sort of Protestants the "contend[ing] for a national sovereignty in every kingdom, over kings, to dispose of them and their kingdoms." It located the intellectual foundations of this contention in continental and Scottish Calvinists, and specifically in their use of "the statesmen of the Roman commonwealth who deposed the emperors which were tyrants and abused their authority" and replaced monarchy with the "new regiment" of republic.[61] Calvin himself, Owen charged, drew on the Roman precedent of "tribunes of the people . . . curb[ing] the Roman consuls" to argue for the power of "estates assembled in Parliament" to "repress the unruliness of licentious kings."[62] For Brownrigg to question this position was in his enemies' view "seditious and treacherous."[63] In their view he might as well have argued the radical position; he embodied precisely the "Puritan" threat that Owen had identified. That Cambridge undergraduates should thus be exposed to theories of regicide and republicanism was intolerable to the conservative heads—in 1618, as it would be in 1627.

Brownrigg was forced to recant or be deprived of his degrees, and the king himself intervened to require a form of recantation "utterly renouncing all private opinions of Mr. Calvin or Mr. Beza wherein they differ from the doctrine or discipline of the Church of England."[64] In addition to Brownrigg's public recantation, Owen was given a chance early in 1619 to buttress his earlier views in a university "determination" published in 1622 by the university press as *Anti-Paraeus*. Brownrigg's later career, however, may have suggested to Wren and his cohort that the heads might better have dealt more harshly with him in the early stages of his dangerous political speculation.[65] In fact Brownrigg, like Ward, claimed loyalty to the king, but the apparent ease with which he cooperated with Parliament during the war years does suggest that the Laudian heads may not have been far wrong in their alarm at his political views.

In any case, resistance theory and occasionally republican ideology were clearly being discussed in the university in the 1620s, they were closely associated with Calvinist theology, and the conservatives on the Vice-chancellor's court clearly perceived it as their own mission to rid Cambridge of these threats to authority.[66] It was bad enough when the ideas were privately read and bandied about in college commons rooms; when they were publicly taught by a chaired lecturer, Wren's and Eden's reaction was predictably severe. The fact that there was no actual groundswell of republicanism in the 1620s—in Cambridge or anywhere else—was not as apparent to them as it is to us. It was quite clear to them, however, that the ideas were being made available.

Another case heard by the Vice-chancellor's court just a few weeks after Dorislaus had left Cambridge also suggests that the Laudian heads may not have overreacted. Wren's worst fears were that the auditors of Dorislaus's lectures would take his praise of both the ancient Roman and the modern Dutch citizenry so to heart that they would come to disdain all constituted authority. Whatever Wren's English sympathies with the enemies of Spain, the Dutch war against an anointed monarch was most alarming. Rejection of monarchy meant, to Wren, rejection of patriarchy and episcopacy, indeed, of the hierarchical structure that held the social order together.

Wren's fears seemed to be realized when, in January of 1628, a then obscure fellow of Christ's College (another very Calvinistic and Puritan foundation), Thomas Edwards, appeared before the Vice-chancellor's court to explain a sermon that he had preached at St. Andrew's on the religious nature of authority. Edwards had argued that a true and reliable authority was "one in whom the Spirit of God dwells." He suggested that if one has a question about the gospel or any other matter of significant truth, it is not appropriate to "go unto thy carnal master, thy carnal father, thy carnal tutor" for the answer; rather, the believer ought to seek out a truly godly individual, that the answer given might reflect the authority of God.[67] Edwards was charged with error by one Mr. Duncan, who seems to have made a hobby out of hounding Puritans before the consistory.[68] After weeks of hearings, depositions, investigations, and heated discussion in the court, Edwards was told to recant in a second public sermon at St. Andrew's. That sermon, preached in April, satisfied the Calvinist auditors assigned by Vice-chancellor Bainbridge to assess the apology; however, it failed to satisfy Duncan and two other self-appointed deponents.[69] Edwards quickly "left the town and made no certification," but he was still not free of his enemies: he wound up suspended by Archbishop Laud from his parish of St. Botolph's, Aldersgate, London, in 1635 and eventually fled to Holland.[70] Edwards was as Calvinistic as they come, and a Puritan to boot. Once again, then, Calvinist Puritanism was publicly associated with a questioning, if not an outright rejection, of constituted authority.

The response of the Laudians to all of this was a clear association of religious with political nonconformity. Those who decried ceremonies and denounced Arminian bishops had proved politically suspect as well, and the conformist preachers of the 1620s and 1630s were quick to come up with an explanation for this correlation. John Donne said it best, perhaps, when he associated Puritan failure to "distinguish places" with their alleged denial of "distinctions of persons."[71] John Cosin, Wren's successor at Peterhouse and archenemy of Puritans during his term as Vice-chancellor of Cambridge (1639–40), built on this presupposition in his 1633 warning that those who oppose formal distinctions of religious times and places "will not only shake the universal fabric of all government and authority, but instantly open a gap, nay set open the flood gates to all confusion and anarchy."[72] That royal authority, divine in origin, was not to be questioned—any more than the authority of fathers and masters—was the theme of many Laudian preachers in the decades before the war: Roger Mainwaring denounced the Calvinist tendency to evaluate even the behavior of kings and sought to instill obedience by pointing out the king's position in the cosmological hierarchy: "Relations and respects challenge duties correspondent," he said, and George Meriton followed suit with a discussion of the superiority of inherited to elective kingship, let alone to republicanism.[73]

The downfall of the Laudians in the 1640s was in one sense their vindication—or at least a confirmation of their ideas. The threat to monarchy that they had found in Dorislaus's lectures proved real enough in 1649. And almost without exception, the people whom they had associated with the threat were associated in one way or another with the reality.

Thomas Edwards was rewarded for his suffering under Laud not only by readmission to parochial ministry in the 1640s, but also by invitation to the Westminster Assembly of Divines. He became an ardent supporter of Samuel Ward's former student, Oliver Cromwell.[74] He is perhaps best known for his evaluation of religious diversity in the war years, the *Gangraena*, which reveals his own alarm at religious antiauthoritarianism once he had become a member of the establishment; however, his uncompromising support for Parliament against the king would not have surprised Wren or Eden.[75]

Samuel Ward, never the republican sympathizer that Wren suspected him to be, refused financial aid to the parliamentary forces that occupied Cambridge in 1643. But he also refused the king a donation when he needed it most.[76] His private journals include emphatic criticism of the king—for "prodigality," for "want of courage and resolution," and for "not looking to matters of state," as well as for more religious offenses such as failure to enforce Sabbath observance and "indulging papists notwithstanding God hath given them into his hand"; of the queen—for "want of religion"; of noble counsellors—"many backward in religion"; and of bishops—for nonresidency, "great ignorance in many," "contempt of godly men," covetousness, and being "pontifical and papistical."[77] Ward, too, was invited to the Westminster Assembly, though he died before it commenced.[78] And Ralph Brownrigg cooperated with parliamentary committees in the government of Cambridge University from 1642 to 1645.

The works of David Pareus, Tacitus's *Annals*, and the *Vindiciae contra Tyrannos* became the handbooks of the regicides and republicans. Among their readers—and among the probable auditors of Dorislaus's lectures—was John Milton of Christ's College, whose comments on Junius Brutus as "that second founder of Rome and great avenger of the lusts of Kings" have plausibly been attributed to the effects of Dorislaus's lecture.[79] Edwards, Ward, Brownrigg, Milton—all of these had been bred up as Calvinists; all had heard and some had succored Isaac Dorislaus; all to some degree lived up to the Laudians' fears.

Dorislaus himself proved the most culpable of the lot. In 1642 the House of Commons appointed him Advocate of the Army to serve as prosecutor in cases of royalist conspiracy.[80] In 1648 he was appointed Judge of the Admiralty, and later in the same year he served with Walter Strickland on a diplomatic mission to Holland.[81] In December of 1648, Cromwell himself went to some lengths to secure housing in London for Dorislaus and his family.[82]

In the following month, Parliament brought about the event to which, in Wren's view, Dorislaus's ideas had logically led: the trial and execution of the king. As the Laudians might have predicted, Dorislaus was at the center. In the position of counsel for the prosecution, Dorislaus put together an argument against the king that condemned him on precisely those grounds used to justify the deposition of Tarquinius Superbus in Tacitus's account. Legitimate rule was construed as an agreement between people and ruler in which the ruler is bound to preserve the rights and liberties of the people or to forfeit the rule that they have bestowed.[83] This was precisely the theory articulated in Dorislaus's fateful Cambridge lectures of 1627.

The following spring, Dorislaus was sent on his second diplomatic mission to the United Provinces.[84] He arrived in The Hague in April and took rooms in an inn. Three days later, twelve armed Englishmen appeared at the door of the inn and asked for wine. As soon as the door was opened, they forced their way down the corridor to the room where Dorislaus was dining. There they stabbed Dorislaus and one of his servants to death. The assassins were never apprehended.[85]

Dorislaus's body was transported to London and laid in state at Worcester House. Here, clearly, was a hero of the republic. The House of Commons issued a *Declaration on their just Resentment of the Horrid Murther perpetrated on the body of Isaac Dorislaus*, placing the blame for the murder squarely on "that party from whom all the troubles of this nation have formerly sprung."[86] "That party" was the party of monarchy—or in the Commons' view, of tyranny and absolutism. It was also the party of episcopacy— Arminian, Laudian episcopacy, denouncing Calvin and venerating places and signs as part and parcel of supporting the political order. It was the party of Matthew Wren and Thomas Eden. It was the party that failed in 1649, and with its failure came political disorder, regicide, and republicanism. Wren and Eden may have handled the Cambridge situation badly in 1627. But they had not altogether misjudged it.

NOTES

1. Thomas Hobbes, *Behemoth, or The Long Parliament*, ed. Ferdinand Tönnies (Chicago: University of Chicago Press, 1990), 56, 58; John Aubrey, *Brief Lives*, ed. Oliver Lawson Dick (London: Secker and Warburg, 1960), 203.

2. Kevin Sharpe, "The Foundation of the Chairs of History at Oxford and Cambridge: An Episode in Jacobean Politics," *History of Universities* 2 (1982): 127–52.

3. Matthew Wren to William Laud, 16 December 1627, Public Record Office (hereafter PRO) SP 16/86/no. 87, f. 175; J. B. Mullinger, *The History of Cambridge University* (Cambridge: Cambridge University Press, 1911), 3:674–77. There is minimal discussion of the Dorislaus lectures and ensuing troubles in John Twigg, *The University of Cambridge and the English Revolution, 1625-1688* (Cambridge: Boydell Press, 1990), 13; a fuller treatment is provided by Mullinger's account (3:81–89).

4. Peter Burke, "Tacitism," in *Tacitus*, ed. T. A. Dorey (New York: Basic Books, 1969), 149–71; Blair Worden, "Classical Republicanism and the Puritan Revolution," in *History and Imagination: Essays in Honour of H. R. Trevor-Roper*, ed. Hugh Lloyd-Jones, Valerie Pearl, and Blair Worden (New York: Holmes and Meier, 1981), 182–200; Zera Fink, *The Classical Republicans*, 2d ed. (Evanston, Ill.: Northwestern University Press, 1962); Margo Todd, *Christian Humanism and the Puritan Social Order* (Cambridge: Cambridge University Press, 1987), 62–67, 81–82, 84–90; Justus Lipsius, *Ad Annales Corn. Taciti liber commentarius* (Antwerp, 1581). Camden's first history lecturer at Oxford also treated Tacitus "for his precepts"—see Sharpe, "The Foundation of the Chairs," 127–152, 132. As for Lord Brooke himself, J. G. A. Pocock, *The Machiavellian Moment: Florentine Political Thought in the Atlantic Republican Tradition* (Princeton: Princeton University Press, 1975), 352–53, notes that his *Treatise of Monarchy* treats kingship as a response to the corruption of creation.

5. Quentin Skinner, *The Foundations of Modern Political Thought* (Cam-

bridge: Cambridge University Press, 1978), 1:83–84, 168; Burke, "Tacitism," in *Tacitus*; Lipsius, *Ad Annales Corn.*, f. 3.

6. PRO SP 16/86/no 87.1, f. 177: "aliquando <u>Populus</u> sui Juris, ita se uni addicat, ut summū regendi sui Jus in eum transcribat, nulla Juris <u>parte sibi retentā</u>" [sometimes a people, by its own law, so commits itself to one man that it transfers the complete right of ruling itself to him, no part of this right being kept for itself]. Underlining is in the original manuscript, in a different ink from that of the text, and so may be Bishop Laud's. In this and all quotes from the manuscript, original underlining is retained. Marginal notes, also in a contrasting ink, seem to be in Laud's hand. All translations are the author's. SP 16/86/no. 88, f. 179–179v, is a fair copy of 16/86/no. 87.1, with slight differences, mostly errors in transcription.

7. SP 16/86/no. 87.1, f. 177: "et memoriā nostrā Belgae obtulere se Elizabethae, nec recepti sunt" [and in our memory the Dutch offered themselves to Elizabeth, but were not received]. The Greek term for this category shows up in Dorislaus's second lecture, f. 177v.

8. Ibid., f. 177: "Saepe Populus Regem eligens <u>quosdam actus sibi servat</u>, alios autem Regi defert pleno Juri" [often the people in choosing a king preserve certain business of the state for themselves, but give over other transactions in full right to the king]. (Again, emphasis is in original.) The Greek term is on f. 177v, in the second lecture, where it is described as "impeditum et difficile" [difficult and complicated].

9. David Cressy, *Bonfires and Bells: National Memory and the Protestant Calendar in Elizabethan and Stuart England* (Berkeley and Los Angeles: University of California Press, 1989), chap. 8.

10. SP 16/86/no. 87.1, f. 177. The reference is to the *Iliad* (12,243): "εἰς οἰνός ἄριστος ἀμύνεσθαι περί πάτρης," [The one best omen is to fight for one's country]. I am grateful to Dale Sweeney for identifying this citation.

11. PRO SP 16/86/no. 87, f. 175. Wren admitted to Laud that most of the other heads did not share his alarm: "His first lecture Dec. 7th did pass unexcepted at by any that I could meet with. But yet I forebore not to shew the heads in private that it contented not me."

12. SP 16/86/no. 87.1, f. 177: "diis hominibusque plaudentibus donatum fuit."

13. Samuel Ward to James Ussher, archbishop of Armagh, 16 May 1628, *The Whole Works of the Most Rev. James Ussher* (Dublin: Hodges and Smith, 1843; hereafter *UW*), 15:403.

14. Ibid.

15. PRO SP 16/86/no. 87.1, f. 177.

16. SP 16/86/no. 88.1, f. 180: "fatigata principum injuriis subditorum patientia in perniciem et suam et dominantium erumpit" [those patient subjects, wearied by the injustices of princes who had subdued them into ruin, seized their own power]. This phrase occurs on f. 177v of SP 16/86/no. 87.1, but without "principum." Dorislaus stressed the importance of prudent timing in the pursuit of liberty and made it clear that such action against earlier kings would not have secured liberty (SP 16/86/no. 87.1, f. 177v).

17. PRO SP 16/86/no. 87.1, f. 177v.

18. Ibid., f. 177v: "Populus Romanus, à quo reges habuere quicquid sibi juris vindicarunt, regibus fuit potentior; et jus idem in reges habuit populus, quod illi in singulos a populo habuerunt" [The Roman people, from whom the kings held whatever rights they claimed for themselves, was more powerful than the kings, and the people had the same rights against the kings that the kings had against individual people]. Cf. John Milton, *The Readie and Easie Way to Establish A Free Com-*

monwealth (1660), in *The Complete Prose Works of John Milton*, ed. Don M. Wolfe et al. 8 vols. (New Haven: Yale University Press, 1953–82), 7: 340–88. Milton cites book 3 of Aristotle's *Politics*, which Dorislaus may have had in mind as well.

19. Ibid., f. 177v.

20. PRO SP 16/86/no. 87.1, f. 177–177v. The most extreme example he proffers of a king gone wrong is Gaius Caligula "casting off his humanity" by desiring the death of his whole people. It is with this example that he introduces the notion that a good citizen's *duty* is to overthrow such a tyrant: "Subit et illa dubitatio, quod sit boni civis officium si rex hostili animo in totius populi exitium feratur, ut G. Caligulam accepimus, qui toti populo unam cervicem optabat, etc. Equidem si quis hominem exuens in talem immanitatem degeneret, ut nolit cum hominibus nisi in eorum perniciem convenire, ne quidem hominem appellandum puto" [There arises a doubt as to what the duty of a good citizen should be if the king is brought by his hostile mind to (desire) the death of his whole people, as we have witnessed of Gaius Caligula, who desired one neck (execution) for the whole people, etc. To be sure, anyone who, shedding his humanity, has deteriorated into such great cruelty that he does not wish to meet with men except to bring about their ruin, I certainly do not think that he ought to be called a man].

21. Ibid., f. 177v: cf. Ward's summary in *UW* 15:403: "Among other things, [he] descended to the vindicating of the Netherlanders for retaining their liberties against the violences of Spain."

22. Ibid., f. 178.

23. Ibid.

24. PRO SP 16/86/87, f. 175.

25. Wren reported that the Vice-chancellor "came in late and heard him [Dorislaus] not" (ibid.).

26. E.g., in the trial of William Clarke for recusancy in 1624, Cambridge University Library (CUL) MS VC Ct. III.27, fols. 66–67, and in the case of William Fawcett's 1626 violation of the Sixth Article, tried in the Monday courts, and recorded in CUL MS Mm 2.23, f. 198, and in CUL MS CUR 6.1, it. 39, fols. 2, 17. Bainbridge had come to mastership of Christ's College in 1622.

27. *UW* 15:403.

28. The phrase from the lecture is on f. 177v of SP 16/86/no. 87.1.

29. He reported to Laud (SP 16/86/no. 87, f. 175v), "I was urgent with the Vice-chancellor to advise what were fit to be done, and Dr. Eden joining stiffly with me, at last he promised to call for the copies of his lectures, out of which I privately gathered the passages which I send here to your honor in the enclosed paper" (now SP 16/86/no. 87.1 and 88).

30. PRO SP 16/86/no. 87, f. 175v; cf. *UW* 15:403.

31. Calling for copies of lectures or sermons for examination by the heads in consistory was the usual first step to full-fledged prosecution by the Vice-chancellor's court. Records of proceedings in consistory in 1627 and 1628, however, include no reference to proceedings against Dorislaus: I have examined CUL MSS VC Ct. I.11, I.47, I.49, I.50, I.51 and I.75; CUR 6, 16, and 18; Com.Ct. I.18; Mm 2.23; the Deposition Books (VC II and Com.Ct. II series) and the Exhibita Files (VC III and Com.Ct. III series) for relevant dates, and the only possible reference to the Dorislaus affair is a cryptic note in MS VC Ct. I.51, fols. 40v–41 about a call for copies of an unspecified lecture. Dorislaus's name is never mentioned, and copies of the lecture are not to be found in the exhibita files. (The only surviving copy of his lectures is in fact the excerpts appended to Wren's letter to Laud in the PRO.) Dorislaus did offer to give public satisfaction, but in other such cases the apology

or satisfaction is included in the court registers. There are two possible explanations for this: (1) Dorislaus may have been immune to prosecution because of his Dutch citizenship or because of Lord Brooke's patronage, or (2) records of his prosecution may have been removed from the Vice-chancellor's court registers by the Long Parliament's subcommittee on religion in the universities when that committee examined the registers in 1641, given the high regard in which Dorislaus was held both by Puritan zealots in Parliament and by parliamentary opponents of the king. See David Hoyle, "A Commons Investigation of Arminianism and Popery in Cambridge on the Eve of the Civil War," *The Historical Journal* 29 (1986): 419–425; cf. BL MS Harl. 7091, f. 53. The first option seems most likely, given survival of rough as well as fair copies of many of the registers: the registrar, James Tabor, would not have turned over both to the committee examiners, and the rough copies are as devoid of reference to Dorislaus as are the fair copies.

32. PRO SP 16/86/no. 87, f. 175.

33. Wren to the Duke of Buckingham, 16 December 1627, printed in C. H. Cooper, *Annals of Cambridge*, ed. J. W. Cooper (Cambridge: Cambridge University Press, 1908), 5:370–71.

34. PRO SP 16/86/no. 87, f. 175–175v.

35. Ward to Ussher, *UW* 15:403.

36. Wren to Laud, PRO SP 16/86/no. 87, f. 175–175v, and Wren to Buckingham in Cooper, *Annals of Cambridge*, 5:370–71, original spelling and capitalization retained in view of the pun. The reference in the latter passage is to 1 Chr. 16:22 (Authorized Version).

37. Bodl. MS Tanner 72.105, f. 233 (Dorislaus to Ward, 4 January 1628). Ward sent the report on to Archbishop Ussher (*UW* 15:403) that Brooke "suppressed the letters and said he would see an accuser before any excuse should be made."

38. Bodl. MS Tanner 72.105, f. 233 (Dorislaus to Ward, 4 January 1628): "Spero me brevi rediturum ad vos" [I hope that in a short time I will be returning to you all].

39. Ibid. Mansell was "acrem illum innocentiae meae propugnatorem officiosissime" [a relentless and most obliging defender of my innocence].

40. *UW* 15:403.

41. "Very bad, getting worse." Bodl. MS Tanner 72.113, f. 248 (Dorislaus to Ward, 13 February 1628).

42. Bodl. MS Tanner 72.113, fols. 248–49 (Dorislaus to Ward, 13 February 1628): "Dissidet enim a me patronus et me res mihi meas habere iussit" [for my patron is distant from me and instructs me to keep my affairs to myself]; cf. MS Tanner 72, fols. 250–51, 257–58 (Dorislaus to Ward, 29 February and 7 March 1628).

43. Ibid., f. 248: "You alone," he told Ward, "have the power to restore my fortunes."

44. Bodl. MS Tanner 72.114, f. 250 (Dorislaus to Ward, 27 February 1628): "Nihil interim apud patronum evaluit tam accurata et diligens deprecatio. Videtur esse ex eorum genere qui plumbeas iras gerunt. Ego patientia concoquo senis morositatem" [In the meantime, your careful and diligent prayers have not prevailed with my patron. He seems to be of the sort which maintains heavy anger. I endure with patience the peevishness of the old man]. He asked Ward at the end of the letter to remind Wren of his integrity and to deny the "evil things" (*Calumnia*) apparently being said about him in Cambridge.

45. Bodl. MS Tanner 72.117 (Dorislaus to Ward, 7 March 1628). He calls Brooke "pervicacissimus Baro" [most obstinate Baro], although Brooke's Calvinism was well known, presumably because of his unwillingness to go to bat for him (Dorislaus). He also complains again of Brooke's unjust anger and moroseness.

46. Bodl. MS Tanner 72.132, f. 284 (Dorislaus to Ward, 16 May 1628, from London); Huntington MS HM 371.

47. CUL MS Mm 1.47, 136–38; cf. Dorislaus to Ward, Bodl. MS Tanner 72, f. 304. Brooke was stabbed to death by a disgruntled servant. His provision for Dorislaus suggests that his failure to keep the historian at Cambridge may be a symptom less of ideological conflict with Dorislaus's republicanism than of his political insecurity. Brooke, already out of favor and known as a patron of Puritans, was in no position to defend a Calvinist republican in the court now dominated by Buckingham and his Arminian cohort.

48. E.g., in Huntington Library MS HM 371 (Dorislaus to Ward, undated), Dorislaus apologizes for giving himself over to wrath, comments on "what you gave me to read," and thanks Ward for a "sumptuous and splendid breakfast," which he enjoyed "as a spice to the rest of your humanity." Frequent greetings to Ward's wife include commiseration for her toothache on 27 February 1628, even in the midst of his own sufferings (Bodl. MS Tanner 72.114, f. 250).

49. Bodl. MS Tanner 72, f. 286 (Jan de Laet to Ward, 4 July 1628). De Laet reported that having just written a "little book" about the princes of Italy, his next project would deal with the trickery of the kings of Spain. An elder in the Leiden consistory, he had met Ward at the Synod of Dort, and he had sent his son to be taught by Ward at Sidney. He was commissioned by the South Holland synod in 1619 to deal in the case of Gerardus Vossius, and also to write a history of the church from 1600 to the present. I am grateful for background on de Laet to Ben Kaplan.

50. E.g., Huntington MS HM 371 (Dorislaus to Ward), undated, but with internal evidence suggesting a mid- to late-1628 date.

51. He wrote to Ward from France in 1629 with news of the war and continental politics, civil and ecclesiastical, and also with a note indicating that he was still appealing to Bainbridge: Bodl. MS Tanner 71.12, f. 25. On contemporary events in Cambridge, see my " 'An Act of Discretion': Evangelical Conformity and the Puritan Dons," *Albion* 18, no. 4 (1986): 595–99. An apparent rumor of Dorislaus's restoration to the lectureship in December of 1628 had proven unfounded but had raised his hopes: "Benignitate Dei et ope vestra redditus sum Academiae a qua Patroni morositas me tam diu avulsit . . . spero me visurum optatissimam matrem, ἀγαθήν κουροτρόφον' " [By the kindness of God and your influence I have been restored to the Academy from which my patron's peevishness alienated me for so long . . . I hope that I will see my most welcome mother, "a good nurturer of youth"] Bodl. MS Tanner 72.141, f. 304 (Dorislaus to Ward, 4 December 1628). The Greek at the end of his Latin sentence is a quote from Homer, *Odyssey*, 9. 27.

52. Bodl., MS Sancroft 18, 11 (Ussher to Laud, 5 April 1630). Vossius's son studied at Sidney: CUL MS Oo 7.45, f. 12 (Vossius to Ward, 9 October 1628); from Leiden, Ward asks, standing *in loco parentis*, to exhort the young Vossius to piety, modesty, and industry. F. 13 (7 August 1627) is a cover letter sent to Ward with Vossius's commentaries on the Latin historians.

53. Bodl. MS Tanner 71.74, f. 188–89 (Dorislaus to Ward, 24 January 1634).

54. Mullinger, *History of Cambridge*, 3:89–90; Sharpe, "Foundation of Chairs."

55. Booksellers' depositions are found in CUL MS VC Ct. 111.26, fol. 3749.

56. Recounted in Mullinger, *History of Cambridge*, 2:563–64. Cf. CUL MS VC Ct. 111.26, fol. 3749.

57. *Books in Cambridge Inventories: Book-lists from Vice-Chancellor's Court Probate Inventories in the Tudor and Stuart Periods*, ed. Elisabeth Leed-

ham-Green (Cambridge: Cambridge University Press, 1986), vol. 1, 1630s lists, passim.

58. Thomas Birch, *The Court and Times of Charles I* (London: Henry Colburn, 1849), 42–45 (Joseph Mede's account of this affair); Thomas A. Walker, *Peterhouse* (Cambridge: W. Heffer and Sons, 1935), 101–3. Mawe moved to Trinity in 1625 to continue John Richardson's Arminian and ceremonialist tradition there.

59. PRO SP 16/86/no. 87, fols. 175 ff. A few years later, Mawe would appear among the accusers of Samuel Ward when Ward was under investigation by his colleagues for possession of forbidden books: CUL MS VC Ct. 1.51, fols. 167–68v (8 April 1629). The outcome of this investigation is not recorded in the registers.

60. *Herod and Pilate Reconciled. Or, The Concord of Papist and Puritan ... for the Coercion, Deposition, and Killing of Kings* was published in Cambridge in 1610, with no apparent controversy.

61. Owen identified Goodman, Danaeus, Pareus, Hotman, Beza, and Buchanan as the crucial thinkers (sig. 2v of Dedicatory Epistle); quotations from ibid., 41 and 44.

62. In Owen's account of the Calvinist position, if magistrates fail to repress kings who violate the "fundamental laws," they "betray the liberty of the People. . . . Thus far Calvin," (ibid., 51, 47). He identified Goodman, Knox, Beza, and Buchanan as the intellectual heirs and expanders of this position (47–48).

63. Depositions of Robert Bing and Humphrey Henchman, fellows of Clare College, CUL MS Mm 2.23, 196–97.

64. James Montagu to the Vice-chancellor [John Richardson], 10 March 1618, CUL MS Mm 2.23, 198.

65. CUL MSS Mm 2.23 and CUR 6.1.

66. It is worth noting that at the same time, the Vice-chancellor's court was being rocked by division between Arminian ceremonialists and Calvinist precisians on more narrowly religious matters. See, e.g., the cases of the Arminian Simpson (CUL MS Ff 5.25, fols. 80–93) and the Puritan Preston (CUL MSS VC Ct. 1.9, fols. 173v–174, VC Ct. 111.24, Com. Ct. 1.13, and CUR 6.1, it. 39, f. 22). These may have reinforced the theological lines drawn in conflicts over the articulation of political theories.

67. Sworn copies of Edwards's sermon and accounts of his trial are found in CUL MSS VC Ct. 1.49, fols. 24–26; Mm 2.23, fols. 198–99; CUR 6.1, it. 39, fol. 2, 21–25, 28; and VC Ct. L51, fols. 26–28, 174 f.

68. Duncan also issued the complaint against John Barcroft of Sidney Sussex College for an anti-Episcopal sermon in 1633: see CUL MSS Com. Ct. 1.18, fols. 110–110v, and CUR 18.6 (7).

69. CUL MS CUR 6.1, it. 39, fols. 21–28. The officially designated auditors were Laurence Chaderton, William Bridge, Thomas Goodwin, Thomas Ball, and Thomas Marshall (f. 22v). Duncan's two friends were John Vaughan and John Cornelius (f. 28). Edwards's statement that we ought to obey ungodly authorities "to win them and stop their mouths," citing 1 Peter 3.1 and 2.18, must have sounded at best condescending to constituted authority, and Edwards continued to insist that one must obey God first if the authority commands an ungodly act (f. 22v).

70. J. A. Venn, John Venn, eds., *Alumni Cantabrigienses. Part I: From the Earliest Times to 1751* (Cambridge: Cambridge University Press, 1922), 1: 4.

71. John Donne, *Sermons*, ed. G. R. Potter and E. M. Simpson (Berkeley and Los Angeles: University of California Press, 1957), 4:377–78.

72. John Cosin, *The Works of John Cosin*, ed. John Henry Parker (Oxford, 1843–45), 1:51; cf. 170.

73. Roger Mainwaring, *Religion and Allegiance* (London, 1627), 2, 8; George Meriton, *A Sermon of Nobilitie* (London, 1627), sig. Eiiii.

74. Venn and Venn, *Alumni Cantabrigienses*, 1: 4.

75. Thomas Edwards's *Gangraena: or a Catalogue and Discovery of many Errours, Heresies, Blasphemies and pernicious Practices of the Sectaries of this Time* was published in London in 1646; cf. Richard Baxter, *The Autobiography of Richard Baxter*, ed. N. H. Keeble (London: Rowan and Littlefield, 1974), 56, 283.

76. See CUL MS Mm 2.25, f. 160, Ward's letter refusing personal financial contribution to the king.

77. Sidney Sussex College, Cambridge, MS Ward B, f. 47v (31 from the back). He adds as one of the sins of the land "want of courage and spirit in the defense of good men and good causes" (f. 30v from the back).

78. *The Names of Orthodox Divines, presented by the Knights and burgesses . . . as fit persons to be consulted with by the Parliament, touching the Reformation of Church Government and Liturgie* (London, 1642), the Sidney Sussex Library copy annotated in Ward's hand.

79. Christopher Hill, *Milton and the English Revolution* (New York: Viking Press, 1978), 35; cf. Milton, *Complete Prose Works of John Milton*, 1:267–68. Blair Worden questions Hill's conclusion (from Prolusion 5's references to Roman history) that Milton heard Dorislaus's lectures: "Milton among the Radicals," review of *Milton and the English Revolution*, by Christopher Hill, *Times Literary Supplement*, 2 December 1977, 1394. Cf. also Martin Dzelzainis, "Milton's Classical Republicanism," in *Milton and Republicanism*, ed. David Armitage, Armand Himy, and Quentin Skinner (Cambridge: Cambridge University Press, 1995), 3–24.

80. *Army Lists of the Roundheads and Cavaliers*, ed. B. Peacock (London, 1874), 21; BL MS Add. 29974, f. 369.

81. Bulstrode Whitelocke, *Memorials of the English Affairs* (London, 1682), 299; *Calendar of State Papers, Domestic Series*, 1648–49, 279, 293.

82. Oliver Cromwell, *The Writings and Speeches of Oliver Cromwell*, ed. Wilbur Cortez Abbott (Cambridge: Harvard University Press, 1937), 1:712.

83. C. V. Wedgewood's *The Trial of Charles I* (London: Collins, 1964) is the best account; T. B. Howell, ed., *A Complete Collection of State Trials* (London, 1816), 4:990–1154, Whitelocke, *Memorials*, 362.

84. *CSPD* 1649–50, 97, 99–100, 103.

85. CUL MS Mm 1.46, 161. Clement Walker's version of the story is a bit different: publishing as Theodorus Verax (*Anarchia Anglicana* [London, 1649], 173), he recorded "about 18. Scotsmen (friends to Hamilton) repairing to his [Dorislaus's] lodging. 6 of them went up the stairs to his chamber, whilst 12 of them made good the stair-foot, where expostulating with him concerning the unjust condemnation and execution of the duke, they stabbed him to death, and escaped." (I am grateful to Joyce Chaplin for this reference.) A good account of the murder and its investigation is given by P. Alessandra Maccioni and Marco Mostert in "Isaac Dorislaus (1595–1649): The Career of a Dutch Scholar in England," *Transactions of the Cambridge Bibliographical Society* 8 (1984): 438–47.

86. Published in London, 1649, and recounted by Maccioni and Mostert, 442; cf. Whitelocke, *Memorials*, 388.

The Emmanuel College, Cambridge, Election of 1622: The Constraints of a Puritan Institution

Steven R. Pointer

In a recent article, C. John Sommerville cites the advantages to be gained by considering English religious groups of the seventeenth century as movements, rather than the church or sect typology of Ernst Troeltsch or other such alternatives. Instead of focusing on church politics, denominational structures, doctrinal debates, or popular responses, attention to the movement character of a group would rather concentrate on its mission, "the goals, strategies, and tactics characteristic of a movement." In so doing, the dynamic character of movements is emphasized and the resulting stories that are told will "have more drama."[1]

This approach, Sommerville acknowledges, builds upon Patrick Collinson's classic study, *The Elizabethan Puritan Movement*. Rightly (if hesitantly) recognizing first generation Puritanism as a movement to effect political and ecclesiastical reform, Collinson's story ends in the early 1590s with Elizabeth having defeated this Presbyterian movement. Nonetheless, a second generation emerges, Sommerville contends, "a more diffuse Puritanism" still worthy of study as a movement, and continuing that status until sometime after the Restoration of 1660, when "Puritanism ceased to be a movement" and was transformed into the sects of various dissenters.[2]

Sommerville's perspective for understanding the Puritan phenomenon (and other English religious groups) is a helpful one. An investigation of a movement's hopes, its resources, and its leadership can shed important light on a subject. However, his assertion that "a defining mark of a movement" is "organization, without recognized institutionalization" raises other questions. Specifically, what about those murky areas where movement and institution intersect? Must movements mean "the deauthorization of the establishment"?[3] This essay will examine one such collision of movement and institution with the hope that the particularity of the case study will heighten the drama of the episode and also illumine the turmoil of such conjunctions.

Jeremiah Burroughes (1599–1646), educated at Emmanuel College, Cambridge, and tutored in his early ministry by the former Emmanuel fellow Thomas Hooker, spoke for many of the English "godly" when he declared: "Singularity is cast upon Gods servants as their disgrace, but certainly it is their glory; they are singular, and their waies are singular, it is true, and they avouch it, they rejoyce in it, and blesse God for it; it is impossible but that it should bee so, for they are of another spirit, a peculiar people, separated from the world, set apart for God, their separation is a wonderful separation, Exod. 33.16."[4] Burroughes's ready embrace of the "singularity" of the godly well reflects his movement to nonconformity and subsequent flight to Holland in the 1630s. It is less certain, however, that his alma mater was as willing to rejoice in its reputation of "singularity." Being different was not always an unmitigated blessing. For Emmanuel College, being part of the University of Cambridge automatically thrust it into a complex world of power, privilege, and interconnected relationships. Emmanuel's leadership—its master and fellows—would have been hard-pressed to identify the "world" from which Burroughes so confidently extolled separation.

This essay, then, will focus on the constraints and maneuvering that characterized Emmanuel College as it attempted to connect the worlds of the Puritan movement and the English establishment. The all-important, albeit mysterious, election of a new master of Emmanuel in 1622—the transition from the founding master, Laurence Chaderton, to his Puritan successor, John Preston—will serve as a crucial episode in illuminating the dynamic of a Puritan institution in early Stuart Cambridge.

To be sure, the notion of Emmanuel's "singularity" by virtue of its Puritan identity has been a persistent one. Early-seventeenth-century contemporaries such as Oxford's Richard Corbett helped establish the popular perception of Emmanuel. In Corbett's ballad, the "Distracted Puritane" sang of himself:

> In the howse of pure Emanuel
> I had my Education;
> Where my friends surmise
> I dazeld mine Eyes,
> With the Light of Revelation.

> Boldly I preach, hate a Crosse, hate a Surplice,
>   Miters, Copes, and Rotchets:
> Come hear mee pray nine times a day,
>   And fill your heads with Crotchets.[5]

Or again, King James I's visit to Cambridge in 1615 provided Corbett with another occasion to mock Emmanuel's haughty singularity:

> But the pure house of *Emanuel*
> Would not be like proud *Jesabel,*
> Nor shew her self before the King
> An Hypocrite, or *painted* thing:
> But, that the wayes might all prove faire,
> Conceiv'd a tedious mile of Prayer.[6]

Nor could Corbett resist a poke at the north-south orientation of Emmanuel's chapel:

> Here noe man spake ought to the point,
> But all they sayd was out of joynt;
> Just like the Chappell ominous
> In th' Colledge called *God with us*
>   Which truly doth stand much awry
> Just North and South, *yes verily.*[7]

A misaligned chapel, unconventional worship, and hypocritical piety constituted Emmanuel's badge of shame, according to critics such as Corbett.

Members and supporters of the college also asserted its distinctiveness, though, of course, more charitably. John Ward, parent of an Emmanuel student, pledged himself to prayer for "that famous Seminary . . . the renowne wherof makes every man that looketh Heaven-ward desirous to crowd his children into it."[8] Or again, Cotton Mather, grandson of an Emmanuel fellow, described the college as "that seminary of Puritans in Cambridge" and claimed that "Immanuel College contributed more than a little" to make New England "in some respects Immanuel's Land."[9]

Not surprisingly, historians ever since have repeated and extended this tradition of Emmanuel's uniqueness. The standard works on the University of Cambridge invariably link Emmanuel with Puritanism, thereby reiterating its distinctiveness.[10] This unquestioned association has thus been a commonplace for British and American scholarship for much of the twentieth century.

In recent decades, however, more focused study of Emmanuel itself (principally in the form of three American doctoral disserta-tions) and continued scholarly attention to the vexing problem of defining Puritanism suggest a need for a more nuanced character-ization of their joint relationship.[11] Richard Tyler's recognition that "a peculiar ambiguity" attended to Emmanuel's Puritanism and Peter Lake's depiction of Laurence Chaderton as the epitome of the "moderate Puritan," combining the zeal of the godly with loyal ser-vice to the establishment of crown, church, and university, helped suggest the direction of this study.[12] Most recently, Tom Webster's study *Godly Clergy in Early Stuart England* positions Emmanuel College as a vital part of a network coherent enough to constitute "an early Stuart Puritan movement."[13] Taken together, these stud-ies point to an institution whose stated mission of providing a learned and godly clergy for a parochial and preaching ministry within a national church required more of an angularity than a "sin-gularity." That is to say, retaining the good graces of its double con-stituency required careful positioning on Emmanuel's part.

On the afternoon of 2 October 1622, the Cambridge University community was stunned by the sight of a triumphal processional making its way from Queens' College to Emmanuel to mark the elec-tion of John Preston as the new master, replacing Laurence Chader-ton. Then, as now, speculation focused on the obvious questions: why the change and why such secrecy? In fact, Chaderton—the only master Emmanuel had known since he was handpicked for the job by founder Sir Walter Mildmay in 1584—had resigned his position on 25 September. The stipulated seven-day period between vacancy and election required by the college statutes was observed, but no public notice was given. Technically, such announcement was only called for if any of the fellows were absent: "And that the vacancy in the Mastership may the more easily come to the notice of those who are absent, a notice concerning the day and hour of the coming election shall continuously during those seven days be posted on the door of the Chapel."[14] Since all of the fellows—eleven in number, one position being open—were in residence at the time, no notice was posted; though, as we shall see, other motives accounted for the maintenance of secrecy.

On the morning of 2 October, as mandated by chapter 11 of the statutes, both the fellows and students were gathered, first, for "the usual prayers," second, for a sermon by the senior fellow exhorting the other fellows to do their duty well, and third, for the celebration of the Lord's Supper: "When all these exercises of piety and religion are ended, by the which the electors may be roused to the more lively and religious performances of their duty, the aforesaid senior

Fellow (all others except the Fellows being first excluded) shall read before them all our statutes concerning the qualification of candidates for the Mastership."[15] Implementing the stated wishes of the founder, crafted thirty-eight years earlier and now for the first time being invoked, the fellows heard the requirements that the new master be "by birth an Englishman," be at least thirty years old, have studied at the university for sixteen years (at least eight of which be in theology), be an ordained minister with experience in preaching and lecturing, and be one who "sincerely abhors and detests Popery, heresy, and all superstitions and errors"—though without elaborating any further on what those might entail. Chapter 9 of the college statutes went on to state a clear priority in the search for the right candidate: "If any such be found among the Fellows of the College, we enjoin in the Lord's name that the same be elected. But if not, let such a one be sought amongst them that have at some time been Fellows of the same College. But if neither among these can a fit person of such kind be found, then it shall be permitted one from Christ's College (which we desire to be given first preference), or failing that, from the whole University of Cambridge."[16] The selection of John Preston from Queens' College, then, as the next master of Emmanuel indicated not only the lack of a suitable candidate from within the ranks of the Emmanuel fellows, but even more strikingly, the fellows' clear preference for Preston over all other possible candidates, even those scoring higher according to the founder's search priorities. In particular, contemporaries immediately interpreted Preston's election as an obvious rebuke of Elias Travers.

Travers had only recently left the ranks of the Emmanuel fellows, having been forced to do so by the distinctive and controversial statute *De mora sociorum*. The statute had been added by the founder in 1588 to safeguard the college's mission of supplying a learned ministry to the church. Mildmay wanted to make clear "that none of the Fellows suppose that we have given him a permanent home in that College," convinced "that the over-long residence of Fellows in other Colleges has done no little hurt both to the affairs of the commonwealth and to the interests of the church." Thus, Mildmay expected that fellows would proceed as expeditiously as possible to the degree of doctor of divinity and then leave the college for pastoral work. Such was the case for Elias Travers. Having secured his doctorate, he was obliged to give up his role as Emmanuel's senior fellow.[17]

Why Travers was so unacceptable to his former Emmanuel colleagues is still a mystery. Was this a case of familiarity breeding contempt? One may surmise that the differences were probably more personal than theological, but in any case the snub was unmistakable. A letter from Joseph Mede (holder of the Greek lectureship at Christ's College) to Sir Michael Stuteville colorfully recounts the episode:

> On Wednesday last in the forenoon Mr. Preston was chosen Master of Emmanuel, it being the seventh day after the *Vacatio agnita* by the resignation of the Old Doctor. Yet so secretly did they carry their business, that not any of the town no nor any of the Scholars of their own College, did so much as suspect any Vacation or Election, till all was done and finished. Dr. Travers himself whom some might suppose likely to hear of such a matter heard not the least jot till all was past, notwithstanding all the acquaintance and relations he left behind him. Never did I believe till I now see it experienced, that so many as twelve could keep counsel a week together, and Fellows of a College too: who would have thought but there would have been a Judas among twelve. But they jest at Emmanuel, and tell us that Judas was gone, and they had but eleven, for one fellowship was void.[18]

Similarly, Emmanuel graduate William Bedell commented upon the surprising developments from his parish in Bury St. Edmund's: "The news of Dr. Chaderton's resigning and the election of Mr. Preston to the Mastership of Emmanuel was altogether unexpected in these parts: wherof I doubt not there were secret motives and perhaps conditions more than the world knows of."[19] Bedell's observations were shrewder than he could have known.

In point of fact, the most surprising aspect of the whole episode for contemporaries of these events was that there was a need to select a new master for Emmanuel in the first place. Apparently, no one had seen the change coming. Why, then, did Chaderton resign, and why so suddenly? The seventeenth-century sources for answering that question offer quite varying accounts. William Dillingham—a former student, fellow, and master of Emmanuel himself—presents the situation in the best possible light, denying that Chaderton was pressured to resign and, instead, attributing his decision simply to the realities of his advanced age. Already an octogenarian, Dillingham's Chaderton makes his decision independently, confessing "I cannot, owing to my age, do my duty." In a scene allegedly recounted to Dillingham by one of the fellows then present (though his source is not named), Chaderton resigns despite the protest of the senior fellow and "amidst the silent sorrow of the [other] fellows." With an appropriate biblical analogue, Chaderton's tearful farewell is likened to the apostle Paul's "saying farewell to the elders at Ephesus."[20]

How very different is the version of this episode told by Thomas Ball. Ball, a student of Preston at Emmanuel and his biographer, emphasizes the fellows' concern for the reputation of the college, their clear preference for Preston and the influence he might command, and the need to convince Chaderton to resign:

> Some of the fellows of Emanuel College were very eminent for pts & learning, & yet clowded & obscured (as they thought) by an oppinion that lay upon the college, that they were Puritans; that is, not only godly and religious, for so they were, & were content to be esteemed, but Nonconformists, and averss to government; for wch cause there had bin lately some alteration made, both in their chapple and manner of diet. They thought, therefore, that, if they could prevaile wth Dr. Chaderton their present master to resigne (who was established in it by ye founder, and named in ye statute, but growne very old, & had outlived many of those great relations wch he had before), they might phaps procure that Mr. Preston might succeede him, & bring ye college into reputation. For Mr. Preston was a good man (though a courtier), the Prince his chapline, & very gratious with ye Duke of Buckingham. But this was sooner said than done.[21]

Ball continues his account by describing Chaderton as "exceeding wary & jealous," not just for himself, but also for the well-being of the college if the plans of the fellows were thwarted. After all, "there were divers lay in wayt to get a mandate & come in against the mynds of the fellows."[22] But, according to Ball, one of the fellows answered this objection by countering that the succession to Chaderton could be more easily masterminded while he was alive, rather than waiting for the unknown time of his death: "for his resignation might be carryed privately, but his death could not; and, if all ye fellows were agreed, the election might be past before the resignation was discovered."[23]

Ball's version of the story extends the conspiracy of machinations beyond the Emmanuel fellows to include, of course, John Preston, and even the court of James I. Presumably, Preston had been approached as to his interest, and there is no reason to doubt Chaderton's affection or high regard for him as a suitable successor. Chaderton's hesitancy to embrace the scheme, according to Ball, was for both personal and political reasons. Chaderton is described as something of a pathetic figure: "The poore old man knew not what to doe; to outlive the mastership he thought was to outlive himselfe, & to goe into his grave alive."[24] Beyond his personal dilemma, however, Chaderton also wanted political assurances that Preston's election would not be blocked by the Crown. Thus, Ball includes the text of a letter purportedly from the Duke of Buckingham to Chaderton that Preston had been able to secure, giving the king's blessing and thereby easing Chaderton's fears.[25]

In comparing Dillingham's and Ball's versions, it would seem that the latter deserves greater credence. Although Chaderton was well into his eighties, it is difficult to accept the notion that he voluntarily stepped aside because of his age. No one, of course, could have known that he would survive another eighteen years and outlive Preston by twelve years, when already in 1622 he was more than twice Preston's senior. Yet, given Chaderton's robust health and passionate commitment to Emmanuel, Ball's account of an anguished Chaderton facing the possibility of the mastership being wrested from him rings more true. Furthermore, Ball's account has the advantage of having been written much closer to the events he was reporting (1628) than Dillingham's, which he was just preparing for publication when he died in 1689. Moreover, Dillingham's revisionist agenda is manifest in his less-than-subtle reference to Ball as "some vulgar English writer" who resorted to "invention or imagination" to concoct his version of Chaderton having been pressured to resign.[26] Thus, while Dillingham is usually a reliable source, in this case he apparently felt that Ball's account demeaned one whom he esteemed so highly.

If the initiative for change of leadership did lie with the fellows, what were their motives? As cited previously, Ball points to the concern of the fellows over the college's reputation and its political influence in high places. It is not evident that Emmanuel was suffering politically in 1622 because of Chaderton's leadership. Of course, years earlier it was well known that Chaderton had been rebuked by the king at the Hampton Court Conference for "sitting Communions in Emanuel Colledge." The publication in 1604 of William Barlow's *The Summe and Substance of the Conference . . . at Hampton Court* had widely advertised the king's warning to Chaderton that he "must conforme, and his irregular Colledge to weare the Surplice, and receive the Communion knelinge or els to be putt out of it."[27] Thereafter, the master and fellows worked assiduously to overcome the Crown's suspicions, yet apparently without conforming Emmanuel's liturgical practices to the prescribed norms. Perhaps Chaderton's friendship with Archbishop Richard Bancroft protected the college from any official action. At any rate, by 1622 Bancroft had been dead for over a decade and the conclusion may well have been reached that Chaderton's political clout was on the wane. While not dissatisfied with Chaderton, then, the fellows might have thought that they could improve their lot with Preston.

Additionally, Ball highlights the feeling of the fellows that certain of the college statutes "greatly pintched them." In particular, the statutes limiting income from other sources and restricting absences constrained their opportunities to "make themselves known unto such as had it in their power to prefer them."[28] Elections to fellowships are a reliable index of the ability of Emmanuel's students to secure preferment in the university. Richard Tyler has found that between 1596 and 1645 only 7.2 percent (187 of 2602) of Emmanuel men became dons compared to 12.5 percent (556 of 4433) of the students at King's, St. John's, and Jesus Colleges, and most of those were fellowships at Emmanuel. (Among 98 future dons admitted to Emmanuel before 1635, 68 were elected fellows at Emmanuel and only 30 at other colleges.)[29] Clearly the fellows at Emmanuel were acutely aware that association with their college made the road to preferment within the university a difficult one. At the same time, the *De mora* statute, as previously discussed, hung over the heads of fellows like the sword of Damocles, ready to oust them from their fellowships in due time. In sum, job security was tenuous and opportunity for placement elsewhere was regarded as unnecessarily hindered; no wonder that the fellows felt "greatly pintched" and, once again, entertained fond hopes that Master Preston would prove sympathetic to their plight.[30]

Taking into account the personal and social circumstances of the fellows helps explain the otherwise remarkable situation of the fellows lamenting the Puritan reputation of the college and then seeking redress by replacing Chaderton with John Preston. One would be hard-pressed to dispute the card-carrying credentials of either in the Puritan cause. Eschewing the Puritan appellation, of course, was not to deny the agenda of the godly in service to church and nation, but only to avoid the negative liabilities of a pejorative epithet. Life and career were already fraught with enough pitfalls; no need to give unnecessary offense—even better to secure an advocate whose popularity and influence might bring a public relations coup.

John Preston's still young but rapidly ascending career certainly beckoned with that kind of promise. A fellow at Queens' College since 1609, Preston's conversion in 1612 under the preaching of Emmanuel's John Cotton secured his services for the Puritan cause. Thereafter, his star only increased in its brightness as he enjoyed sparkling popularity as a lecturer in Cambridge, established formidable connections in Parliament, became the special protégé of the Duke of Buckingham, and favorably impressed King James.

At Queens' College, Preston was so popular a tutor that Thomas

Fuller called him "the greatest pupil monger in England in man's memory."[31] Ultimately he became both Dean and Catechist at Queens', with his lectures achieving such notoriety that townsmen as well as scholars from other colleges flocked to hear him. The overcrowding that resulted led to an edict prohibiting any "stranger" from attending lectures intended for members of a college.[32]

While at Queens', Preston also became involved in a controversy that almost resulted in his expulsion from the university for "nonconformity." An incident at St. Botolph's Church in Cambridge sometime in the years 1618–19 aroused the ire of the Bishop of Ely, Lancelot Andrewes, who accused Preston of opposition to set forms of prayer. Called to account before the Chancellor and the heads of the colleges, Preston managed to extricate himself by offering to clarify his views in another sermon. Back at St. Botolph's, far from recanting, Preston gave a rousing performance—defending both written and extemporaneous prayers as having their rightful place in the worship of God—that left his detractors unable to find fault and even the "indifferent hearers praised all."[33] Undoubtedly, this episode would have impressed the Emmanuel fellows, even as it also showed Preston's remarkable ability to work—or to learn how to work—within the establishment without actually moderating his views.

By 1622 Preston had established not only his popularity but also his political connections. He had significant ties with both houses of Parliament and a new relationship with the Duke of Buckingham. In the midst of the controversy over the "Spanish match" for Prince Charles, a document linked to Preston (the "Alured letter") urged the Duke to use his influence to discourage the match and to persuade the king to be guided by Parliament, not foreigners, in such matters. The letter was clever and affirming enough to do its work; Irvonwy Morgan concludes that this episode marked the beginning of the unlikely alliance among the Puritan party, Preston, and Buckingham.[34] When Preston added the royal favor to his credentials after an impressive sermon defending the lawfulness of liturgies and set prayers, he identified himself as a force with which to be reckoned. Clearly, as Ball put it, "if he must be a Puritan. . . . He would not be one of the lower rank, but would get places if he could."[35]

Preston's election as Master of Emmanuel in October 1622 culminated a banner year for him, as he had earlier been appointed court chaplain to Prince Charles and elected preacher to Lincoln's Inn.

Small wonder, then, that the Emmanuel fellows would seek to hitch their fate, and that of the college, to this rising star.

One other factor may have motivated the Emmanuel fellows in their desire to replace Chaderton with Preston: the college's enrollment figures. The admission of new students had reached a high under Chaderton in 1619 with seventy-one freshmen but had declined to only forty-four in 1621 (Chaderton's last full year). Was this decrease simply part of the normal fluctuating cycle in enrollment patterns, or was it an ominous sign that change was needed to forestall disaster? Actually, it is remarkable how quickly Emmanuel became one of the larger colleges in the University of Cambridge. In spite of its recent origins (1584), its relative poverty, and its lack of prestige—at least in comparison to other Cambridge colleges— Emmanuel had enrolled sixty-one new students as early as 1596. For the next quarter century (with one notable exception), the overall tendency for Emmanuel, as for the university, was numerical growth. By the early 1620s, however, perhaps because of worsening economic conditions, the years of university expansion ended, and overall admissions declined slightly during the decade.[36]

The low point of Emmanuel's enrollment had come in 1605 when only twelve new boys had begun studies. With this decline coming in the aftermath of the disappointments of the Hampton Court Conference, it is hard to resist the conclusion that Emmanuel's admissions were adversely affected by the religious and political controversies of the time, as the numbers dropped from forty-one in 1603 to twenty-eight in 1604 to twelve. Conversely, rising enrollment numbers thereafter (forty-two in 1606, forty-six in 1607, etc.) are a solid indication that Emmanuel's leadership had successfully weathered the storm and that confidence in the school had returned.[37]

Yet there was that significant downturn in students again in 1621, and that had been preceded by an alarming trend of more Emmanuel students migrating to other colleges. (The years 1617–21 saw the percentage of transfers increase to 10.5 percent of the total admitted, compared to only 5.7 percent for the years 1612–16.) Presumably such a trend indicated disenchantment on the part of a growing minority with Emmanuel's mission and its leadership; a school with a fledgling endowment could not afford to be indifferent to such trends.

If concerns about enrollment at all affected the thinking of the Emmanuel fellows, our sources offer nary a whisper. But again, it is difficult to imagine that the fellows were not aware of such problems with Chaderton and hopeful for improvement under Preston, that great "pupil monger." In fact, if the fellows did entertain such hopes, they were quickly realized. In 1623 Emmanuel enrolled sixty-six new students and surpassed that the next year with a new high of eighty-two. Under Preston, Emmanuel passed Trinity and St. John's as the largest college in the University.

The Preston years not only brought Emmanuel more students, but they were also "the wealthier class of undergraduates."[38] Richard Tyler's extensive analysis of Emmanuel's social composition in comparison to selected other Cambridge colleges has revealed something of the school's social "singularity." Tyler has found Emmanuel to be a "comparatively homogeneous society," with 63 percent of its students by birth belonging to the gentry, especially to the two lower ranks of this wide class, esquires and gentlemen. As a result, the percentage of Emmanuel students who were fellow commoners or pensioners increased and that of sizars (the poorest category of students) decreased. Moreover, almost half of Emmanuel students came from just six counties (Essex, Kent, Suffolk, Norfolk, Sussex, and Northamptonshire), limiting the geographical draw of the college and emphasizing the deliberateness of the choice of the school.[39]

Having fastened their attention on Preston, the Emmanuel fellows devised a plan to secure him. Their strategy placed a premium on secrecy. We have seen earlier the amazement of contemporaries at the secrecy of events in the week between Chaderton's resignation and Preston's election. However, no less amazing is the secrecy of the plan in the days, weeks, or even months prior to its implementation. We have no clues as to which fellow or fellows first conceived the idea, with whom and when it was shared, how long it took to evolve, or when Chaderton was first approached with the scheme.

What we do know is that the campaign of secrecy existed, in large measure, because of Emmanuel's neighbor, Christ's College, and that for two reasons. First, Christ's College was now the home of Elias Travers, late fellow of Emmanuel and erstwhile aspirant to its mastership. Thomas Ball's *Life of Preston* confirms our other sources as to his designs. Although in one place he describes Travers as "a man of great worth," elsewhere Ball elaborates on his presumed intentions and the expectations of the Emmanuel fellows: "They all knew that Dr. Traverse lay in wayt for this preferment; for being outed by the statute of Emanuel college, he soujorned as a fellow Comoner at Christ's College, & presumed, either by his friends at Court to get a mandate, or be chosen in ye college by a pty of ye fellows whom he thought his owne; therefore great care was taken to keepe all secret."[40] Again, Ball offers no insight into

Travers's inadequacies (or was it only Preston's perceived advantages?). But in addition to whatever political clout and personal friendships Travers could wield, he had the double "home court" advantage over Preston if the Emmanuel fellows strictly followed the stipulated preferential priorities of their own college statutes: he was a former Emmanuel fellow who met the stated criteria for the mastership *and* he was now in residence at Christ's College (to be given preference over all other Cambridge colleges).

Secrecy was required, second, because of what had happened at Christ's College in 1609. The memory of an election by the fellows that had been declared void by royal intervention and the subsequent imposition of a master (Valentine Cary) deemed hostile to Puritan interests was all too vivid. Those events had elicited a cry of alarm from Samuel Ward, "Woe is me for Christ's College. Now one is imposed . . . who will be the utter ruin and destruction of that college."[41] The departures, soon thereafter, of the more fiery Puritan types (especially William Ames) seemed to confirm, if not Ward's prediction of Christ's College's destruction, at least the "pacification" of its venerable Puritan tradition.[42]

That precedent was all the more painful for the godly at Emmanuel because of the intimate connections between the two schools. Christ's College had been the educational home of Emmanuel's founder and first master; it had been the model for the crafting of Emmanuel's own statutes; and, of course, Christ's had been an example of Puritan activism in the attempted further reformation of the English Church, from Edward Dering to William Perkins to William Ames. We can well imagine, then, Emmanuel's fellows treading carefully as they negotiated the first significant transition in the college's history.

We can hardly fault the Emmanuel fellows for their mixed motives in masterminding this plot. Their actions show a combination of commitment to the college's mission and an attempt to improve their own standing in it. With John Preston secured as master, they hoped to perpetuate Emmanuel's leadership in providing godly ministers, to take advantage of his political leverage at court to mitigate any criticisms, and, if possible, to exploit his good will to address their grievances. In sum, they wanted to have their cake and to eat it too. But wasn't that reflective of the tension the godly experienced whenever one hand scratched the back of the English establishment while the other tilled the ground? Individual Emmanuel men, desiring the use of two hands on the plow, could and often did move further down the path of nonconformity as a way of alleviating that tension. But the very positions of master and fellow required the extension of a trusting hand in two directions simultaneously: to the establishment nexus of university, national church, and crown, as well as to the network of reform-minded, godly brethren.

To complicate matters still further, the college's commitment to its mission of providing a learned clergy through an ongoing rotation of students and fellows meant that Emmanuel's very structure dictated change and not stability. Emmanuel College was not intended to be, nor could it become, a stable Puritan enclave within a hostile establishment. On the contrary, its position within the university structure and its very design presumed an establishment receptive to its contributions. Yet one senses a growing dissonance for the Emmanuel fellows between such ideals and their realities in the early 1620s.

Peter Lake has rightly declared that if we must persist in our definitional attempts at Puritanism then it must be in terms of its "spiritual dynamic," especially of the presumed ability of the godly to recognize one another in a fallen world.[43] To that insight, Tom Webster has helpfully added the recognition of a complementary "social dynamic," emphasizing the solidarity that existed especially among the godly clergy.[44]

The fascinating episode of the 1622 election of a new master at Emmanuel College suggests that a "realism dynamic" also characterized "establishment Puritans" such as the fellows at Emmanuel. The constraints of political realities, collegiate statutes, and past precedents all required careful repositioning of Emmanuel's "singularity." The angular posture of Emmanuel, necessary to serve its double constituency, belies the "wonderful separation" from this world enjoined by the likes of Jeremiah Burroughes. Indeed, there is a wonderful irony in the discontent of the Emmanuel fellows: their concern over the Puritan reputation of the college hindering the advancement of their own careers while at the same time carefully and secretly negotiating the transition from Chaderton to Preston so as to continue the Puritan mission of the school dramatically illustrates their dilemma in serving two masters simultaneously.

NOTES

1. C. John Sommerville, "Interpreting Seventeenth-Century English Religion as Movements," *Church History* 69, no. 4 (December 2000): 749–69.

2. Ibid., 756, 752.

3. Ibid., 755, 767.

4. Jeremiah Burroughes, *A Gracious Spirit a Choyce and Pretious Spirit* (London, 1638), 151, as cited in Tom Webster, *Godly Clergy in Early Stuart En-*

gland: The Caroline Puritan Movement, c. 1620-1643 (Cambridge: Cambridge University Press, 1997), vii.

5. Richard Corbett, "The Distracted Puritane," in *The Poems of Richard Corbett*, ed. J. A. W. Bennett and H. R. Trevor-Roper (Oxford: Clarendon Press, 1955), 57.

6. Corbett, "A Certaine Poeme," in *The Poems of Richard Corbett*, 13.

7. Ibid., 16.

8. John Ward to William Sancroft, 19 October 1634, British Library, Harleian MS 3783, Letters to William Sancroft, 1, 39r.

9. Cotton Mather, *Magnalia Christi Americana or, The Ecclesiastical History of New England* (1852; reprint, New York: Russell and Russell, 1967), 2: 355, 589–90. For additional testimonies about Emmanuel, see also Joseph Hall, *The Works of the Right Reverend Joseph Hall*, ed. Philip Wynter (Oxford: Clarendon Press, 1863), 1:xxv; Richard Rogers and Samuel Ward, *Two Elizabethan Diaries*, ed. Marshall M. Knappen (Chicago: University of Chicago Press, 1933), 130; Samuel Clarke, *The Lives of Sundry Eminent Persons in this Later Age* (London, 1683), 3; and Emmanuel College Archives, COL. 9.1, "William Bennet's Book, Containing Anecdotes Relative to the College, or to Persons Connected with It," 1:78.

10. See especially C. H. Cooper, *Annals of Cambridge,* ed. J. W. Cooper, 5 vols. (Cambridge: Cambridge University Press, 1908), and J. B. Mullinger, *The History of Cambridge University*, 3 vols. (Cambridge: Cambridge University Press, 1873–1911).

11. The dissertations on Emmanuel are Richard Tyler, "The Children of Disobedience: The Social Composition of Emmanuel College, Cambridge, 1596–1645" (D. Phil. Thesis, University of California, Berkeley, 1976); Rebecca Seward Rolph, "Emmanuel College, Cambridge, and the Puritan Movements of Old and New England" (D. Phil.Thesis, University of Southern California, 1979); Joan Schenk Ibish, "Emmanuel College: The Founding Generation, with a Biographical Register of the Members of the College, 1584–1604," (D. Phil. Thesis, Harvard University, 1985). Also of great value for research on Emmanuel has been the publication of *The Statutes of Sir Walter Mildmay . . . for the government of Emmanuel College founded by him* (Cambridge: Cambridge University Press, 1983), trans. and ed. Frank Stubbings. I am grateful to Dr. Stubbings, fellow and retired librarian of Emmanuel, for his kindness in conversing with me about some of the substance of this paper.

12. Tyler, "Children of Disobedience," 12; Peter Lake, "Laurence Chaderton and the Cambridge Moderate Puritan Tradition" (D. Phil. Thesis, University of Cambridge, 1978), and also his *Moderate Puritans and the Elizabethan Church* (Cambridge: Cambridge University Press, 1982).

13. Webster, *Godly Clergy in Early Stuart England*, 43, 338.

14. Stubbings, *Statutes of . . . Emmanuel College*, 41.

15. Ibid.

16. Ibid., 39.

17. Ibid., 95. Stubbings notes the controversies this statute caused at Emmanuel as early as 1595 and most severely in 1627 (97–98). See also the discussion of the relevant documents in "William Bennet's Book," Emmanuel College Archives, COL. 9.1.

18. Joseph Mede to Michael Stuteville, 5 October 1622, as cited in Bennet's Book, 1:74, Emmanuel College Archives, COL. 9.1.

19. As cited in E. S. Shuckburgh, *Emmanuel College* (London: F. E. Robinson and Co., 1904), 54.

20. William Dillingham, *Laurence Chaderton, D.D.*, trans. E. S. Shuckburgh (Cambridge: Macmillan and Bowes, 1884), 14–15.

21. Thomas Ball, *The Life of the Renowned Doctor Preston*, ed. E. W. Harcourt (Oxford and London, 1885), 79–80.

22. Ibid., 80.

23. Ibid., 81.

24. Ibid., 82–83.

25. The letter is dated in Ball's text as 20 September (which fits the chronology of events), 1662 (an obvious error for 1622). Ibid., 84–85.

26. Dillingham, *Chaderton*, 15–16.

27. The full title of Barlow's book is *The Summe and Substance of the Conference, which, it pleased his Exceelent Majestie to have with the Lords, Bishops, and other of his Clergie (at which the most of the Lordes of the Councell were present) in his Majesties Privy-Chamber, at Hampton Court, January 14, 1603* (London, 1604).

28. Ball, *Life of Preston*, 81.

29. Tyler, "Children of Disobedience," 217–18.

30. Ball, *Life of Preston*, 81–82. When, in fact, King Charles did abrogate the controversial statute in 1627 in response to a petition to do so by some of the Emmanuel fellows, it was not because of Preston's support. Apparently both Preston and Chaderton were in agreement that the statute should not be changed. The petitioners questioned the validity of the statute and the "great inconveniences" it imposed on them. Chaderton responded swiftly and forcefully in a paper entitled "Reasons offered to the heads to show why the statute of Emmanuel College, *De mora sociorum*, may not be altered," arguing that any change would be a violation of the wishes of the deceased. Indeed, Chaderton went so far as to say that "I am fully persuaded . . . that he [Sir Walter Mildmay] had rather not have founded the College, than have omitted this statute" (Cambridge University Library, Add. MS. 22, f. 9v, f. 13).

31. As cited in Rolph, "Emmanuel College," 260.

32. Ball, *Life of Preston*, 40–43.

33. Ibid.

34. Besides Ball's biography of Preston, the only substantial work on him is Irvonwy Morgan's *Prince Charles's Puritan Chaplain* (London: George Allen and Unwin Ltd., 1957), 57–60. See also Rolph, "Emmanuel College," 258–72.

35. Ball, *Life of Preston*, 22.

36. Tyler, "Children of Disobedience," 41–44, 75.

37. Ibid., 83.

38. Ibid., 75–76.

39. Ibid., 140, 147, 157, 193–99.

40. Ball, *Life of Preston*, 82, 85.

41. Knappen, *Two Puritan Diaries*, 133. See also Stephen Bondos-Greene, "The End of an Era: Cambridge Puritanism and the Christ's College Election of 1609," *The Historical Journal* 25, no. 1 (1982): 197–208. For a comprehensive discussion of other mastership elections, see V. Morgan, "Country, Court and Cambridge University, 1558–1640: A Study in the Evolution of a Political Culture" (D. Phil. Thesis, University of East Anglia, 1983). I am indebted to Professor John Morrill for this last source.

42. Bondos-Greene, "The End of an Era," 208.

43. Lake, *Moderate Puritans*, 282.

44. Webster, *Godly Clergy*, 335–38.

The Fabric of Restoration Puritanism: Mary Chudleigh's *The Song of the Three Children Paraphras'd*

Barbara Olive

O ALL ye works of the Word, bless ye the Lord: Praise him, and
magnify him for ever
> —"Benedicite, Omnia Opera," Book of Common Prayer

I will sing of the mercies of the Lord for ever—my dear second
son Richard Chudleigh born October 18 [1685] died 10 Juli
[16]88 buried in the hope of the Resurrection—he is not born in
vain who dies well [for me] death is the birth of immortal glory
and eternal life[.] I shall rise again.
> —Inscription on ledger stone in Ashton Church, Devon

THE CONTRAST IN TONE BETWEEN THESE TWO OPENING PASSAGES, THE
exalted yet controlled and distant voice of the first, and the personal, evangelical voice of the second, suggests that they belong in
different churches—yet they are both part of the same parish
church in Higher Ashton, Devon. The first passage occurs as the
opening of a canticle in the Book of Common Prayer, the second as
a memorial inscription on a worn stone in the nave of the church. A
1984 description of the history and architecture of Ashton Church
refers to the latter as "a statement of faith," suggesting that even
today its piety stands out as unique in the austere country parish
church known for its unchanged medieval rood screen.[1]

The inscription on the ledger stone was very probably authored
by Mary, Lady Chudleigh (1656–1710), whose son Richard's dates
of christening and burial correspond to dates of birth and death on
the ledger stone.[2] If Mary Chudleigh found herself out of place in the
conservative Ashton parish to which she moved with her husband
in the late 1680s, she was not alone in her experience. Given the
large number of people influenced in some manner by "godly" ideals both before and during the Interregnum and the relatively small

number of nonconformists after the Restoration, one can conclude that many people who chose to conform during the Restoration nonetheless were shaped by or continued to hold certain Puritan values.[3] It was this group of conforming Puritans whose construction of identity was most profoundly complex during a time preoccupied with drawing clear divisions between those who did and those who did not conform to the Church of England, a preoccupation that continues in scholarly studies even into our own time.

The relatively small numbers of nonconformists during the Restoration can be attributed to a number of factors. The Conventicle Acts of 1664 and 1668–70 made those who worshipped outside of the Church of England part of a new category of offenders against civil law. And nonconformists found themselves under strong—even scathing—attack by community as well as church leaders. The arguments of some moderate churchmen such as John Tillotson and Gilbert Burnet for broader comprehension brought only critique.[4] Daniel Defoe summarizes the criticism against these moderate churchmen when he describes them with his typical irony as "complying too far with the Dissenters and . . . giving up the decent ceremonyes and settled discipline, in exchange for a slovenly rude way of worship."[5] For many years after the Restoration, those who had former associations with Puritanism or Cromwell's regime found themselves under attack. Mary Chudleigh's uncle, Colonel William Sydenham, who had served in the Cromwellian government, was arrested in December 1660 along with a number of other Cromwellian officers, accused of a plot that appears to have had little basis.[6] Years later, a second uncle, Dr. Thomas Sydenham, a physician and researcher, found himself accused of sectarianism when his innovative medical practices brought him into conflict with his peers.[7] Indeed, a general fear of sedition and loss of peace held strong sway after the Restoration. As John Marshall points out, even John Locke, a theorizer and supporter of toleration, displayed in his early writings an uneasiness with nonconformity, and texts as late as the first drafts of his *Essay on Toleration* show Locke's continuing fear of sedition.[8]

In this new climate, most former Puritans conformed. As described by Richard Baxter, those clergy who chose to conform included not only those "zealous for the Diocesan Party and the Cause" but also former Puritans, whether Presbyterians, who conformed out of their wish for a strong church government or out of their own economic necessity, or Latitudinarians, those "Cambridge Men" who chose to pursue a course of "moderation" from within the church.[9] Many of the latter kept their ties to dissenters following the Restoration, the most prominent of whom, John Tillot-son, had himself "thought hard before conforming."[10] As Donald Davie explains, the phenomenon of Puritanism did not lie only in nonconformists, for after 1700 as before "a remarkable number of the most devoted Puritans and iconoclasts have been in fact mem-bers of the Established Church."[11]

Not only did conforming dissenters find themselves with ambigu-ous religious identities following the Restoration, but so, appar-ently, did those parishes that continued to practice some forms of comprehension after 1660. Such, at least, appears to have been the case of the Devonshire parish of Clyst St. George, home parish of Mary Chudleigh's parents, Richard Lee and Mary Sydenham Lee. For despite their associations with dissent, the Lees appear to have retained connections to the Clyst St. George parish.[12] These connec-tions with the parish may have been made palatable by the nature of the parish, for the Clyst St. George church itself appears to have links to dissent in both its patrons and its clergy through the Resto-ration period and beyond.[13] Thus, when in the late 1680s Mary Chudleigh moved with her husband from her family's home to the Chudleigh estate at Place Barton in the Ashton Church parish, she would likely have found herself in a significantly more conservative religious climate.[14] Although the Chudleighs had not themselves es-caped the influence of Puritanism, the Teign Valley where Ashton is located, separated as it is from Exeter by a prominent land ridge, did not have available the moderating influences on its conserva-tism as did a commercial city such as Clyst St. George.[15] The expec-tations of the parish would surely have played on Mary Chudleigh's life at Ashton as wife to the third baron, George Chudleigh.

It is at Place Barton, Ashton, that Chudleigh composed *The Song of the Three Children Paraphras'd*, a long poem of multiple themes weaving together contemporary religious issues from the point of view of a conforming dissenter.[16] While *The Song* para-phrases a canticle from the Book of Common Prayer, its subject, the persecution of the three young men in Daniel, is a story long claimed by Puritans, one kept alive during the Restoration by John Bunyan among others. In Bunyan's *Seasonable Counsel*, written in 1664 at the height of the persecution of nonconformists and some years before Chudleigh composed *The Song*, Bunyan employs the story of Daniel and its theme of suffering under a king's law to con-vince nonconformists of the "necessity" of demonstrating their fi-delity to God alone despite the consequences. The "three children," Bunyan explains, "run the hazzard of being *turned to ashes, in a burning fiery furnace*, for so doing. But *necessity* has a loud voice, and *shrill* in the case of a tender conscience."[17]

Although in the preface to *The Song*, Chudleigh asserts her allegiance to the Church of England, she explains at the same time her own indifference to its ceremonies, which she sees as "no longer obligatory than they are made so by the sanction of a Law." Unless the rule of "Divine Precepts" in conjunction with "inward Principles" and "internal Honours" is primary, Chudleigh argues, forms of worship are useless.[18] Even more striking is the contrast between Chudleigh's opening protestation of allegiance to the church and the poem's forceful narrator, who functions as worship leader in the poem, leading praise and prayer in the stead of authorities and proclaiming eschatological visions of the world beyond the reign of any single church or government.

In *The Song*, Chudleigh acknowledges the established clergy as priests of Israel; however she also elaborates at length on God's deliverance from bondage of the children of Israel, a story employed by Restoration Puritans, John Bunyan among others, for the way it paralleled the nonconformists' persecution by the church. In his *Seasonable Counsel*, Bunyan aligns the narrative of Israel with the particular circumstances of the Restoration by pointing to those Israelites who were murdered on account of the religion of their parents. Similar was the suffering, albeit not death, of the persecuted nonconformist clergy and laity in the Restoration period.[19] Bunyan claims that the victims of these persecutions, those children who defended their parents' religion, "died for righteousness."[20]

Finally, at the same time as Chudleigh concedes that the established clergy are more "Learned, Orthodox, and Ingenious" than ever before and that many demonstrate piety and virtue, she turns the poem into a statement of instruction directed at the clergy.[21] In the poem's preface, Chudleigh excuses herself for the boldness with which she instructs the clergy in their duty: "I beg them to do me the Justice to believe, that I would not have assum'd so great a Boldness had not my Subject led me to it."[22] The very act of implying that such instruction is necessary, however, suggests that Chudleigh sees a spiritual ignorance in religious leaders of the church in the same manner as did Bunyan. Chudleigh appears to be suggesting in the poem that the church would do well to accommodate those who have challenged its traditions—and that it should open itself to the spirit, to the boldness and faith, of more godly worshippers.

We cannot be sure of Chudleigh's publication intentions for *The Song* when she first wrote it. The poem was likely composed in the 1690s, though it was not published until 1703, when it appeared as a part of Chudleigh's collection of poems, retaining a separate preface. Whatever her original intentions for publication, Chudleigh appears to position herself carefully in the poem by insisting upon her allegiance to the church and thus countering possible accusations of enthusiasm. Given the experience of her close relatives—uncles and father—Chudleigh would have known well how perceived enthusiasm could lead to accusations of sectarianism and vulgarity.[23] Following the restoration of Charles II, as Spurr explains, those clergy who spoke in favor of reducing punishments for nonconformists were accused of being secret supporters of dissenters and "betrayers of the church." By the 1670s, dissenters had few friends and were the object of biting censures.[24] Even with the ascent of William III and the Toleration Act, attitudes toward nonconformists remained negative, with the clergy particularly hostile until long after 1689.[25]

For these reasons, Chudleigh's long paraphrase is a bold endeavor, with its elaborate tapestry of themes shared by dissenters and helping to constitute their identity during the Restoration. One sees ambitious efforts in the poem to signal this identity through tone and allusions and central tropes, techniques that carry the poem's meanings indirectly and ambiguously—yet unmistakably. That these meanings are contained in a paraphrase of a canticle of the church is a telling sign of Chudleigh's effort to carry out her reform within the church. The partial masking of her intentions in the poem is a tactic one can imagine was used in numerous ways by former Puritans throughout the decades of the Restoration. Two threads of *The Song*—in particular, its emphasis on the creator God and on innovation—signal Chudleigh's statement of a dissenting religious identity. I would suggest that these two dominant motifs function by metonymy to represent Puritan ideals as intact even in this time of repression. By representing indirectly the preoccupations and themes of Restoration Puritanism, Chudleigh can suggest the continuation of a shared understanding among a physically and socially dispersed people. This implied understanding in the poem includes a reminder of God's promises for continued protection of the godly together with a claim of their continuing viability. However indirectly, these themes continue to express the spirit of Puritan reform from laity within the church despite the opposition of leaders in church and state.[26]

PRAISE OF THE CREATOR GOD

The most profound quality of Chudleigh's ambitious paraphrase is its lofty tone, whose sounds of praise resound far beyond those of the canticle of praise, the "Benedicite, Omnia Opera" from the Book of Common Prayer, on which it is based.[27] The first forty-two stanzas of the poem focus without interruption on a call for all within a vast universe to join the song of praise to God: the vision is comprehensive in the largest sense; the tone, already celebrative in the canticle, moves to a level of Pindaric rapture in the poem. In the preface to *The Song*, Chudleigh explains her choice of a Pindaric Ode as one fitting the exalted subject of the poem as well as one providing the poet "a great Scope to the Fancy" and freeing her from "the stricter Rules of other Poetry."[28] This aesthetic of grandeur and lofty praise of "enthusiasm" that Chudleigh chooses for *The Song* exemplifies the preferred quality for poetry of a number of poets of dissenting background during the Restoration.[29] Poet and critic John Dennis articulated most directly the aesthetic argument for employing "enthusiasm" in poetry. Dennis saw the quality of enthusiasm as most apt for religious subjects, which, in his view, "necessarily produce these great and strong Enthusiams that can produce passions that other topics cannot."[30]

The object of Chudleigh's elaborate praise in *The Song* is the creator God. Although an emphasis on God as creator is implicit in the "Benedicite, Omnia Opera," which begins, "O all ye Works of the Lord, bless ye the Lord," Chudleigh makes explicit and develops extensively numerous references to God as creator:

> And thence to their first Cause thy Admiration raise
> In sprightly Airs, and sweet harmonious Lays.
> Assist me, all ye Works of Art Divine,
> Ye wondrous Products of Almighty Pow'r.
>
> . . . .
> Adore his Goodness, whose unweary'd Love
> Call'd into Act that great Design.
>
> . . . .
> Extol his Wisdom, who such Wonders wrought,
> Who made, and like one individual Soul
> Fills ev'ry part, and still preserves the Mighty Whole.
>
> . . . .
> In lofty Strains your kind Creator bless:
> In unforc'd, grateful, and exalted Lays.
> (ll. 9–12, 32–33, 67–69, 115–16)

Of possible explanations for Chudleigh's emphasis on the creator God in *The Song*, one surely cannot disregard the emerging theology of natural religion in the late seventeenth century. Nor can one ignore Chudleigh's genuine concern with moving beyond "party" or division, the goal as well of the Cambridge Platonists by whom she was influenced.[31] In this second light, one can read the many allusions to the creator as suggesting a grandly comprehensive vision of a God in whom all reside and whom all can worship, thus mitigating divisions in the religious fabric of England.

Less obvious than these explanations, but more closely aligned with the poem's central narrative of the "three children" of Daniel, is a reading of the poem's trope of the creator God as conveying a particular message to those under persecution. Such an appeal by nonconformists during the Restoration to the absolute, unqualified power of the creator God was not unique to Chudleigh. Owen C. Watkins points out that Bunyan's focus on God as creator rather than on God's presence or promises of love is deliberate and purposeful.[32] It is from the perspective of the creator God that Bunyan can best offer the promise for protection to those under current persecution. In his *Seasonable Counsel*, Bunyan explains at length this rationale for focusing on the creator God, using imagery of the earth and universe similar to that in Chudleigh's poem:

> Now a *Creation* none can destroy but a *Creator*; wherefore here is comfort. But again, God hath created us in *Christ Jesus,* thats another thing: the *Sun* is created in the *Heavens*; the *Stars* are created in the *Heavens*; the *Moon* is created in the *Heavens*, who can reach them, touch them, destroy them, but the *Creator*? Why, this is the case of the Saint, because he has to do with a *Creator,* he is fastened to Christ: Yea, is in him by an act of Creation (Eph 2.10) so that unless Christ and the creation of the holy Ghost can be destroyed, he is safe that is *suffering according to the will of God, and that hath committed the keeping of his Soul to him in well-doing, as unto a faithful Creator.*[33]

Although Bunyan acknowledges the paucity of biblical references to God as creator, he argues that the unlimited power of the creator is a necessary emphasis for those who live in adversity. How, Bunyan asks, can one be fearful in the light of God the creator?[34]

As part of their emphasis on the creator God, both Bunyan and Chudleigh invoke the Old Testament narrative of God's intervention in saving the Israelites. Bunyan illustrates this intervention of the creator God explicitly when he describes, again in a tone closer to Chudleigh's than to his own professed "plain and simple" style, God's rescue of Israel from their political and social exile in Egypt: "God the Creator will sometimes mount himself and ride thorough the earth in such Majesty and glory, that he will make all to stand in the Tent doors to behold him. O how he rode in his *chariots of Salvation*, when he went to save his people out of the land of

Egypt; how he shook the Nations."[35] Bunyan argues that it is the power of the creator God that offers both support for the suffering godly—"Wherefore by this peculiar Title of Creator, the Apostle prepareth support for suffering Saints"—and a promise to destroy those who would "seek to *swallow* up and destroy the *Church and People of God*."[36]

Similarly, in *The Song*, Chudleigh makes repeated references to God's protection of Israel. Indeed, the stanza that introduces the narrative of Israel in the poem is filled with such promises:

> Let Israel, that distinguish'd Race,
> Those Darlings of almighty Love,
> Whom Heav'n has bless'd with his peculiar Grace,
> To their great Benefactor thankful prove:
> To him, who in their infant State,
> When they, expos'd and helpless, lay,
> To ev'ry threatening Ill a Prey:
> Obnoxious to the Storms of Fate,
> And their insulting Neighbours Hate,
> Kept them from all approaching Harms
> Secure, in his all-pow'rful Arms.
>
> (ll. 1311–21)

Although Chudleigh's connection of the creator God to the Old Testament narrative is less explicit than Bunyan's, the major role of the two elements in her work is undeniable. Thus, Chudleigh communicates not only through the elevated tone of *The Song* but also through the associations that the emphasis on a creator God may have held for those who were familiar with this trope of promise.

INNOVATION AND GODLINESS

Within the extended, exalted praise of *The Song*, a number of repeated allusions draw attention to themselves through their seeming lack of fit. For instance, regularly breaking into the song of praise are prosaic explanations of the physical universe from the point of view of empirical science. Even more startling are extensive references to the theories of the preexistence of souls and the prior existence of a physically flawless earth. For both of these latter radical concepts, Chudleigh offers explanation and apology in the poem's preface, apologies, however, that instead of mitigating the motifs, draw further attention to them, underscoring their central place in the poem. As with the poem's use of empirical science, the

appeals to the preexistence of souls and a prior flawless earth challenge the current status quo, signaling an implied community of
those who would challenge the Restoration's conservative majority.

Chudleigh alludes regularly in *The Song* to the new empirical
knowledge, whether to knowledge of global weather, the cycle of
condensation and rain, atom theory, or to theories of the universe—
even to the possibility of human life in other parts of a vast universe.
That Chudleigh would have access to discoveries emerging from
empirical studies of the earth and universe is made likely not only
by the general interest in such studies during the Restoration but
also because of a more direct connection through her uncle, Dr.
Thomas Sydenham, her mother's youngest brother from a family of
Dorset Independents, who pursued research and practice in medi-
cine recognized even in our own century for its innovation. The independent thinking of this former Cromwellian soldier, who was
twice wounded in the civil wars and who was later an associate of
Robert Boyle and John Locke, among others, is revealed in his letter
to a fellow physician in which Sydenham defends his proposal for
treating gout: "If this dissertation escape blame both from you and
those other few (but tried and honorable men) whom I call my
friends, I shall care little for the others. They are hostile to me simply because what I think of diseases and their cures differs from
what they think. It could not be otherwise. It is my nature to think
where others read; to ask less whether the world agrees with me
than whether I agree with the truth, and to hold cheap the rumors
and applause of the multitude."[37]

Given the challenge to orthodox medical practice from this former Puritan soldier-turned-physician, it is perhaps not surprising
that, with the publication of his most important and controversial
treatise on the treatment of smallpox, Thomas Sydenham found
himself seeking protection from the first Earl of Shaftesbury, a defender of nonconformists. Sydenham explains in his dedication to
Shaftesbury that in his smallpox research the primary "contest"
had been, not with the disease itself, but with "what is more uncur-
able, the prejudices of Relations and Assistants . . . and the receivd
practice of physitians.[38] In the minds of those who resisted his work,
the concepts of innovation and dissent became linked, as seen in
their charges of sectarianism against Sydenham in response to the
new directions in medical treatment he propounded.

Although Chudleigh's references to the physical workings of the
world in *The Song* may be understood in the context of the excitement over the discoveries of empirical science at the time, the context of the full poem suggests that these allusions may signal

innovation as an understood sign of discontent. For Chudleigh employs other concepts in the poem characterized by their strikingly innovative nature. One of these, the concept of the preexistence of souls, posits the idea that souls exist from the beginning of time independent of the forms of their material embodiment. Chudleigh describes this doctrine in some detail in the poem's preface, attempting to defend it by virtue of those ancient and modern writers who have propounded the idea.

The particular proponent of the preexistence of souls during Chudleigh's time was Henry More, one of the more mystical of the Cambridge Platonists. Like others of this group of former dissenters who worked to calm contention by formulating a broad notion of Christianity, More rejected both the narrow theological construction and elitism of Calvinism and the rigid ecclesiastical practices of the Anglican Church. Employing the idea of the preexistence of souls in part to counter contemporary materialist philosophies, another preoccupation of the Cambridge Platonists, More defended the theory, as did Chudleigh, on the basis of its ancient origins and its congruity with reason: "But that in some sort souls do preexist / Seems to right reason nothing dissonant."[39] Identified by Baxter as a belief held by some Latitudinarians, the concept of the preexistence of souls was popular enough by the 1690s among those with dissenting connections to become a featured theme in the weekly periodical *The Athenian Mercury*, a project of the Whig publisher and friend to nonconformists John Dunton.[40]

The concept of the preexistent soul may have appealed to those of Puritan background for several reasons. Primarily, it offered a way of defining sin without either penalizing individuals or giving up the idea of a deeply flawed world. The latter emphasis is implied in a prefatory dialogue in Dunton's *The Visions of the Soul,* where one of the speakers explains, "incorporation [into a body] is a Penalty inflicted upon Souls for their Extravagance in this World . . . the Body is a Prison, A Clog."[41]

Chudleigh herself employs the idea of the preexistence of souls specifically as a way to reconcile the existence of sin with God's justice to individuals, specifically to the question of the fate of children who die young, an instance to which More also explicitly refers. As Chudleigh explains in the preface to *The Song*: "Its Advocates tell us, that 'tis contrary to the Idea we have of the Justice and Goodness of God, to believe that he would condemn innocent Spirits, such as had never committed any Sin, nor done any thing that could justly Occasion their forfeiting his Favour, to such Bodies as much unavoidably rob them of their Native Purity, and render them ob-

noxious to his Wrath, and its dreadful Consequence, eternal Punishment."[42] For Chudleigh as well as More, the concept of the
preexistence of souls appears to have provided an explanation for
human sin that is more universal and hope filled than the strict Calvinist models of the earlier part of the century. More captures this
optimism in his explanation of the ease with which the soul of the
righteous human rejoins God:

> So nothing now in death is to be dred
> Of him that wakes to truth and righteousnesse.
> The Corps lies here, the soul aloft is fled
> Unto the fount of perfect happiness:
> Full freedom, joy and peace, she lively doth possesse.[43]

Underscoring the emphasis on innovation in *The Song* is yet a
second unorthodox motif that is given significant emphasis in the
poem's structure: the idea of the original smoothness and perfection
of the antediluvian earth's surface. The source of this concept is the
elaborately detailed *The Sacred Theory of the Earth* (1690, 1701)
by Thomas Burnet, to which Chudleigh refers in the poem's preface.[44] Of Puritan background, Burnet was a pupil of Tillotson and a
friend to the Cambridge Platonist Ralph Cudsworth. Like More,
Burnet developed a theory that allowed him to foreground human
sinfulness at the same time as he attempted to satisfy reason. If
More's theory of the preexistence of souls ameliorates the concept
of the consequences of sin for individuals at the same time as it retains an emphasis on human sinfulness, Burnet's theory emphasizes the world's sinfulness while satisfying the reason of science's
laws. In Burnet's theory, sin caused the dramatic change in the
earth from its original perfection to the current chaotic quality of
the earth's surface. Burnet's own chronology of cataclysmic events
moves from an account of the flood to that of a second cataclysm in
the form of fire, whose sources are in natural causes such as volca-
noes and whose origin is Rome, seat of the Antichrist, and then onto
a stage of renovation before a final consummation of all things.

Burnet's emphasis on apocalyptic events is not unique; Neil Keeble points to the millenarian tradition inherited by those of Puritan
background in the Restoration and summarizes the forms this tradition takes on in the literature of the time.[45] Thus, when Chudleigh
chooses an apocalyptic theme as a major structural element in *The
Song*, she appears again to be marking her poem by employing a
motif familiar to the community of Puritans in this time of marginal-
ization and dispersion. As early as the fourth stanza in a poem of

ninety stanzas, Chudleigh outlines a series of apocalyptic-like events closely paralleling those in Burnet's scheme. She uses this sequence of events to structure in striking fashion the long first section of the poem, whose glorious praise becomes broken into intermittently by instances of human sin and its cataclysmic consequences.

At the same time that Chudleigh employs unorthodox, innovative concepts in her poem, she also marks limits to that innovation, thus indicating her own basic Christian orthodoxy. For instance, Chudleigh demonstrates in *The Song* that she was aware of, and taking a stance against, the threat of Socinianism, a movement opposed in particular by John Owen.[46] Signs of Chudleigh's affirmation of a rationalist view of the Trinity and Christ's divinity include the celebration of the Trinity in the final ten stanzas of *The Song* as well as the placing at the heart of the poem a narrative of the New Testament story of Christ's intervention and redemption.

Even in these passages, however, Chudleigh continues to signal the discontent of a dissenting community. In the section that introduces Christ's intervention, Chudleigh suggests a particular sensibility or "Sentiment" (l. 1094) necessary to receive and act out Christ's redemption. Modulating her tone from the poem's earlier rapturous praise to a subdued but compelling voice that carries the message of personal responsibility for Christ's suffering, Chudleigh appeals to the personal emotions of the individual sinner. The move from the prominence of an abstract Creator in the first section of the poem to that of Christ's redemptive act and the reception of that act shifts the focus to the quality of the individual human heart. It is this emphasis on the inward state of the believer that Keeble argues had become a primary theme in the writings of nonconformists during the Restoration period, with the battles that had been fought externally earlier in the century now contained primarily in battles of the internal spirit.[47]

This emphasis on the condition of one's heart is also achieved by the modulation in the poem's middle stanzas from third- to second-person accounts of human sin, moving the reader from observer to one personally implicated in the guilt. Christ's "ignominious Fate" is described in stanza 48 as "the dire Result both of *their* ["cruel Men['s]"] Guilt and Hate" (l. 1083); by the following stanza Christ's pain is depicted as the result of "*our* Sins," a phrase repeated twice to suggest the sermonlike nature of the poem at this point. Completing the movement at the heart of this section is a shift into prayer, delivered in third person plural to reinforce the shared outcome of the lesson for all who receive it: "Ah!, blessed Virgin, let us learn

from thee / To live from all our sinful Passions free: . . . Thy blest
Example shall our Pattern be, / We'll strive to live, to love, to grieve,
like thee" (ll. 1150–51, 1163–64).[48]

The implied audience for this section of *The Song* that stresses
individual response to Christ's redemption are those "suff'ring
Saints" who have been "Follo'wers in the rugged Way" (ll. 1272,
1281). Indeed, the final stanzas of the poem's central section allude
directly to a special "godly" people who take God's gospel into the
world, a "dang'rous Proof of Zeal" (l. 1301).[49] Chudleigh's attitude
toward this group who "cross Seas unknown" (l. 1304) is clear from
her tone of approbation and encouragement:

> Contemning Dangers, still pursue your Way,
> And far as the remotest Bounds of Day,
> The glorious Ensign of your Suff'ring God display.
>
> (ll. 1308–10)

Merging in these lines are the implied motifs of an all-powerful, protecting God, who teaches courage amidst persecution, and of God's
followers, who pursue their own ways and convictions beyond existing boundaries, concepts that would offer comfort and reassurance
to those who found themselves religiously and socially dispos-
sessed.

Prophesy and Preaching

By associating the two tropes of the creator God and innovation
with godliness, Chudleigh positions herself to assume boldly in the
remainder of the poem a Puritan voice of reform in the mode of
prophet and preacher. It is in the context of the poem's two main
narratives of communities under persecution—the Israelites in
bondage in Egypt and the three Jewish youth in Babylon—that
Chudleigh sets out to instruct the established clergy. As mentioned,
Chudleigh's extensive use of Old Testament analogue in the poem
recalls earlier Puritan sermons and exegesis; indeed, the use of prophetic writings such as Daniel continued to be associated with radical thought in the later seventeenth century.[50] One might speculate
that the long narrative in this section of the Israelites' battle for
freedom from Egyptian rule corresponds with the plight of nonconformists as Chudleigh had known it throughout her lifetime. An
even more pointed correspondence to the experience of nonconformists is the poem's primary narrative of the story of the three

persecuted "children" of Daniel. Daniel and his three young Jewish compatriots have been put into the power of enemies and an ungodly king and left with no leader. They have been silenced and given no means or place to worship. And, despite their proofs of godliness and wisdom, they are persecuted by the king for not following his commands to worship idols.

Although Chudleigh does not make explicit in her poem all the narrative details of the story from Daniel, she makes clear her attitude toward the young Israelites who are persecuted because they "would not [their] holy faith conceal" (l. 1881). She depicts the young men as "Jewish heroes" who show courage "amid the tempting Glories of a vicious Court" (l. 1914) by resisting its efforts to force them to compromise their faith:

> You did ev'n the Tyrant's Threats despise,
> And brav'd those Dangers they so much did dread;
> Life, on vile impious Terms you did refuse,
> And, unconcern'd, did all your Honour lose.
>
> (ll. 1917–20)

Indeed, Chudleigh's argument comes across pointedly: those who suffer for the sake of their faith and who "despise" the "Tyrant's Threats" (l. 1917) are to be praised for not compromising their faith. It is the "haughty Tyrant," not those persecuted for their faith, who is to be reprimanded—and instructed.

A number of structural techniques in the last section of Chudleigh's poem help align the Old Testament narratives with seventeenth-century England. For instance, her language echoes that of earlier Puritan texts: the Israelites are saved, the poem suggests, by providence, allowing them to "reach the happy Soil . . . / The promis'd Canaan" (ll. 1494, 1496); the three Jewish youth are told to sing their song to "admiring Saints" (l. 1929) with continued "Zeal" and "Raptures" (l. 1928, 1930). Chudleigh's language is striking here, for texts containing such expressions of enthusiasm could expect to meet with scorn. One senses no hint of reticence in Chudleigh's tone, however, as she employs a language that reclaims the qualities of belief of an earlier age.

Chudleigh further intertwines the Old Testament narratives with contemporary circumstances by paralleling the established clergy with the priests of Israel. Already in the preface to *The Song*, Chudleigh constructs the established clergy explicitly as the recipients of her instruction. It is, Chudleigh suggests, precisely those clergy who exhibit a religious spirit who will understand her intentions: "Such among them as answer this Character, will not, I hope, misconstrue my Words."[51] Chudleigh goes so far as to define the religious spirit she expects in clergy, urging that they be "persons who make doing Good the Business of their Lives, who have no other Design, no other Aim, but that of imitating their great Master, and making themselves shining Examples of Piety and Virtue."[52]

Assuming a moral authority beyond that of the earlier sections of the poem, Chudleigh goes on to teach her audience of "priests" their duties. She would have them substitute a battle against vice for one against parties: "No more a War with diff'rent Parties wage, / But make it your whole Bus'ness to reform the Age / With Vice alone the Combat try" (ll. 1514–16). She asks them to teach forgiveness to the "Revengeful," a group during the Restoration that would include clergy who themselves often led the way in "scorning" nonconformists, a term Chudleigh repeats twice in the passage.[53] Chudleigh also advises the clergy on the virtues she would have them teach. She begins her list of virtues with charity—"Persuade them with a bounteous Mind / To be to the deserving Needy Kind" (ll. 1534–35). Such an emphasis on charity, as Chudleigh would have surely observed through her father's associations in Exeter and Clyst St. George, was often associated during the Restoration with nonconformists. Margo Todd points out that the preaching of charity from Anglican pulpits decreased in frequency during the decades of the Restoration as the increasingly conservative church gradually withdrew from this humanist ideal.[54] Finally, Chudleigh goes so far as to instruct the clergy in the style of their preaching: preach "with Zeal and Clearness," she urges, "banish empty Shews" in favor of "solid Notion" (ll. 1505, 1511). Although the "plain" style of preaching associated with Puritanism had to a degree been adopted by Anglicans as well, Chudleigh's instructions still ring with the voice of an earlier age and ideal.

Given the political and social hegemony of the monarchy and the Established Church during the Restoration, one cannot ignore the social leveling that Chudleigh makes explicit in this section of the poem. Chudleigh contends that many are currently "honoured" who do not deserve it, "while such as merit Empires, live obscure, / And all th' Indignities of Fate endure" (ll. 1551–52). The true test of worth, she suggests, lies not in one's given position in the hierarchy but in one's own virtue. Neither the church's ecclesiastical hierarchy nor its rites have precedent over the piety of the individual believer, for "the true, substantial Wealth is lodg'd within" (l. 1585). Chudleigh's very acts in the poem of locating authority within individuals and placing her own narrative authority over that of the church hierarchy boldly demonstrate her argument. Indeed, despite Chudleigh's emphasis on reason, one sees in this late-seventeenth-century text qualities of the "hotter sort of Protestants" who demanded that those in elevated social positions live disciplined lives.[55] Chudleigh would have clergy increase their piety. She directs them, "priests of Israel" as they are, to live "strict blameless Lives" that will give "pious Lessons" to others and to make their lives an act of praise to God: "No other God, no other Joy, no other Bus'ness Know" (ll. 1755, 1763, 1777).

In her attempt to improve the clergy, Chudleigh may have been referencing the problem faced by the church following the Restoration in supplying qualified clergy. Given the approximate time of the poem's composition, it appears likely, however, that her discontent ranged more broadly than this. Whether Chudleigh was responding to the increasing persecution of nonconformists in the 1680s, to the new promises held out by the ascension of William and Mary, or to the growing conservatism of the Anglican Church and to her own circumstances of changing parishes, the poem suggests that the church had not reformed itself sufficiently for those still influenced by earlier Puritan ideals. Even as Chudleigh describes herself in the poem's preface as conforming to the practices of the church, she implies that these practices are neither sufficiently reformed nor carried out by a sufficiently pious clergy.

In Spurr's concise formulation, separation from the Anglican Church during the Restoration was "an offense against charity, common sense and prudence" and chosen by only a small minority.[56] Although Keeble has documented the inability of legal restrictions to quiet nonconformist literary voices, yet another strategy was to voice discontent from a more socially and politically secure place within the church. Mary Lee Chudleigh offered her contribution to the voicing of this discontent in *The Song of the Three Children Paraphras'd*, bringing her imaginative interpretation of an Anglican canticle into the service of reform. The themes of the poem together suggest an awareness of an identity among Restoration discontents that may have been shared by those, like herself, who attempted to retain Puritan values in a culture and under conditions that forced these values into new shapes and expressions. Like others of Puritan background born at the beginning of the Restoration decades, Chudleigh maintained a spirit of godliness while she helped articulate the new shape of these values.[57] The poet Elizabeth Thomas's description of Chudleigh as the last of three important pious women of her acquaintance is telling. A woman of "pious Words" and "pious Zeal," as Thomas calls her, Chudleigh, together with other poets of Puritan background, continued to model a godly piety that surely influenced the spiritual movements that emerged in the new century.[58] Chudleigh's primary contribution in constructing her ambitious paraphrase, however, was to capture in literary form something of the complex of Puritan values and identity that characterized the twilight of seventeenth-century Puritanism.

NOTES

1. Mark Stoyle attributes the ancient church fixtures characteristic of the churches in the Teign Valley to the valley's physical isolation, an isolation that also accounted for the small number of "godly activists" in this area of Devonshire during the civil wars. See *Loyalty and Locality: Popular Allegiance in Devon during the English Civil War* (Exeter: University of Exeter Press, 1994), 213.

2. In March 1998 I submitted a report to Ashton Church, Devon, that provides evidence for Mary Chudleigh's authorship of the inscription. I would like to thank Annabell Hoffman, Ashton church warden, for welcoming me to St. John the Baptist Church, Ashton, and providing me a copy of *Ashton Church Devon* (Exeter: Ashton PCC, 1984, 1993), in which the ledger stone is described.

3. Allan Brockett, *Nonconformity in Exeter, 1650-1875* (Manchester: Manchester University Press, 1962), 37, estimates the number of nonconformists in Exeter in 1672 as approximately one in twelve or 8 percent, a number somewhat larger than the estimate of 5 percent for all of England offered by John Spurr in *The Restoration Church in England, 1646-1689* (New Haven: Yale University Press, 1991), 72.

4. Spurr, *The Restoration Church*, 83.

5. Daniel Defoe, *King William's Affection to the Church of England Examined*, 5th ed. (London, 1703), 23.

6. Richard L. Greaves, *Deliver Us from Evil: The Radical Underground in Britain, 1660-1663* (New York: Oxford University Press, 1986), 35-40.

7. David Riesman, *Thomas Sydenham: Clinician* (New York: Paul B. Hoebner, 1926), 26.

8. John Marshall, *John Locke: Resistance, Religion and Responsibility* (Cambridge: Cambridge University Press, 1994), 53.

9. Richard Baxter, *Reliquiae Baxterianae* (London: printed for T. Parkhurst, J. Robinson, F. Lawrence, and F. Dunton, 1696), 386–87.

10. Marshall, *John Locke*, 40 n. 13. Chudleigh praised Tillotson as one of the first among clergy.

11. Donald Davie, *A Gathered Church: The Literature of the English Dissenting Interest, 1700-1930* (New York: Oxford University Press, 1978), 6.

12. Mary Sydenham Lee's father and brothers were leading fighters for Parliament in Dorset County; her mother, Mary Jeffrey Sydenham, was reportedly killed in 1643 by royalists in a retributive raid on the Sydenham home. See Kenneth Dewhurst, *Dr. Thomas Sydenham, 1624-1689: His Life and Original Writings* (Berkeley and Los Angeles: University of California Press, 1966), 9.

The dates of Richard Lee's local political activities suggest that he was unable to hold local office until after the Revolution of 1688. Two prominent political leaders from Exeter with whom he appears to have worked most closely, John Elwill and Sir Edward Seaward, had clear ties to nonconformity. As a member of the House of Commons for Barnstaple in 1679/80 and again in 1688, Richard Lee represented one of the most significant strongholds of Puritanism in Devon during the years of the Exclusion Crisis.

13. The patronage of Clyst St. George was held by the Parr family from 1625 until 1738. John Parr, an Exeter merchant who was patron through much of the Restoration, is identified by Burnet Morris as a nonconformist: See "John Parr," *The Burnet Morris Index, 1940–1990* (Exeter: Devon Library Services, 1990). A single clergyman, Robert Parr, M.A., served the parish continuously from 1638 until his death in 1664, suggesting that he was reformed enough to satisfy the leaders of the Commonwealth.

14. Ashton Church was served by William Bowden from an undetermined beginning date through 1662, at which time he was deprived of his position. Bowden was listed without patron; only with his successors did the Chudleigh family again assume its customary role of patron. See George Oliver, *Ecclesiastical Antiquities in Devon, Being Observations on Several Churches in Devonshire with Some Memoranda for the History of Cornwall* (Exeter: W. C. Featherstone, 1840), 197.

15. Mary Strode, wife of the first baronet, Sir George Chudleigh, was the daughter of William and Mary Strode, he a parliamentarian, she known for her exceptional practices of Puritan piety and devotion. Mary Strode's brother, William Strode, was one of a handful of parliamentarians whom King Charles sought to imprison. The Chudleigh's home on the Stretchleigh estate from 1605 until the late 1620s placed them in close proximity to the Strode family and to Plymouth, a city with long exposure to radical ideas and where George Chudleigh himself participated with his father-in-law in sponsoring a lectureship in nearby Mobery. See Mary Wolffe, *Gentry Leaders in Peace and War: The Gentry Governors of Devon in the Early Seventeenth Century* (Exeter: University of Exeter Press, 1997), 96.

16. Hereafter referred to as *The Song*. Passages from the poem will be identified by line number in the text. See *The Poems and Prose of Mary, Lady Chudleigh*, ed. Margaret J. M. Ezell (New York: Oxford University Press, 1993), 177–241. See my discussion of Chudleigh in relation to Queen Anne in "A Puritan Subject's Panegyrics to Queen Anne," *Studies in English Literature* 42, no. 3 (2002): 475–99.

17. John Bunyan, *Seasonable Counsel* and *A Discourse upon the Pharisee and the Publicane*, ed. Owen C. Watkins (Oxford: Clarendon Press, 1988), 52.

18. Chudleigh, preface to *The Song, Poems and Prose*, 174–75.

19. Chudleigh was very likely aware of the stories of the persecution of nonconformist clergy and of the piety and courage often associated with them. In "Early Nonconformity in Bideford," Miss Wickham describes the imprisonment of the nonconformist clergyman Mr. Oliver Peard, whose family was from Barnstaple, the city in which Chudleigh's father won election to the House of Commons in the 1680s. Mr. Peard's sufferings "'brought him to the very point of death.'" Wickam summarizes the fate of other Devon nonconformist clergy: "Some were committed to jail, some were fined, others harassed by the powers in being, two were exiled for nine and ten months, one was led to prison, his hands so tightly bound that 'the blood burst out from the end of his fingers.'" See *Reports and Transactions of the Devonshire Association for the Advancement of Science, Literature, and Art* 34 (1902): 416. Many of these stories about Devonshire nonconformist clergy were recorded in Edward Calamy's *The Nonconformist's Memorial: Ministers Ejected or Silenced in Devonshire* (Samuel Palmer, n.d.).

20. Bunyan, *Seasonable Counsel*, 41.

21. Chudleigh's acknowledgment of the positive qualities of the present clergy is similar in tone to Locke's comment in his "Critical Notes" that he does not intend to criticize the "'many excellent preachers . . . of the Church of England,'" to whose popular sermons even dissenters flocked (quoted in Marshall, *John Locke*, 106). Both Locke and Chudleigh may have had in mind, in particular, John Tillotson's preaching.

22. Chudleigh, preface to *The Song, Poems and Prose*, 173.

23. Most former supporters of the Commonwealth did not wish to draw attention to themselves, subject as they were to blame for the turmoil of the civil wars and Interregnum. Most wished to prove themselves law-abiding citizens during this time when their status was unsure. See J. T. Cliffe, *The Puritan Gentry Besieged, 1650-1700* (London and New York: Routledge, 1993), 175–76, 194; and Keith Thomas, *Religion and the Decline of Magic: Studies in Popular Beliefs in Sixteenth and Seventeenth Century England* (New York: Oxford University Press, 1971), 144.

24. Spurr, *Restoration Church*, 83, 37–38.

25. See Harry Grant Plum, *Restoration Puritanism: A Study of the Growth of English Liberty* (Port Washington, N.Y.: Kennikat Press, 1943), 79.

26. The vital voice of *The Song* illustrates N. H. Keeble's argument that nonconformist writing during the Restoration period was far from anachronistic, but rather, growing out of the persecution of the time, achieved a status beyond that of the preceding decades. See *The Literary Culture of Nonconformity in Later Seventeenth-Century England* (Athens, Ga.: University of Georgia Press, 1987), 22–23.

27. The canticle itself is based on an Apocryphal addition to Daniel 3.

28. Chudleigh, preface to *The Song, Poems and Prose*, 169.

29. Hoxie Neale Fairchild in her study, *Religious Trends in English Poetry*, vol. 1 (New York: Columbia University Press, 1939), 203, suggests that more verse forms than usually acknowledged were employed in the late seventeenth and early eighteenth centuries, including the Pindaric. She finds the religious poetry of this period to be composed primarily by those associated with nonconformity, the Low Church, and the Whig party. One poet of this period who wrote extensively in the Pindaric form was the nonconformist Elizabeth Singer Rowe, who wrote for the *Athenian Mercury* in the 1690s and whose poetry may have influenced Chudleigh's own.

30. John Dennis, *The Advancement and Reformation of Poetry* (London: Rich. Parker, 1701), 218. That the emphasis on enthusiastic praise was shared in wider circles of nonconformists as well is suggested by Cliffe's story of nonconformist Sir Edward Rode, who, at his death in 1704, expressed his confidence that he could be saved if he could but sing praise to God (*Puritan Gentry Besieged*, 195).

31. Richard Baxter identifies as one of five types of nonconformists those "abhorring the very Name of Parties" (*Reliquiae Baxterianae*, 387).

32. Bunyan, *Seasonable Counsel*, xxx, xxvii.

33. Ibid., 80.

34. Ibid., 83.

35. John Bunyan, *Grace Abounding to the Chief of Sinners*, ed. Roger Sharrock (Oxford: Clarendon Press, 1962), 3; *Seasonable Counsel*, 84.

36. Bunyan, *Seasonable Counsel*, 79, 84.

37. Sydenham to Dr. Thomas Short, *The Whole Works of that Excellent Practical Physician, Dr. Thomas Sydenham,* 4th ed., trans. John Pechey (London, 1705), 341.

38. Dewhurst, *Dr. Thomas Sydenham*, 103.

39. Henry More, "The Præexistency of the Soul," *The Complete Poems of Dr. Henry More, 1614-1687,* ed. Alexander B. Grosart (St. George's Blackburn, Lancashire: printed for private circulation, 1878), 127.

40. Baxter, *Reliquiae Baxterianae*, 386. The theory of the preexistence of souls was brought up in several issues of the first volume of *The Athenian Mercury*, and at least one special issue of the periodical was given over to the this topic. Dunton also published a separate book on the topic: *The Visions of the Soul, Before it Came into the Body* (London: printed for John Dunton, at the Raven in the Poultry, 1692).

41. Dunton, *The Vision of the Soul,* 1.

42. Chudleigh, preface to *The Song, Poems and Prose*, 170.

43. More, "The Præexistency of the Soul," *Complete Poems*, 128.

44. Thomas Burnet, *The Sacred Theory of the Earth* (London: Centaur Press, 1965).

45. See Keeble, *Literary Culture of Nonconformity*, 15–17, 192, 197–98.

46. The Socinian debates appear to have reached into the dissenting community in Exeter, as signaled by the publication of *A Letter to a Dissenter in Exeter* (London: printed for John Noon, 1719), which attempted to moderate the debate. The subtitle of the text, "*occasin'd by the late heats in those Parts: Upon Some Difference of Sentiments among the Brethren,*" suggests that the controversy may have been brewing for some time in the Westcounty of England.

47. Keeble, *Literary Culture of Nonconformity*, 197–204. That the idea of the indwelling spirit was still alive among dissenters in the Restoration is also suggested in the attacks on the concept: see, for example, Samuel Park's *A Discourse of Ecclesiastical Polity*, 1669.

48. By the last decades of the seventeenth century, one finds evidence in the writings of those in the church and nonconformists alike of the Virgin becoming a figure of sentiment with whom suffering believers identified. See, for instance, John Norris, "The Passion of the Virgin Mother: Beholding the Crucifixion of Her Divine Son," in *A Collection of Miscellanies* (Oxford: John Crofley, 1687), 92–94, or Nahum Tate, "The Blessed Virgin's Expostulation," in *Miscellanea Sacra, or, Poems on Divine & Moral Subjects,* 2d ed. (London: Hen[ry] Playford, 1698), 30–31. Tate (1652–1715), son of a nonconformist minister, is described by Fairchild as "more of a puritan than a latitudinarian" (Fairchild, *Religious Trends in English Poetry*, 178).

49. Michael Winship points out that although Robert Boyle, the governor of the Corporation for Propagating the Gospel in New England, was Anglican, most of the members were Puritans. Boyle, who was Thomas Sydenham's neighbor and colleague, visited with Increase Mather a number of times in the 1680s and gave Mather copies of his writings. See *Seers of God: Puritan Providentialism in the Restoration and Early Enlightenment* (Baltimore: The Johns Hopkins University Press, 1996), 64.

50. Thomas, *Religion and the Decline of Magic*, 140. Keeble points out that the millennial theme of the book of Daniel, a theme that Chudleigh foregrounds in her poem, had been popular among such radical groups as the fifth monarchists, and that the narratives of Daniel and the Israelites' escape from Egypt continued to be popular allusions in the writings of Restoration nonconformists (*Literary Culture of Nonconformity*, 189).

51. Chudleigh, preface to *The Song, Poems and Prose*, 174.

52. Ibid.

53. In his study of Puritanism and royalism in Devon, Stoyle notes the strong disdain shown toward Puritans by Anglican clergy and explains how this attitude heightened among royalists during the Restoration (*Loyality and Locality*, 208–10).

54. Margo Todd, *Christian Humanism and the Puritan Social Order* (Cambridge: Cambridge University Press, 1987), 158–62, 168–70, 175, 250–53, 258. Such religious and political divisions over charities showed up in Restoration Exeter over the construction and oversight of a workhouse for the poor. A number of nonconformist adherents of the project had close connections to Richard Lee, Chudleigh's father, who himself was involved in a charitable venture of significant scope in Clyst St. George.

55. Todd, *Christian Humanism*, 195.

56. Spurr, *Restoration Church*, 123–24.

57. Fairchild contends that the majority of "pious" poets of the Restoration years were born in the 1650s and earlier (*Religious Trends*, 202).

58. Elizabeth Thomas, "On the Death of Lady Chudleigh: An Ode," in *Pylades and Corinna* (London, 1731–32), 1:276; "To the Lady Chudleigh: On Printing Her Excellent Poems," in *Pylades and Corinna*, 1:149.

Part III
Puritanism and Its Others

From Imitating Language to a Language of Imitation: Puritan-Indian Discourse in Early New England

Richard Pointer

In seventeenth-century New England, Puritans endeavored to re-create Indians in their own image.[1] They wanted Native Americans to follow their lead in embracing the Christian gospel and living in communities dedicated to biblical principles and English cultural ways. That desire was often communicated in a language or vocabulary rife with the notion of imitation. Even as Puritans sought to pattern their lives after first-century Christianity, so they told Indian peoples to remodel their worlds after the Puritans'. Some natives heeded the call, others pretended to, and most preferred to stick with their old ways. Whatever the response, Puritan-Indian intercourse in a "language of imitation" had important effects on Puritan self-identity, sometimes confirming, as often complicating, who these Englishmen saw themselves to be.

The Puritan impulse to transform Indians was expressed right from the beginning of their colonial enterprise. In February 1629, Governor Matthew Cradock of the New England Company wrote a letter of instructions to John Endecott, leader of the first wave of planters in what would become the Massachusetts Bay Colony. Cradock reminded Endecott that "the main end of our Plantation" was to "bring the Indians to the knowledge of the Gospel." That end could be more quickly achieved if Endecott kept a "watchful eye over our own people," for their behavior would be the key to winning Indians to Christ. English settlers should "live unblamable and without reproof, and demean themselves justly and courteous towards the Indians, thereby to draw them to affect our persons, and consequently our religion."[2] A second letter two months later from all the company governors in London reiterated the same point. The governors expressed the hope that there might be "such a union" among all those involved in planting the colony "as might draw the heathen by our good example to the embracing of Christ and his Gospel."[3] Cradock and his colleagues apparently believed that if transplanted English Puritans could practice what they preached, Native Americans would be enticed to follow their exemplary lives and accept Christianity.

Drawing in the native peoples of southern New England to the gospel in the seventeenth century proved more difficult than the colony founders anticipated. However loud actions might speak, words would also be necessary to convince Indians to change their ways, and not just any words would do the job. Eventually, no one knew that better than John Eliot. "The *first step* which he [Eliot] judg'd Necessary," according to Cotton Mather, "was to learn the *Indian* language." Eliot recognized that natives "would never do so much as enquire after the Religion of the strangers now come into their Country, much less would they so far imitate us as to leave off their beastly way of living . . . unless we could first address them in a *Language* of their own."[4] Eliot labored long and hard from the 1640s through the 1680s to master the Massachusett tongue so that he could deliver in word and deed calls for Indians to follow English Christianity and civility. His messages made explicit what Cradock had hoped natives would discover on their own: that the Massachusett should leave the old ways and the old wisdom behind and pattern themselves instead on the biblical models embodied in New England Puritanism.

Massachusett men and women were hardly the only ones told to imitate English ways. Pequots, Narragansetts, Nipmucks, Wampanoags, and all the other Indian peoples with whom Puritans had contact heard the newcomers speak the same message.[5] Interestingly, natives often responded in kind. The result was a discourse, and especially a religious discourse, between Puritans and Indians in the middle decades of the seventeenth century punctuated by the motifs of pattern, model, and example. While clearly only one element of a larger religious discourse, the language of imitation is striking for what it reveals about the aims, assumptions, and anxieties of those on both sides of the cultural divide.[6] That language was firmly rooted in Puritans' views of themselves; imitation was at the heart of their religious self-identity. It was natural for them to frame their hopes and fears about Indians in a familiar vocabulary. But Native American peoples may also have brought imitation to the encounter as they underwent significant cultural transformations in the wake of the English arrival. If words were "at the center of the encounter between the Old World and the New, between the European 'self' and the native American 'other,'" as Jill Lepore has recently argued, then the choice to communicate in a language of imitation is worth examining for the ways in which it shaped both sides' view of themselves and the other.[7]

I

Before speaking to one another of imitation, Indians and Englishmen first had to imitate speech. Initial contacts in the late sixteenth and early seventeenth centuries between coastal natives and English fishermen and traders involved efforts to communicate with signs. Without a common language, Europeans and Indians improvised with gestures in hopes the other would understand their intended meaning. Body language, material gifts, and mimicked sounds were all employed. The case of English merchant John Guy's first encounter with Beothuck Indians is illustrative. When Guy's small trading party in 1612 came upon a temporarily vacated Beothuck village, the English took great care to make sure that the natives knew they had been there, not by stealing anything but by moving all the Indian goods into a different cabin and leaving behind gifts of food and beads. Guy's intent was to win Indian trust, a necessary first step for beginning and carrying on trade relations. His strategy proved effective for before long, two canoes of natives approached the white traders and through a series of reciprocal flag wavings and shouts, the two sides initiated face-to-face contact. A single Englishman and two Beothuck left their vessels and moved toward one another imitating the gestures of the other. When they met, gifts were immediately exchanged to the delight of all. After another Englishman went ashore, "all fower togeather daunced, laughing, & makeing signes of ioy, & gladnes, sometimes strikeing the breastes of our companie & sometymes theyre owne."[8]

As Stephen Greenblatt has explained, the display and interpretation of signs, the exchange of gifts, and the bartering of goods were all critical modes of communication in these early cross-cultural encounters. They in turn paved the way for the learning of language. Europeans were usually inclined to speed up the process of language acquisition by taking Indians back to Europe, often against their will. There they expected that the natives in childlike fashion would quickly assimilate the Europeans' language through imitation. Linguistically equipped Indians would then be returned to the Americas to serve as interpreters and guides.[9] Something like this happened in the case of Squanto. One of over twenty Indian captives of English sea captain John Hunt, Squanto ended up at the English home of merchant John Slaney, where he learned at least a modicum of English. Once back in New England, that language skill allowed him to become an important go-between when Pokanoket sachem, Massasoit, decided that it was a good idea to establish friendly relations with the newly arrived English Pilgrims in 1621.[10]

By the time the much larger Puritan migration occurred in the next decade, some members of each southern New England tribe were conversing well enough with the English (and the Dutch for that matter) to carry on complex diplomatic and trade relationships. Cross-cultural communication expanded apace despite English reluctance to learn much of the Ninnimissinuok's Algonquian languages.[11] Native dialects generally baffled settlers and reinforced European assumptions about the barbarism of native cultures.[12] Nevertheless, sustained exchange with New England's indigenous population convinced many Puritans that though savage, the Indians were educable and capable of both recognizing the superiority of English ways and mimicking them.[13]

While clearly ethnocentric, Puritan pronouncements about the natives' need to follow English models are understandable from a people whose collective religious identity was bound up in the notion of imitation.[14] Governor John Winthrop's sermon aboard the *Arbella*, "*Model* of Christian Charity" (my emphasis), presumed that they themselves would be the exemplar, at least according to Perry Miller's version of the Puritan errand. Winthrop called them to be a holy commonwealth whose light would shine to all nations, but especially to England. Someday the land and the church that had forsaken them might be stirred by their example to complete the reformation begun a century earlier.[15] For the Puritan "city on a hill" to flourish, however, they would also need to do their share of imitating. As Dwight Bozeman has emphasized, Puritans were strong biblical primitivists committed to the "power and exemplary authority of an ancient and 'first time.'" The Old and New Testaments laid out precedents for church and society that were now to be restored. Human additions to scriptural patterns, what the Puritans called "inventions," were to be stripped away in the return to biblical simplicity and purity.[16] Competing versions of Christianity as well as other belief systems were similarly disdained as "invented religions." Thus Roger Williams (admittedly a marginal Puritan himself) thought that Indians, "having lost the true and living God their Maker," had "created out of the nothing of their owne inventions many false and fained Gods and Creators."[17] Today historians recognize that European (including Puritan) views of Native

American religions (and much else) were themselves "inventions."[18] But in the seventeenth century, Puritans saw themselves not as originators or innovators but as imitators of the originals set down in the biblical narrative.

Whether wishing to be the imitated (as in models of Christian charity) or the imitator, New England Puritans operated within a mind-set and language caught up with imitation. That Puritans repeatedly brought that theme into their discourse with Native Americans is therefore not surprising. Before examining that discourse more closely, however, it is worth noting briefly that the Indians of southern New England may have been similarly inclined to speak among themselves and with Englishmen about what patterns they should follow. They were accustomed to conceiving time as "the constant re-enactment of tradition," a sort of perpetual dance in which new waves of dancers continually joined the circle and learned to imitate the steps of those more experienced. This "taken-for-granted character of day-to-day interaction" within Indian communities was becoming far less sure by the 1630s and 1640s, however, as the English presence gradually made it increasingly difficult for natives to count on the dance continuing unabated.[19] Following a smallpox epidemic and amid the Pequot War in 1636–37, for example, Narragansett sachem Miantonimi decided that the best way of protecting his people and their social order was to act more "like an English leader" (and less like his forefathers?) and to place "himself and those associated with him within the English system of rules and government."[20] By 1641, in the face of new circumstances, including English violations of earlier agreements, Miantonimi sought to reverse his earlier act of political imitation and urged the Montauks to unite with them against the English "for so are we all Indians, as the English are, and Say brother to one another, so we must be one as they are, otherwise we shall be all gone shortly, for you know our fathers had plenty of deer and skins, our plains were full of deer, as also our woods, and full of turkies, and our coves full of fish and fowl."[21] Miantonimi's plea for pan-Indian cooperation to rival English unity embodied yet another departure from past Narragansett action. Even more telling though, as anthropologist Kathleen Bragdon has pointed out, was his appeal to the *past*. This appeal reflects a growing tendency among the Ninnimissinuok to view time historically, that is, as a progression of change. Native communities wrestling with the prospect that time as they had understood it would not be endless thus had their own reasons for talking with Puritans about ancient ways.

II

More often than not, when Puritans employed the language of imitation in speaking with or about Indians, they did so in a prescriptive manner. Most typically natives were encouraged, much as lay Puritans were, to follow some good Puritan model. The usual admonition was to heed the righteous example of the local minister. But this style of discourse proved flexible enough for the English to use it to cover a variety of other "imitative" relationships. Sources reveal at least four other prescriptive applications within Puritan-Indian dialogue during the mid-seventeenth century. One involved Puritans upholding themselves as faithful followers of good models in their relations with Indians. Or to put it another way, they presented themselves not only as good models but as model followers of good models. At other times, Puritans placed emphasis on converted Indians as positive examples for whites and natives alike to emulate. Just as readily, however, Puritans warned all Englishmen against the bad models set by unredeemed natives. And conversely, all natives were told not to pattern their lives after one or another of the all-too-readily-available models of wickedness in New England.

Puritan dexterity in communicating through a language of imitation may be seen through briefly sampling each of these prescriptive uses. When it came to being told to emulate Puritan ways, few groups of Native Americans heard the refrain more often than Eliot's band of praying Indians at Natick, Massachusetts. Like later praying towns, Natick's formation reflected the Puritans' own strong impulse to imitate biblical patterns. Eliot instructed natives to construct political and ecclesiastical forms explicitly modeled on precedents found in Exodus 18. Convinced that Indian ways were inadequate in both church and state, Eliot implored these Massachusett men and women to refashion their community life along Old Testament lines.[22] Beyond that, the twin goals of Christianization and civilization that Puritans set out for the Massachusett required that they imitate English ways in matters of individual faith as well as in their dress, hair length, architecture, farming, and much more.[23] How far the Puritans expected Indians to go in copying them is suggested in Charles Cohen's recent analysis of Massachusett church confessions. Indian neophytes were instructed in the elaborate morphology of conversion that New England Puritans had worked out, another sign of their penchant for models.[24] Despite the fact that Waban, Nishohkou, Ponampan, and other Natick residents made confessions in 1652 that echoed "the cries of contrition standard in Puritan narrations," they were turned down for membership. They failed again in 1654. Only in 1659, when their spiritual narratives resembled those of English saints even more closely, did these converts win acceptance into Eliot's Roxbury congregation and the eventual right to form their own church.[25]

Whether church members or not, Ninnimissinuok who embraced Christianity could find themselves quickly upheld as model saints by their English brethren on both sides of the Atlantic. "Sagamore John" was one of the first, celebrated because "he desired to learne and speake our [English] language, and loved to imitate us in our behaviour and apparrell, and began to hearken after our God."[26] Other natives progressed even further in the faith. Early converts of Roger Williams, Thomas Mayhew Jr., and John Eliot became familiar figures to English readers who followed their spiritual journeys in tracts detailing missionary work in the 1640s and early 1650s. Wequash, Hiacoomes, Waban, and an elderly native referred to simply as "an Old Man" were portrayed as dedicated believers worthy of English imitation.[27] So, too, were Nishohkou and Robin Speen. The deathbed testimonies of their young children provided examples of the fruits of Christian fathering at its best.[28] Massachusetts minister Thomas Shepard "frequently chided his countrymen for being outdone [in piety] by the Christian natives." Stephen Marshall and a group of English Puritan pastors went even further. They admonished their charges to "let these poor *Indians* stand up as *incentives* to us . . . who knows but God *gave* life to *New England*, to quicken Old?" Model native lives could function in Marshall's words as an *"Indian Sermon"* to inspire or goad the English on to holier actions.[29] As early as 1651 Eliot believed that Natick as a whole could serve as something of a city on a hill for other native communities, if not for his homeland. In response to requests from other groups of New England Indians for evangelists, he expressed confidence that "the work which we now have in hand [in Natick], will be as a patterne and Copie before them, to imitate in all the Countrey, both in civillizing them in their Order, Government, Law, and in their Church proceedings and administrations."[30]

Thirty years later Eliot and the Mayhews were still publishing accounts of Indian lives transformed by grace.[31] Their positive portrayals of Massachusett and Wampanoag men and women belie claims that Puritan views of Native Americans were wholly negative.[32] Individual Indians could be as holy or devilish as anyone else. In most cases, Puritans were not out to destroy Indian ways because they were Indian but because the newcomers perceived them as wrong and displeasing to God.[33] On the other hand, it is clear that when Englishmen extolled the merits of Indian believers for others to follow, it was usually the natives' saintliness and not their Indian-ness that the English had in mind.[34] Furthermore, in the wake of events such as Metacom's War (King Philip's War) in 1675–76, it became difficult for even pious New Englanders to appreciate any Indians, praying or not. Amid that conflict, it seemed that there were only preying Indians.[35] No wonder second- and third-genera-tion New England Puritans were more inclined to hail the mission-aries rather than the natives as exemplars, although even they came under attack during the war.[36] During quieter times, the work of the first generation in evangelizing Indians, as with much else that it did, was celebrated as a worthy model to follow.[37] This was only one of a number of ways in which Puritans either encouraged each other to imitate or told themselves they were already imitating biblical models in their relations with Indians. Later Puritans hailed the exemplary lives of redeemed Indian captives such as Mary Row-landson and Hannah Swarton. Their narrative accounts of physical survival and spiritual salvation amid harrowing circumstances fol-lowed in the literary tradition of a representative life, a genre well suited for a people enamored with imitation. Their experiences be-came lessons for their neighbors that the same sovereign God who had preserved Daniel and Jonah was still at work in their world.[38]

Puritan fears of being carried away by Indians were part of a longstanding, broader concern that contact with natives might "In-dianize" them. Here the language of imitation took the form of nega-tive prescriptions against native cultures and any influence they might exert on English newcomers. Colin Calloway has suggested that from the earliest settlement, New England Puritans "worried that conquering the American wilderness and coming into contact with American Indians would alter the colonists' English culture and their sense of themselves as English people. Their American experience threatened to give colonists a new identity," one they did not want.[39] Jill Lepore goes even further and insists that the "colonists' greatest cultural anxiety . . . was the fear that they were becoming Indianized." This was especially acute during the bloody fighting of Metacom's War when the English worried that their tac-tics too closely resembled those of their cruel foes. Puritan histories of the war became instruments of reassurance that their own ac-tions had in fact been justified and that they had remained English-men throughout the conflict.[40] The words of those narratives added to a long line of Puritan defenses against Indianization, for as Alden Vaughan and Edward Clark have explained, "Puritan society had abundant legal and social structures against imitating or admiring the Indians' 'prophane course of life.' Indian ways were to be shunned, not emulated."[41] When those strictures were not obeyed, the results were disastrous, at least according to Increase Mather. "God is greatly offended," Mather wrote in the 1670s, "with the *Heathenisme* of the English People. How many that although they are *Christians* in name, are no better then *Heathens* in heart, and in Conversation? How many Families that live like *profane Indians* without any *Family prayer*? . . . Now there is no place under heaven where the neglect of *Divine Institutions* will so highly provoke and incense the displeasure of God as in *New-England*, because . . . *Religion is our Interist* and that which our Fathers came into this Land for."[42]

Mather was hardly alone in raising the specter of divine judgment on New England if the right models were not followed. Nor were such warnings only addressed to the English. Indian listeners no doubt grew weary of Puritans telling them to flee from the pagan paths of their fathers. In one such conversation in 1646, Thomas Shepard and other Puritan ministers were asked by a group of Massachusett, "how came the English to differ so much from the Indians in the knowledge of God and Jesus Christ seeing they had all at first one father?" The ministers tried to make a case that the English had descended from sons of Adam who had heeded God's counsel, whereas "Indian forefathers were a stubborne and rebellious children, and would not heare the word, did not care to pray nor to teach their children, and hence Indians that now are, do not know God at all." Shepard and company went on to say that there were plenty of Englishmen who similarly "did not know God but were like to . . . drunken Indians." Avoiding the "prophane and ignorant" example of this other sort of Englishmen was equally important for natives.[43]

III

What did the native peoples of southern New England think of all this Puritan advice offered up in the language of imitation? While a full answer to that question is beyond the scope of this paper, it is possible to note here how Puritans also used the language of imitation in descriptive ways to characterize Indian responses to their Christian message.

In the half century between the Puritans' arrival and Metacom's War, somewhere between one thousand and two thousand Indians converted to Christianity in New England.[44] Puritan accounts of how those natives appropriated and practiced their new faith once again made use of the words and motifs of pattern, imitation, and example. Praying Indians were commended for following godly English models in Sabbath observance, administration of the sacraments, church discipline, and family prayer.[45] Even more striking are the cases in which the English noted the Indians' ability to mimic their oral modes of religious expression. Europeans had long marveled at how the peoples of the Americas could rapidly imitate new languages.[46] In seventeenth-century New England, the Massachusett and other Indian groups proved adept at echoing the substance and style of Puritan religious discourse. In the 1640s, for example, Thomas Shepard reported on how quickly native children learned catechetical answers, largely because they mimicked the responses given by more experienced catechumens.[47] John Eliot was not disappointed to find that Massachusett preachers and teachers he had earlier evangelized now followed his sermon style in trying to win over fellow natives. "They imitate me," Eliot asserted; the "manner of my teaching them" through inductive questions and answers was borrowed intact.[48] Indians also apparently imitated Puritan styles of public prayer. When Governor John Endecott attended a worship service in Natick, he was brought to tears by an Indian prayer despite not understanding most of it. What he admired was the way it had been offered with "such reverence, zeale, good affection, and distinct utterance." Endecott knew a good prayer when he heard one, even if spoken in an incomprehensible tongue.[49] Pastor Richard Mather had a similar experience listening to and watching Natick residents offer spiritual testimonies. Though again understanding little of what they said, Mather and others "heard them perform their duties . . . with such grave and sober countenances, with such comely reverence in gesture, and their whol carriage, and with such plenty of tears . . . as did argue to us that they spoke with much good affection, and holy fear of God, and it much affected our hearts."[50] Lack of comprehension did not keep men like Endecott and Mather from "using native speech patterns to distinguish a 'good' Indian from a 'bad' one." As Jane Kamensky has noted, "good Indians were good speakers, cherishing rules for right speaking similar to those the English prized. Pliant, generous, polite, respectful—some Indians spoke in ways that confirmed their 'civility,'" and apparently also their Christian faith.[51]

Sometimes even nonbelieving natives seemed to know of the need to follow the right rhetorical models in talking to or about the Christian god. At least that is how John Eliot depicted one such Algonquian speaker in his *Indian Dialogues*, a series of fictional conversations based on his long experience of trying to convert the

Massachusett and designed to train native missionaries to evangelize fellow Indians more effectively. Peneovot was spiritually moved by the counsel of Waban, who encouraged him to pray for other natives and for God's work in the world as a whole. "I feel your heart to answer your words like an echo," said Peneovot. But his imitative impulse needed guidance: "I am ignorant of fit words in prayer, and therefore I do request of you, first do you pray, and set me a pattern." After they had spent the night in prayer together, Waban pointed the new convert beyond any mortal model: "Christ himself hath set us an example, who spent whole nights in prayer."[52]

Eliot's construction of Waban as a model convert and teacher who had learned to imitate the language of imitation logically flowed from Puritan hopes and observations. Eliot made Waban who he wanted him to be. Similar acts of invention took place in representing Indian figures such as Philip, a character based on the Narragansett sachem. In the *Dialogues,* he initially resists Christianity but eventually sees the light.[53] Whatever liberties Eliot took with the end of the story (and within five years of writing this, Eliot did see a very different end—the real Philip went to war with the English), he may have been most historical in recording the kinds of objections Philip and others voiced to the evangelists' overtures.[54] After all, if Eliot hoped the *Dialogues* could prepare native missionaries well, he would have to portray the verbal exchanges they could expect to encounter with recalcitrant brethren as realistically as possible. Those exchanges in the *Dialogues* are, in fact, remarkable because they reveal that Indian resistance to Puritan evangelism could be voiced as eloquently in the language of imitation as any embrace of the new faith had been. Very likely, the Ninnimissinuok derived such language in part out of their own cultural traditions and needs. But they also might well have appropriated it from listening to Puritan pleas and then turning them on their heads in discontented replies.

Indian opposition in the language of imitation manifests itself in the *Dialogues* in two principal ways.[55] On the one hand, natives responded to Puritan calls that they leave their old "fleshly" ways behind by in essence retorting, "why should we follow the examples of your fathers rather than our own?" To do so would be an act of intellectual arrogance and cultural disobedience. As one Indian "kinsman" explained it, "Our forefathers were (many of them) wise men, and we have wise men now living. They all delight in these our delights. They have taught us nothing about our soul, and God, and heaven, and hell, and joy and torment in the life to come. Are you wiser than our fathers?" Another sachem pointed the finger directly

at natives themselves: "As for this new way of praying to God, I like
it not. We and our forefathers have through all generations lived in
our religion, which I desire not to change. Are we wiser than our
forefathers?" To deviate from long-set patterns of belief and practice would "make trouble and disturbance unto us [and disrupt]
those old ways in which we and our forefathers have walked." Better for the Indian and Englishmen alike to follow the separate sets
of ancient wisdom passed down to them. Or as one native woman
put it, "we are well as we are."[56]

Eliot's fictional Indians were not even always sure about how ancient or wise Puritan Christianity in fact was, and they used the language of imitation in a second way to say so. In words that cut to
the heart of Puritan identity as biblical imitators, an Indian pointedly asked why he and others could not "think that *English* men
have *invented* these stories to amaze us and fear us out of our old
customs [my emphasis], and bring us to stand in awe of them, that
they might wipe us of our lands, and drive us into corners, to seek
new ways of living, and new places too?"[57] To be accused of *inventing* their faith was for Puritans the strongest indictment possible.
It was the very weapon they used against Catholics, Baptists, Antinomians, and all other religious opponents. As Dwight Bozeman has
put it, in the Puritan "world of discourse, no combatant's thrust
could gouge a deeper wound."[58] In a later dialogue, Philip used the
same verbal knife: "I pray tell me what book that is? What is written
in it? And how do you know that it [the Bible] is the Word of God?
Many say that some wise Englishmen have devised and framed it,
and tell us that it is God's word, when it is no other than the words
of wise men."[59] No wonder Piumbukhou, a Christian Indian, felt
compelled to respond to such accusations by insisting, "The Book
of God is no *invention* of Englishmen [my emphasis]." He and other
native Christian apologists were well trained to defend Puritan
views of Scripture and to warn against all those who would "add
their own wicked inventions unto the pure and perfect Word of
God."[60]

Among those "wicked inventors" were Catholic missionaries. Puritan denunciations of their Jesuit competitors give interesting
hints of a third type of Indian response to Puritan admonitions to
imitate them, one that fell between positive embrace and outright
opposition. In the *Indian Dialogues,* native evangelists Anthony
and William deride "popish teachers and ministers" for on the one
hand keeping the Bible from their proselytes, and on the other hand,
adding to the Scriptures.[61] What they (and Eliot) feared were shal-
low "converts" who not only were taught false doctrine but whose

Christianity was only a "mere imitation" of the real thing. Puritan leaders throughout the century insisted that in contrast to Catholic methods, they offered Indians the "whole Bible" and a *"Thorough-paced Christianity"*; anything less and they would not have "imagined our Indians *Christianized*."[62]

And yet Puritans clearly worried about how deep the Ninnimissinuok were drinking at the waters of English religion and civility. How many of the natives who appeared to be following the newcomers' ways were merely playing a role rather than internalizing a message? When Matthew Cradock expressed his hope that Indians would "affect" Puritan Christianity and culture, he surely used that word to mean "to be drawn to" or to "have affection or liking for." But was it possible that some natives could "affect" the English in the more negative sense of that word, that is, "to put on a pretence of; to assume a false appearance of, to counterfeit or pretend"?[63] Certainly some New Englanders thought so. Roger Williams worried that if he or other ministers concentrated on teaching Indians to observe church ordinances without them first experiencing a "true turning to God," natives could not help but be like the baneful "million of soules in England" who were brought into the church without "the saving work of Repentance."[64] Williams pointed the finger at himself for the Indians' predicament: "woe be to me if intending to catch men . . . I should pretend conversion and the bringing of men . . . into a *Church-estate*, . . . and so build them up with *Ordinances* as a converted Christian People, and yet afterward still pretend to catch them by an after conversion."[65] Others were more inclined to point the finger at the Indians themselves. Increase Mather rehearsed the story of Squando, "a strange *Enthusiastical Sagamore* . . . who some years before pretended that God appeared to him." After that supposed divine visitation, Squando had left off his evil ways and "with great seeming Devotion and Conscience" practiced the Christian disciplines of prayer, attendance at worship, and Sabbath observance. Recently, however, he had led an attack on the town of Saco, thereby revealing "himself to be no otherwise then a childe of him, that was a Murtherer and a Lyor from the beginning."[66]

Squando's deception had been too subtle for Puritan detection. That was not always true. Sometimes there was no mistaking Indian mimicking for the real thing, as when during Metacom's War a band of warring Nipmucks entered a Congregational church and mockingly "made an hideous noise somewhat resembling singing." They shouted derisively at nearby soldiers to "Come and pray, & sing Psalmes."[67] Such "theater" might have reminded Puritans of the satirical attacks leveled in print and onstage against their for-bears in England and in the colonies.[68] That kind of overt mockery could be easily countered, linguistically if not militarily. Far more pernicious were cases like Squando's, where a believable Christian facade masked political intrigue. Missionaries such as Eliot, the Mayhews, and Daniel Gookin became accustomed to defending the validity of Indian conversions, perhaps to allay their own fears as well as those of others. They also got used to dispelling suspicions of the sort Eliot reported in 1653 when the Praying Indians were rumored to be "in a conspiracy with others, and with the *Dutch*, to doe mischief to the English." Eliot called the accusations "ground-less" but indicated that his own course of action was accordingly more cautious thereafter.[69]

Puritan anxieties over the authenticity and depth of Indian imita-tion thus fueled, and were fueled by, a recurrent English belief that Indians of all types were secretly plotting against them. Time and again in seventeenth-century New England, rumors circulated that natives were about to attack. English vulnerability to such rumors and misinformation stemmed in part from their ignorance of native languages and from the difficulty of verifying information. Not un-derstanding what Indians said or fear of misinterpreting their signs left Puritans suspicious. They were inclined to believe the worst, succumbing in the process to the "mere imitations" of the truth em-bodied in those rumors. Such a fate was ironic for a Puritan people convinced that "right speech" (including truthful speech) was cru-cial for the godly social order they wished to maintain in New En-gland. Whatever the case, shrewd Indian leaders such as Uncas, a Mohegan sachem, took advantage by repeatedly spreading stories that his enemies, the Narragansetts, were conspiring with the Mo-hawks against the English.[70]

That other equally shrewd Indians engaged in religious forms of mere imitation in interacting with the English there is little doubt. And even when natives were entirely genuine in embracing the En-glish faith, it is important to note that what the Puritans saw as simple imitation was sometimes from the Indian standpoint acts of incorporation, as they added Puritan elements onto existing pat-terns of worship and belief.[71] The Ninnimissinuok knew their own needs and proved capable of using the words and deeds of "imita-tion" to suit their own ends.

IV

If Eliot's *Indian Dialogues* and other written sources are any kind of reliable guide to how Indians and Puritans actually conversed about religion in the seventeenth century, then it is hard to avoid the conclusion that an essential component was what I have called the language of imitation. Whether consoling or cajoling natives, Puritans usually spoke in a prescriptive manner that appealed to good models and bad, to communicate what they wanted Indians to do and who they hoped Indians would be. Meanwhile, whether confessing or critiquing Puritanism, natives spoke back to the English in ways and words that made equally common use of "imitation" in one form or another.

What did the choice to use this style of discourse mean for people on both sides of the cultural divide? Recent historians of Puritan-Indian relations have paid increased attention to how cross-cultural interaction shaped or reshaped communal and individual identities in New England. Taking note of both sides' use of the language of imitation opens another window onto how contact with the other changed native and English selves in early America. Space limitations dictate that I leave aside the impact on the Indian self and conclude with a few observations regarding New England Puritans. It is perhaps first worth noting that the Puritans' very preoccupation with imitation reveals much about their values and view of the self.[72] For the godly, the upholding of models meant that life was to be derivative not innovative. Direction about those things that mattered most in life had been set out long ago in the Bible. The task before individuals and the whole community was to follow or, more precisely, to recover; little value was placed on the act of discovery. Fidelity to communal testimony or declarations was therefore far more important than individual expression, no matter how creative. How one measured up to community standards was what counted. Puritan introspection consequently entailed regular evaluation of oneself against an external standard, not a self-invented one. And given the perfection of that standard or model, there was little chance that a person or a group could fail to see their inadequacies. By nature, then, the Puritan bent toward imitation produced a discontented self, one routinely brought low by the high examples set out before it.

Even so, Puritans were entirely capable of self-righteousness and self-congratulation, as their spiritual diaries and relations with Indians attest.[73] In the Puritan mind, no matter how low they needed to be brought, Native Americans needed to be "reduced" that much more.[74] The language of imitation proved immensely useful in conveying that message. More broadly, it allowed Puritans to fit their encounter with Indians into the same framework within which they understood themselves. Put simply, Indians were to imitate them as they imitated the "first ways" laid out in scripture. In Puritan minds, what they asked of natives ran parallel to what they asked of themselves. Being able to communicate for several decades with Indians about religion in a language whose central theme was at the core of who Puritans thought they were and what they thought they were doing, therefore, reinforced Puritan self-perceptions as imitators and the imitated. And whenever Indians appeared to learn their lessons well, those self-perceptions were all the more confirmed.

In retrospect, it is clear that what Puritans asked of natives was not what they asked of themselves but instead its precise opposite. Rather than recovering the purity and simplicity of some "primitive" past, the call to convert to Christianity and English ways for the Ninnimissinuok entailed breaking with the past, being innovative and adaptive, standing at odds with one's community and its standards. For Indians to undergo the kind of cultural transformation that the Puritans wanted demanded that they embrace the very values that Puritans usually rejected for themselves. That irony seems to have escaped most colonists and, as a result, contributed to the misunderstanding and miscommunication that so often plagued cross-cultural relations.

Amid the upheavals of the seventeenth century, some southern New England native people heeded English pleas. Their positive response, as noted above, confirmed Puritan convictions about themselves. More troubling, of course, were those cases of "mere imitation" in which Indians simply pretended to embrace Puritan ways. Such mimicking, carried on by natives for their own reasons, might in retrospect be seen as a subversive form of imitation. As James Axtell has put it, "in the face of great need or desire, some Indians were capable of masterly dissembling, even over long periods of time."[75] When Puritans occasionally "discovered," sometimes after fatal consequences, that one or more Indians had feigned civility or Christianity, they were forced to question their own ability to read others. Under such circumstances, it was often easier to dismiss all natives as beyond the pale. At the very least, it meant keeping up one's guard against an untrustworthy lot. Those who worked hardest at and cared most about Indian Christianization held out for the possibility that natives could be genuinely changed. But even they were forced to consider that within the imitative world the Puritans had constructed, no one might be quite who they seemed.

Resistant Indians knew how to make that precise point. When Native Americans, consciously or not, employed the language of imitation to ward off Puritan approaches, they leveled attacks where

Puritans may have been the most vulnerable. Charges that Christianity was a "human invention" and the Bible a work of clever Englishmen could not be simply dismissed as pagan nonsense. They came too close to expressing doubts Puritans had about themselves, if not about the Bible. Those doubts were especially acute during times of crisis when Puritans wondered individually and collectively whether God had abandoned them.[76] Were they in fact inventors of human religion rather than imitators of biblical faith? Were they no different from those in the Church of England from which they had fled, or from those dissenters who threatened to spoil the purity of the church in colonial New England? For Puritans to hear Indians express what others discontent with Puritanism had said on both sides of the Atlantic was for Puritans to come face-to-face then with their own religious identity. Those voices made clear that conversing with Indians in a language of imitation just as easily complicated as confirmed Puritan notions of who they were in colonial New England.

Perhaps that fact alone was reason enough for Puritans to grow even less enthusiastic about reaching Indians with the gospel in the last quarter of the seventeenth century. By that point, English settlers were less sure about the founders' imitative project for themselves or for the region's native peoples. And they worried that their own behavior during Metacom's War had been far from exemplary.[77] If Ninnimissinuok did "affect English persons" in the wake of the conflict, Indian actions would likely be a far cry from the Christian civility Matthew Cradock originally envisioned. That was one form of mimicry that Puritans could do without.

NOTES

1. I do not mean to imply here that the missionary impulse was the sole or, at times, even the primary way Puritans thought about or acted out their relations with Indians. For the best recent discussion of Puritan missionary efforts, see Richard W. Cogley, *John Eliot's Mission to the Indians before King Philip's War* (Cambridge: Harvard University Press, 1999).

2. Matthew Cradock to John Endecott, February 16, 1629, in Alexander Young, ed., *Chronicles of the First Planters of the Colony of Massachusetts Bay from 1623 to 1636* (Boston: Little and Brown, 1846), 133–34.

3. The New England Company to John Endecott, April 17, 1629, in Ibid., 149. By that point, the New England Company had become the Massachusetts Bay Company, following the issuing of a charter under royal seal in early March.

4. Cotton Mather, *The Triumphs of the Reformed Religion: The Life of the Reverend John Eliot* (Boston: Benjamin Harris and John Allen, 1691), 85. Cogley, *John Eliot's Mission to the Indians*, 5–6, suggests that the Cradock-Endecott ap-

proach to missions (what Cogley calls the "affective model") was especially important in the years preceding Eliot's more formal missionary labors, which began in 1646.

5. Helpful introductions to the experiences of each of these peoples in the colonial era are provided in Robert S. Grumet, *Historic Contact: Indian People and Colonists in Today's Northeastern United States in the Sixteenth through Eighteenth Centuries*, Contributions to Public Archeology (Norman, Okla.: University of Oklahoma Press, 1995), 55–193.

6. Scholarly interest in the words with which Indians and Puritans spoke to and about one another continues to grow. Samples of that scholarship may be found in Henry W. Bowden and James P. Ronda, introduction to *John Eliot's Indian Dialogues: A Study in Cultural Interaction*, ed. Henry W. Bowden and James P. Ronda (Westport, Conn.: Greenwood Press, 1980), 3–45; Robert James Naeher, "Dialogue in the Wilderness: John Eliot and the Indian Exploration of Puritanism as a Source of Meaning, Comfort, and Ethnic Survival," *New England Quarterly* 62 (1989): 346–68; and Jill Lepore, *The Name of War: King Philip's War and the Origins of American Identity* (New York: Alfred A. Knopf, 1998).

7. Lepore, *Name of War*, xiv. For a discussion of recent scholarship on how encountering the Indian other affected the Puritan self, see my "Selves and Others in Early New England: Refashioning American Puritan Studies," in *History and the Christian Historian*, ed. Ronald A. Wells (Grand Rapids, Mich.: Eerdmans, 1998), 149–58.

8. My discussion of Guy's encounter with the Beothuck in Newfoundland is based on Stephen Greenblatt, *Marvelous Possessions: The Wonder of the New World* (Chicago: University of Chicago Press, 1991), 91–93, 99–102.

9. Ibid., 105–9; James Axtell, *Beyond 1492: Encounters in Colonial North America* (New York: Oxford University Press, 1992), 102–3. Axtell explains that the natives similarly saw the newcomers as childlike; to accommodate them, Indians "devised simplified pidgin languages." Such tongues might be called "imitation languages" and be seen as a stage between imitating speech and a language of imitation.

10. The earliest account of Squanto's role is provided in *Journall of the English Plantation at Plimoth* (1622; reprint, Ann Arbor, Mich.: University Microfilms, 1966), 35–36. Also see Neal Salisbury, "Squanto: Last of the Patuxets," in *Struggle and Survival in Colonial America,* ed. David G. Sweet and Gary B. Nash (Berkeley and Los Angeles: University of California Press, 1981), 228–46.

11. I am following Kathleen J. Bragdon in using the term "Ninnimissinuok" to refer to the Native American peoples of southern New England. Kathleen J. Bragdon, *Native Peoples of Southern New England, 1500-1650* (Norman, Okla.: University of Oklahoma Press, 1996), xi.

12. Lepore, *Name of War*, 29.

13. There is a substantial literature on Puritan views of Indians. For two quite different interpretations of those views see Karen Ordahl Kupperman, *Settling with the Indians: The Meeting of English and Indian Cultures in America, 1580-1640* (Totowa, N.J.: Rowman and Littlefield, 1980) and Alfred A. Cave, *The Pequot War* (Amherst, Mass.: University of Massachusetts Press, 1996). Several early works from New England note natives' abilities to imitate English practical skills. See William Wood, *New England's Prospect*, ed. Alden T. Vaughan (1634; reprint, Amherst, Mass.: University of Massachusetts Press, 1993), 81, 96–97, and Roger Williams, *A Key into the Language of America*, 5th ed. (London: Gregory Dexter, 1643), 19.

14. Puritans were certainly not alone in their bent toward imitation. Historians of early America have long noted a strong mimetic impulse among many colonists as they sought to pattern life in the New World after what was customary or fashionable in the Old. What perhaps set Puritan imitation apart from other colonial varieties was its intense biblical primitivism. At a more purely literary level, some Puritans may have been drawn to a language of imitation through familiarity with uses of imitation in Renaissance literature. For one discussion of the latter see G. W. Pigman III, "Versions of Imitation in the Renaissance," *Renaissance Quarterly* 33 (1980): 1–32.

15. Perry Miller's seminal statement on the Puritan mission is in "Errand into the Wilderness," in Perry Miller, *Errand into the Wilderness* (Cambridge: Harvard University Press, 1956), 1–15. Alternative interpretations of that mission have been offered in Andrew Delbanco, "The Puritan Errand Re-Viewed," *Journal of American Studies* 18 (1984): 343–60, and Theodore Dwight Bozeman, "The Puritans' 'Errand into the Wilderness' Reconsidered," *New England Quarterly* 59 (1986): 231–51.

16. Theodore Dwight Bozeman, *To Live Ancient Lives: The Primitivist Dimension in Puritanism* (Chapel Hill, N.C.: University of North Carolina Press, 1988), 4–19 (quote on 14).

17. Williams, *Key into the Language of America*, 139.

18. John F. Moffitt and Santiago Sebastian, *O Brave New People: The European Invention of the American Indian* (Albuquerque, N.Mex.: University of New Mexico Press, 1996).

19. My discussion of Indian concepts of time is based on Anthony Giddens, *Central Problems in Social Theory: Action, Structure, and Contradiction in Social Analysis* (Berkeley and Los Angeles: University of California Press, 1979), 219–22 (quotes on 222 and 220), and Bragdon, *Native People*, 246.

20. Paul A. Robinson, "Lost Opportunities: Miantonimi and the English in Seventeenth-Century Narragansett Country," in *Northeastern Indian Lives, 1632-1816*, ed. Robert S. Grumet (Amherst, Mass.: University of Massachusetts Press, 1996), 25–26.

21. As quoted in Bragdon, *Native People*, 246.

22. Bozeman, *To Live Ancient Lives*, 139, 153, 268.

23. Dane Morrison, *A Praying People: Massachusett Acculturation and the Failure of the Puritan Mission, 1600-1690* (New York: Peter Lang, 1995), 76–87; Harold W. Van Lonkhuyzen, "A Reappraisal of Praying Indians: Acculturation, Conversion, and Identity at Natick, Massachusetts, 1646–1730," *New England Quarterly* 63 (1990): 396–428. Daniel Mandell, " 'Standing by His Father': Thomas Waban of Natick, circa 1630–1722," in *Northeastern Indian Lives*, 170–71, argues that praying Indians in Natick and elsewhere made substantial cultural changes in the second half of the seventeenth century, but those changes were still "moderated by the persistence of aboriginal ideas and customs." The result was something of a cultural "middle ground." Cogley, *John Eliot's Mission to the Indians*, 241–42, concludes that Eliot wanted Indians to change their cultural ways in three main areas: personal grooming, sexual behavior, and settlement patterns. Cogley finds that over the long run, Eliot came to tolerate many traditional native ways within the praying towns.

24. Edmund S. Morgan, *Visible Saints: The History of a Puritan Idea* (Ithaca, N.Y.: Cornell University Press, 1963), 64–80, gives the classic account of the Puritan morphology of conversion.

25. Charles L. Cohen, "Conversion among Puritans and Amerindians: A Theo-

logical and Cultural Perspective," in *Puritanism: Transatlantic Perspectives on a Seventeenth-Century Anglo-American Faith*, ed. Francis J. Bremer (Boston: Massachusetts Historical Society, 1993), 248–54. Cohen makes the important point that despite the close parallels with English confessions in 1659, Indian narratives still were distinctive in a number of ways, thanks to the natives' own "socio-psychological backgrounds" that shaped their appropriation of Christianity (255). Eliot recorded the Indian narratives offered on these three occasions in tracts printed in London between 1653 and 1660: John Eliot and Thomas Mayhew Jr., "Tears of Repentance: Or, a further Narrative of the Progress of the Gospel Amongst the Indians in New England" (orig. pub. 1653; reprinted in Massachusetts Historical Society, *Collections*, 3d ser., 4 [1834]: 197–260); John Eliot, *A Late and Further Manifestation of the Progress of the Gospel amongst the Indians in New-England* (London: M.S., 1655); [John Eliot], *A Further Account of the Progress of the Gospel amongst the Indians in New England* (London: John Macock, 1660).

26. *New England's First Fruits: with Divers other Special Matters Concerning that Country* (1643; reprint, New York: Joseph Sabin, 1865), 5.

27. J. William T. Youngs Jr., "The Indian Saints of Early New England," *Early American Literature* 16 (1981–82): 243–48.

28. Eliot and Mayhew, "Tears of Repentance," 259–60.

29. As quoted in Youngs, Jr., "Indian Saints," 247.

30. As quoted in Henry Whitfield, *Strength Out of Weakness: or a Glorious Manifestation of the Further Progress of the Gospel among the Indians of New England* (1652; reprint, New York: Joseph Saban, 1865), 12–13.

31. John Eliot, *The Dying Speeches of Several Indians* (Cambridge, [1685?]); Matthew Mayhew, *A Brief Narrative of the Success which the Gospel hath had, among the Indians* (Boston: Bartholomew Green, 1694); James P. Ronda, "Generations of Faith: The Christian Indians of Martha's Vineyard," *William and Mary Quarterly*, 3d ser., 38 (1981): 369–94, discusses the profiles of 176 Indian converts provided in Experience Mayhew's tract, *Indian Converts*, published in London in 1727.

32. Here I take exception to the depiction of Puritan views of Indians as unrelievedly negative found in works such as Roy Harvey Pearce, " 'The Ruines of Mankind': The Indian and the Puritan Mind," *Journal of the History of Ideas* 13 (1952): 200–17; G. E. Thomas, "Puritans, Indians, and the Concept of Race," *New England Quarterly* 48 (1975): 3–27; William S. Simmons, "Cultural Bias in the New England Puritans' Perceptions of Indians," *William and Mary Quarterly*, 3d ser., 38 (1981): 56–72; and Cave, *Pequot War*.

33. Bowden and Ronda, introduction to *Indian Dialogues*, 36.

34. That these were *Indian* converts made a difference to Puritan authors speculating about the eschatological significance of New World mission work.

35. Lepore, *Name of War*, 156–58.

36. Ibid., 138–41.

37. Richard Slotkin and James K. Folsom, eds., *So Dreadfull a Judgment: Puritan Responses to King Philip's War, 1676-1677* (Middletown, Conn.: Wesleyan University Press, 1978), 61–63. Puritan excitement over early Indian missions may be sampled in [Thomas Shepard], *The Day-Breaking if not the Sun-Rising of the Gospell with the Indians in New-England* (London, 1647; reprint New York: Joseph Sabin, 1865); Thomas Shepard, *The Clear Sunshine of the Gospel Breaking Forth upon the Indians in New-England* (London, 1648; reprint New York: Joseph Sabin, 1865); Henry Whitfield, "The Light Appearing More and More towards

the Perfect Day" (orig. pub. 1651; reprinted in Massachusetts Historical Society, *Collections*, 3d ser., 4 [1834]: 100–47); and Whitfield, *Strength Out of Weakness*.

38. Alden T. Vaughan and Edward W. Clark, "Cups of Common Calamity: Puritan Captivity Narratives as Literature and History," in *Puritans among the Indians: Accounts of Captivity and Redemption, 1676-1724*, ed. Alden T. Vaughan and Edward W. Clark (Cambridge: Harvard University Press, 1981), 4–6.

39. Colin Calloway, *New Worlds for All: Indians, Europeans, and the Remaking of Early America* (Baltimore: The Johns Hopkins University Press, 1997), 7. Not all Puritans shared these worries. According to Cogley, *John Eliot's Mission to the Indians*, Eliot never "used pagan natives as symbols of what 'Indianizing' colonists might or had become—lazy and lustful degenerates who lived beyond the pale of civilized institutions. In fact, Eliot betrayed no fear that he might be corrupted by the native 'heart of darkness' " (248).

40. Lepore, *Name of War*, 5–8, 11, 88–89, 112–13, 129–31, 175 (quote on 6). Lepore emphasizes the colonists' special disdain for the Indians' "skulking way of war" (112–13), but it is interesting to note that John Eliot wrote rather approvingly of the English learning it in a letter to Robert Boyle in 1677: "Now we are glad to learn the skulking way of war. And what God's end is, in teaching us such a way of discipline, I know not." "Letters of Rev. John Eliot of Roxbury, to Hon. Robert Boyle," Massachusetts Historical Society, *Collections*, 1st ser., 3 (1794): 178.

41. Vaughan and Clark, "Cups of Common Calamity," 17.

42. Increase Mather, "An Earnest Exhortation," in *So Dreadfull a Judgment*, 174–75.

43. [Shepard], *Day-Breaking*, 6, 12–13.

44. Naeher, "Dialogue in the Wilderness," 346–47.

45. For two examples from after the 1670s, see "Letters of Eliot to Boyle," 183–84, and [Increase Mather, Cotton Mather, and Nehemiah Walter], *A Letter, about the present state of Christianity, among the Christianized Indians of New-England* (Boston: Timothy Green, 1705), 6–9.

46. Greenblatt, *Marvelous Possessions*, 105.

47. [Shepard], *Day-Breaking*, 10.

48. Whitfield, *Strength Out of Weakness*, 22.

49. Ibid., 48.

50. Richard Mather, "Introductory Note" to Eliot and Mayhew, "Tears of Repentance," 223.

51. Jane Kamensky, *Governing the Tongue: The Politics of Speech in Early New England* (New York: Oxford University Press, 1997), 51.

52. *Indian Dialogues*, 107–8.

53. Ibid., 120–44; Lepore, *Name of War*, 68, 219.

54. Eliot told Richard Baxter that the "instructive dialogs" were "p[art]'ly historical." F. W. Powicke, ed., *Some Unpublished Correspondence of the Reverend Richard Baxter and the Reverend John Eliot, the Apostle of the American Indians, 1656-1682* (Manchester: Manchester University Press, 1931), 62.

55. Indians used many "languages" and arguments to express their rejection of Christianity. For an overview of that opposition, see James P. Ronda, " 'We Are Well As We Are': An Indian Critique of Seventeenth-Century Christian Missions," *William and Mary Quarterly*, 3d. ser., 34 (1977): 66–82.

56. *Indian Dialogues*, 71, 73, 134–35.

57. Ibid., 71.

58. Bozeman, *To Live Ancient Lives*, 137.

59. *Indian Dialogues*, 134. Eliot could have based Philip's challenge upon the

confession he had heard Natick convert Poquanum make two decades earlier: "When the Indians first prayed to God, I did not think there was a God, or that the Bible was Gods Book, but that wise men made it" (Eliot and Mayhew, "Tears of Repentance," 253).

60. *Indian Dialogues,* 71, 141.

61. Ibid., 135–41.

62. Mather, *Triumphs of the Reformed Religion,* 124–35 (quote on 128). James Axtell, *After Columbus: Essays in the Ethnohistory of Colonial America* (New York: Oxford University Press, 1988), 114, argues that contrary to Protestant accusations at the time and the skepticism of some modern scholars, Jesuit missionaries were as demanding as the Puritans in holding "Indians to a high standard for baptism and church admission."

63. Both of these definitions were in use in the seventeenth century. *Oxford English Dictionary,* 2d ed., s.v. "affect."

64. Williams, *Key into the Language,* 137–38.

65. As quoted in Margery Ruth Johnson, "The Mayhew Mission to the Indians, 1643–1806," (D. Phil. Thesis, Clark University, 1966), 78. Williams made this point in his tract, *Christenings Make Not Christians,* published in London in 1645.

66. Increase Mather, *A Brief History of the War with the Indians in New-England* (Boston: John Foster, 1676), 13.

67. As quoted in Lepore, *Name of War,* 105.

68. Harold E. L. Prins, "Chief Rawandagan, Alias Robin Hood: Native 'Lord of Misrule' in the Maine Wilderness," in *Northeastern Indian Lives,* 102–5, offers the intriguing suggestion that non-Puritan English settlers in Maine may have staged "comical burlesques" (103) that would have satirized both the local Abenaki people and the standard English targets such as the Puritans. See Stephen Woolsey's essay in this volume for one Puritan's (Cotton Mather) response to satirical ridicule of fellow Puritans in print and on stage.

69. Eliot, *Late and Further Manifestation,* 4.

70. Eric S. Johnson, "Uncas and the Politics of Contact," in *Northeastern Indian Lives, 1632–1816,* 37; Kamensky, *Governing the Tongue,* 52–55.

71. Axtell, *After Columbus,* 116–18, provides a helpful analysis of Indian syncretism, arguing that too often syncretism has been a "red herring dragged across the discussion of the quality of native conversions" (117).

72. Discussions of the Puritan self are legion. The places to begin remain Perry Miller, *The New England Mind: The Seventeenth Century,* 2d ed. (Cambridge: Harvard University Press, 1954), Perry Miller, *The New England Mind: From Colony to Province* (Cambridge: Harvard University Press, 1953), and Sacvan Bercovitch, *The Puritan Origins of the American Self* (New Haven and London: Yale University Press, 1975).

73. David Lyle Jeffrey, *People of the Book: Christian Identity and Literary Culture* (Grand Rapids, Mich.: Eerdmans, 1996), 276–81.

74. James Axtell, *The Invasion Within: The Contest of Cultures in Colonial North America* (New York: Oxford University Press, 1985), 131–78.

75. Axtell, *After Columbus,* 106.

76. Lepore, *Name of War,* 104–5. Lepore's concern is with demonstrating how the encounter with Indians endangered the colonists' cultural identity as English. My point here is that the encounter could also endanger the colonists' religious identity as Puritans. While closely related, the two identities were not identical.

77. Ibid., 8–10, 175. Lepore argues that the English sought to alleviate such fears by writing accounts of the war that fashioned the colonists as just and *English* in their actions.

"A plain Turkish Tyranny": Images of the Turk in Anti-Puritan Polemic

Glenn Sanders

In *OBSERVATIONS UPON THE ARTICLES OF PEACE WITH THE IRISH REBELS* (1649), John Milton uses a negative image commonplace in many seventeenth-century treatments of political power—the "Turkish tyranny": "[The Earl of Ormond] passes on in his groundless conjectures, that the aime of this Parlament may be perhaps to set up first an elective Kingdome, and after that a perfet Turkish tyranny."[1] Milton defends the Rump and its regicide leaders by taking the offensive: "Of the latter certainly there needed no other patterne then that Tyranny which was so long modelling by the late King himself, with *Strafford,* and that arch Prelat of *Canterbury,* his chief Instruments; whose designes God hath dissipated. Neither is it any new project of the Monarchs, and their Courtiers in these dayes, though Christians they would be thought, to endeavour the introducing of a plain Turkish Tyranny."[2] As evidence he cites discussions in the French court, where such tyranny "is a Monarchicall designe, and not of those who have dissolvd Monarchy."[3]

Milton blasts the Earl of Ormond for using the image of the Turk against Parliament. Then he deploys it himself to taint monarchy under Charles I and his agents, suggesting that God had "dissipated" their plans because of their false faith.[4] Why this image of the Turk? What complex of ideas did the image represent? Why was the image meaningful to seventeenth-century Britons and thus able to serve in both political and religious polemic? Finally, and most important, what does the image suggest about the dynamic of political and religious change—the conflict and interplay between republican and royalist opinions, Puritan and non-Puritan?

The many pamphlets of the Commonwealth and early Stuart Restoration suggest that, after the regicide, opponents of Oliver Cromwell's military rule used the image of the Turk to recast the political debate and to establish the polemic and ideological initiative for a popular audience. For three decades, Puritanism had been a radical force, contributing to republicanism.[5] Events and conditions after 1649 encouraged a move away from such political and religious extremism. Charges of "Turkish tyranny" against Cromwell and the godly helped discredit their political and religious policies. After the Restoration the charges contributed to the reinvigoration of the monarchy, one based on tradition, reason, and true faith.

THE NATURE OF "TURKISH TYRANNY"

Scholars of early modern Europe have long recognized the potent symbolism attached to the image of the aggressive and violent Turk as the Ottomans expanded into the Mediterranean and South-Central Europe.[6] Ottoman expansion affected the English on two fronts in particular. First, the Ottoman regencies along the North African coast readily enslaved English captives taken at sea. This practice complicated early diplomatic contacts and an expanding trade between London and the Turkish Empire. Second, increased contacts with Muslims during the century or so after the Reformation led to serious questions about Christian faith and eschatology.[7]

In an important recent study, Nabil Matar suggests that English captives enslaved to the Ottomans between 1550 and 1685 numbered in the thousands during any particular year. The threat of violent attack was a dominant reality, not only for traders in the Mediterranean but also for anyone who lived along the British coast. Especially before the strengthening of the English navy under the Commonwealth, raiders could even penetrate along the Thames and the Severn and as far north as Edinburgh. The economic and social effects were substantial: the cost of supporting and ransoming captives; the breakup of families; and the destitution of wives and children that followed the loss of a breadwinner.[8]

The establishment of the Levant Company and William Harborne's mission to the Porte in the 1580s had opened up regular commercial exchanges.[9] English trade with the Ottomans steadily increased throughout the next century. Continuing threats of enslavement destabilized this trade, however, potentially damaging domestic production, especially given the claims of the Levant Company in 1605 to employ forty thousand workers in the production of fustian alone.[10] Ambassadors, including Henry Hyde and Thomas Bendysh, had regularly to deal with the redemption of captives.[11]

Enslavement sometimes led captives to renounce their Christian faith, "turn Turk," and embrace Islam. They did so for various reasons, including relief from torture, the material benefits that followed integration into Ottoman society, the possibility of freedom, and sincere religious desire. Such apostasy created many problems for English Christians. It suggested the failure of efforts to educate Christians about true belief. Apostasy pointed to a decline in the Protestant faith that had produced the Marian martyrs only a generation before. It removed the apostate from the jurisdiction of English law. It represented treason, especially when "renegades" helped the Muslims capture and enslave more Britons. Given Muslim rejection of Christ's divinity, apostasy reinforced anti-Trinitarian opinions. In general, apostasy called the superiority of Christendom and Christianity into question.[12]

The "Turk plays" of the late Tudor and early Stuart periods represent a popular English exploration of the reasons behind apostasy and the effects of conversion.[13] But ecclesiastical and specifically religious responses are of greater significance for understanding Puritanism and mid-seventeenth-century politics. Archbishop Laud set up formal processes to rehabilitate repentant apostates who were willing to admit their sin. This process allowed the renegade, his family, and his community to cope with the problems that followed his return.[14] Publication of the first translations of the Qur'an aimed to improve public knowledge of Muslim belief. Arabic scientific and religious treatises remained accepted if esoteric parts of early modern English scholarship.[15]

At the level of public debate, however, the image of the Muslim or Turk remained controversial, a figure to use in polemic whenever conflict heated up within the church. Especially prominent in mid-seventeenth-century pamphlets was a linkage between Turkism and popery. The sultan and the pope were frequently Gog and Magog, both Antichrists, both opponents of the true church.[16] They both violated body and conscience. A news sheet of August 1642 reported that intercepted letters from Algerian pirates to the pope proved an agreement between the two. They had common interests: "they are both enclined to thrust Christ out of the Church, and the one of them hath entertained *Mahomet*, and as for the other hee hath Sants and Reliques enough of his owne making to patch up such a religion as neither Christ nor his Apostles ever knew of."[17] As Milton's comments in the *Observations* suggest, this linkage between popery and Turkism was in part a response to the growth of Catholic absolutism on the continent. But no hard and fast rules existed to govern the image of the Turk. Sometimes opponents of the established church contrasted Catholicism and Islam by praising the latter for its toleration toward Christians and Jews.[18] That the

Turk could represent both enslavement and freedom (although this last much less frequently) suggests the flexibility of usage.

Within such a context of fear—about enslavement, apostasy, and challenges to true faith—the notion of "Turkish tyranny" thrived. While uses of the image of the Turk could be extremely fluid, and while writers sometimes praised Islam, by and large the "Turkish tyranny" was portrayed negatively. After Richard Knolles's *General Historie of the Turkes* appeared in 1603 with its description of the Turks as "the present terrour of the world," a regular stream of public and private reports came from Constantinople to London.[19] Travel accounts multiplied.[20] In addition, early-seventeenth-century scholars gleaned observations from continental writers in particular to compile lengthy descriptions of the Turkish Empire and Muslim ways.[21] Most of these accounts circulated basic, accurate knowledge about the Turk. Nonetheless, in part because late medieval crusading ideals continued to have influence,[22] writers on the East still filtered their observations through popular preconceptions, and the Turk remained "a cosmic enigma," "identified with everything strange, peculiar, and bizarre."[23] Fears about enslavement and the decline of Christianity joined with popular unfamiliarity to create the image of "Turkish tyranny."

The image of the Turk might appeal to all parties in seventeenth-century political debates because it neatly linked together a variety of ideas on improper government: arbritrariness, perfidy, irrationality, violence, and servility. The image was especially serviceable because it mixed political and religious ideas in a way common to the age. William Bates's purely religious characterization of "Turkish tyranny" suggests the common usage. The moderate nonconformist gave five points on the alleged failings of Islam.[24] First, Muhammad was a sensual robber, ill-suited to deliver revelation. Second, Muslim beliefs are foolish, debasing, and violent. Third, Islam spread first through Muhammad's deceit, then through violence, and deceit and violence maintain the faith. Fourth, Muslim believers are barbarous, and "absolutely forbid to make an inquiry into the matters of religion."[25] Finally, Islam promises an afterlife "fit for swine," making the faith "repugnant to the dictates of clear religion."[26] Bates's charges distill to three: Islam is perfidious, is violent to both body and conscience (individually and collectively), and is a perversion of good reason.

Two engravings suggest these charges by linking arbitrary power, cruelty, perfidy, religious darkness, and servile obedience together in the image of the Turk. The frontispiece to the several mid-century editions of George Sandys's *Travells* contains an alle-

Figure 1. Frontispiece to George Sandys, *Sandys Travells: Containing an History of the Original and Present State of the Turkish Empire,* 1670. This item is reproduced by permission of The Huntington Library, San Marino, California. RB no. 433459.

gory of temporary Christian defeat but final victory over the idolatrous eastern tyrant.[27] From bottom to top, the Sibyl (bottom center
medallion) has read in her leaves about the subjugation of the cross
(bottom left medallion) to the Turk and his corrupt foreign gods
(Isis and Osiris, on the right). "Achmet, or the tyrant" (*Achmet sive
tyrannus*) appears left center, with the orb of temporal power in
his left hand and a yoke in his right; he tramples books, scientific
instruments, and other signs of civilization. The superstitious
thought control of "Turkism" binds men and disregards the tools of
modern enlightenment. But above all in this hierarchical representation is the returning Christ (center top medallion), flanked by his
agents Truth (*Veritas*) and Constancy (*Constantia*). All three define the "Turkish tyranny" by presenting its opposite: a reasonable
Christianity linked to classical ideals (in the proper fashion of
Christian humanism).[28] The apocalyptic second person of the Trinity triumphs over all (in stark contrast to anti-Trinitarian Islam).
Truth appears nude with appropriate draperies, armed with sun-
light, book, and giant quill (the very things on which the tyrant
tramples), which represent an enlightened, understandable, discursive faith, productive because it is reasonable. Helmeted in Athena-
like splendor, with armor, fire, and hefty column, Constancy adds
physical might and wisdom to the true Christian faith. The central
inscription concludes: "You are great and shall prevail" (*magnae
estis et praevalebitis*)." The armed might of the Muslim empire
proves so frightening because the sultan wields a temporal power
built on ignorance. Nonetheless, despite temporary setbacks,
Christ's cause will triumph because it is true.

   This opposition of true Christianity to "Turkish tyranny" also appears in Henry Marsh's *A New Survey of the Turkish Empire and
Government*. After presenting a history of the Turkish Empire,
Marsh describes social conditions. The illustration at the beginning
of the section summarizes his view. Four slaves appear yoked to
the plow, Christians beaten by Turkish plowmen. The steeple on the
building in the background suggests a church, but now it is a
mosque, crescent atop the steeple and muezzin on the minaret to
the side.[29] The caption is ambiguous. "God will give these also an
end" suggests both the effect of Turkish rule—slavery—and the
possibility of future redemption. There follows a section on "the af-
flictions of Captives, and Christians under the Turkish Tribute."[30]

   Marsh had spent thirteen years among the Turks and spoke Arabic. His reflections would have borne weight with contemporaries.
Marsh first published the *Survey* in 1633, but it appeared again
twice during the early Restoration, a clear sign that his views on

Figure 2. Scene of Turks plowing from Henry Marsh, *A New Survey of the Turkish Empire,* 1663. This item is reproduced by permission of The Huntington Library, San Marino, California. RB no. 377077.

"Turkish tyranny" resonated with readers who had recently experienced political turmoil.[31] He suggests how "Turkish tyranny" had become a problem for contemporary Englishmen. After the treatment of Turkish slavery comes "A Narration of a dispute with a Turk," in which Marsh shows how easily the Lord could use his own puny efforts to turn a prideful Turk toward Christianity.[32] The unadulterated gospel is naturally convincing. But this interesting example of cross-cultural dialogue is only a lead-in to "A Lamentation for the loss of Christians destroyed."[33]

Marsh agrees with practically every writer since the Middle Ages that Christian failure against the Turks arises from a lack of unity. But he frames his comments in nationalistic terms, with Frenchmen, Spaniards, Italians, and Englishmen mentioned separately. Given seventeenth-century concerns, he worries about slavery and the renegade: "And in the mean season, the Turk laughs at us."[34] The English bring such tyranny upon themselves, becoming slaves no better than Turkish captives:

> Why should Christ remain with us, whom we have rent and torn in far more pieces then the Souldiers did his garment, by our hideous Sects, Schisms and Heresies? Besides his Name, what of him is dear unto us? The very Plow-man these times is impudent and factious, the Citizen fraudulent & avaricious; the Magistrate seeks retributions and rewards; the Nobility is riotous and lazy, the Gentry contentious and proud. The Souldier, beyond his pay and spoil, craves nothing from the war; let Scepters fall as they will, he is no less grievous to friends and companions, then Enemies. Some Church-men, besides the due pomp Ecclesiastical, have little of the Church, not sanctity, not piety, and some but little erudition, seeking their own, not Christs advancement. That we may say with the Prophet, *All have declined the ways of God, and are unprofitable; there's none that doth good, not even one.*[35]

Instead of promoting true Christian liberty by fighting the real "Turkish tyranny" through the "righteous and divine" gospel—the clarity and effectiveness of which Marsh's own discussions with the Turk have suggested—Englishmen embrace "the *Alcoran*, a book of stuff as foolish, as full of vanity," and "turn Turks in our minds and approbations, sooner then in our bodies to their Dominion."[36]

Thus, popular fears about Turks and Islam, as well as the economic packaging of negative ideas in the stereotype, go far to explain the general popularity of "Turkish tyranny" as a polemical metaphor. It remains to consider how writers would use the image in particular instances, especially against Oliver Cromwell and the rule of the godly.

"Turkish Tyranny" during the British Civil Wars

As political tensions heated up during the early 1640s, and in the absence of strict censorship, writers of many persuasions charged their enemies with "Turkish tyranny" at one time or another.[37] An easy target were the rebellious Catholic Irish. An inflammatory 1641 pamphlet describes the Irish march of 14 December as "the Rebels Turkish Tyranny": "Shewing how cruelly they put [the Protestant settlers] to the Sword, ravished religious women, and put their Children upon red hot Spits before their parents eyes, throw them in the fire, and burn them to ashes, cut off their eares, and nose, put out their eyes, cut off their armes, and legges, broyle them at the fire, cut out their tongues, and thrust hot Irons down their throats, drown them, dash out their brains, and such like other cruelty not heard of amongst *Christians*."[38] (And that is only the subtitle.)

Charges that Charles I and his advisors advocated a "Turkish tyranny" and some form of Turkism were especially significant, both as an indicator of public opinion and in light of later attacks upon Cromwell and the major-generals. In 1642 some writers still hesitated to label the king a tyrant, let alone one of the distasteful Turkish variety, and instead couched their comments in general diatribes against tyranny. Two pamphlets, *A Brief Discourse upon Tyrants and Tyranny* and *Certain Considerations upon the Duties Both of Prince and People,* suggest this sort of guilt by association. The soldiers of the Turkish tyrant are slaves or mercenaries, without proper loyalties to a commonwealth.[39] Their false religion reinforces their servility: "And the *Turks,* to worke their security and continuance, have wholly put out the light of knowledge from among their people, and have subdued them to a false Religion, that has in it selfe no other end, nor office, than onely to keepe men in subjection; so that they having deprived themselves of the principall of all conditions of humanity, and made themselves (in a manner) an Empire of beasts."[40] Under such conditions, temporary earthly successes are meaningless. In contrast, good Christian rulers are to lead their subjects to a higher level, to live as "supernaturall men."[41]

Even direct attacks on the king continued to equivocate. One writer attacked the "boysterous and violent" advisors who would create "a *Thraldom* of meer servile and slavish Vassals": "For although we think so well of His Majesty, and honour him so much, that we cannot find in our hearts to make any culpable comparison betwixt him and the Turke, we must needs think so ill of them, who have not only withdrawn him, and do yet with-hold him from his most wise and faithfull Councell (the High Court of Parliament) but abuse his power, to manage a most pernicious hostility against them, and (in them) against the whole state and people of *England*, that they would prove no better than the worst sort of Turkish Janizaries."[42] The janizaries formed the sultan's select army. They were child converts to Islam taken as a tribute (*devshirme*) in conquered Christian territories. While technically the sultan's slaves, seventeenth-century janizaries were notorious usurpers of political power who controlled the Ottoman succession and tyrannized Ottoman subjects. Several times they enslaved their own master. To call Charles I's advisors janizaries was thus a pointed shorthand attack. In another pamphlet Charles I is "the greatest Adventurer," embarking on "the ship of the Commonwealth." But his "malignant Councellours" are the primary cause of trouble. They convince him that "what he shall be advised by them is right; that is (in many cases) what ambition, hatred, covetousnesse, luxurie, lecherie suggest to be right; that is, flat tyrannie, more absolute than the Turks."[43] In a similar vein, Pym described Strafford publicly as a sultan's minister.[44] Milton's attack on monarchy in the *Observations* hence followed established practice.

While insinuations that Charles I was a "Turkish tyrant" were limited and were directed primarily at the king's advisors, the links between the image and the besieged monarchy suggest that "Turkish tyranny" resonated with pamphlet readers. Given the aggressive Turkish threat on the seas and in Christian hearts, the allusion made sense. It communicated in one phrase the claim of anticourt forces that the king and his men aimed at a tyranny (an arbitrary limitation of freedom) based on Charles's isolation from the English people and his "true counsellors." Preexisting, deeply entrenched "oriental" stereotypes of lust, greed, and hatred reinforced this view by suggesting that Charles's isolation among the court faction had demoralized and debilitated him just as isolation in the seraglio hurt the sultan.

But by 1642 supporters of the king and his church had started deploying charges of "Turkish tyranny" for their own polemical ends. The appearance of *Luther's Alcoran* pointed the way. While apolitical in tone and content, it nonetheless drew out a correspondence between Puritanism and Islam important for later attacks on Cromwell and his supporters. In 1618, the Cardinal Jacques Davy du Perron had aimed to discredit the Huguenots by demonstrating fundamental similarities between Islam and Protestantism on one hundred and twenty points. His Catholic translator had other quarry in mind; in a preface he attached a letter specifically "to the Puritan Reader."[45] But his goal was more to convert the *"English Precisians"* to true faith than to call them "Turkish tyrants." The translation remained essentially a learned treatise on the visibility of the church, the honor of the Virgin, and other theological points on which moderate Englishmen and Catholics already supposedly agreed.[46] Its two hundred pages include symbolic correspondences, parallels, and direct identities. Islam and Protestantism are said to be similar, for example, because the supposed writer of the Qur'an was the apostate monk Sergius, and the monk Luther "after forsaking his Religion, coyned your Ghospell."[47] The writer thus upbraids the reader: "Do you meane to peseuer in your *Reformed Religion* . . . and yet not to be reputed *Turks,* in many Points of fayth? With as much probability may a man desire to be an *Ethiopian,* and yet not to be black, or couet to put his naked hand into a hoat fyer, and withall couet to auoyd burning. For it is euer euident, . . . your *Beliefe* consists in *Misbeliefe,* your *Fayth* in *Infidelity,* and your *Creede* in *Miscreancy,* you making the *Turkish Alcoran* your Catechisme, for your instruction in many Points thereof."[48] Whether "Turkish" or "Puritan," the religion of rebellion is unnatural apostasy, the willful following of a false belief based on a collection of legalisms, not faith in the Church's guidance.

By 1644 the militant aspects of Puritanism had advanced far enough to encourage direct attacks. John Doughty could write in defense of the king's faith, "I have read of Religion in the Primitive times planted, yea propagated in blood, under *Pagans* and *Infidells*; but for *Christians* amongst themselves, professing one and the same faith, to advance the supposed purity of Gods worship by such harsh meanes, I have *not so frequently* heard of, untill these later and frantick daies of ours. It is the fruit of a doctrine well becoming the *Turkish Alcoron,* and *there* accordingly ofttimes inculcated, but no where surely to be found in the *Gospell* of Christ; not taught by his Apostles, nor afterwards abetted by any of the Orthodox Fathers."[49] The allegation here is that Muslims practice *jihad*—holy war—to convert unbelievers by force, a practice also common to the Puritans but alien to the true church of the apostles and fathers.

In the mid-1640s, polemical tracts increasingly targeted Puritan-inspired acts of violence against the established order. James Howell's *Dendrologia: Dodona's Grove, or the Vocall Forrest* (1645) is an intricate political allegory in which all states have the names and characters of plants. The Turkish Empire is "Alcharona" (described as a giantess) and the Great Turk "Bramble," suggesting impediments to the true faith. The third edition minces nothing in its criticism of Puritans: "Yet for all the specious fruits of sanctity these *Dotard Trees* outwardly beare, they are found commonly rotten at the heart, they are like *putrified Wood* shining in the darke."[50] Christ's consignment of both the Puritans and the extreme loyalists to the flame would be fit punishment for those who believe as quasi-Muslims: "they would propagate Pietie as *Alcharona* doth hers, with the sword, and so make Religion to be *Gladii pedissequa,* and which is worse, the Mantle to palliate all their designes, so that if one should prie narrowly into the carriage of their actions, it would put him in mind of that damnable tenet of the Atheist, *in nomine Domini fit omne malum.*"[51] With a step beyond the irony of *Luther's Alcoran, Dendrologia* makes Puritan sanctity a rotten, heartless atheism promoted by the sword. Its surface propriety keeps thinking people from digging too deeply into its true nature.

The military victories of parliamentary forces in the mid-1640s encouraged similar attacks on Puritans as hypocritical legalists ready to impose their will through violence. According to a 1648 "History of Independency," extreme Puritanism combines the worst features of Judaism, Christianity, and Islam, the first two in its arrogant phariseeism, the last in its appeal to force: "they subject all things, even *Religion, Laws,* and *Liberties* (so much cried up by them heretofore) to the power of the Sword ever since. By undermining practises and lies they have jugled the *States sword* into the *Independent scabbard.*"[52] These Puritan-atheists are notorious liars as well. *The Downfal of Dagon* (1653)—its title parodying excessive Puritan zeal against idolatry—attacks "Parliament and Army" for perjury: "They imitate their elder brother the Turk, who holds that there are no Oathes to be kept with Christians, any longer then they serve for their advantages. Nay, these Independents go beyond the Turks: for they are heathens, but these are Atheists; these acknowledge not Christ, many of them."[53]

By the time of the regicide, comparison of Puritans to Muslims or Turks was a common and often biting way to deride the godly. In *A Description of the Grand Signor's Seraglio, or Turkish Emperour's Court*, taken from an earlier Italian version, the translator is none too complimentary of *sufis,* generally described today as Muslim mystics. They are "Professours of Religion, and devotion" who "do commonly read, as they walk along the streets, and have their beads longer then other men, carrying them in their hands into the *Moscheas,* and are ever busie with them as they walk up and down the streets, that the world may take notice of their fained zeal." At least these latter-day Pharisees utter their devotions in only two or three words, unlike the long-winded papists. But how best to gloss this description in the text? The translator chooses the single word "Puritans," evoking the usual picture of the godly hypocrite.[54] Another critic compares Puritan legalists to *qadis*, local Muslim judges: "They think they have an inerring spirit, and that their *Diall* must needs go true, howsoever the Sun goes. They wold make the *Gospell*, as the *Caddies* make the *Alchoran*, to decide all civill temporall matters under the large notion of *slander*, whereof *they* to be the Judges, and so in time to hook in all things to their *Classis*."[55] The proud godly distort the true faith by making the Scriptures a law book. Hoping to gain complete control in both religious and political matters, they reduce every controversial issue to the public one of slander against themselves. Indeed, such desire for control led these men, "worse then any *Turkes*," to the wanton destruction of organs and stained glass.[56]

CROMWELL AND HIS SUPPORTERS AS "TURKISH TYRANTS"

Thus as the political and military conflicts heated up through civil war, regicide, and republic, so too did polemical references to "Turkish tyranny." Antimonarchist John Milton deployed the stereotype in both his *Observations upon the Articles of Peace* and *Eikonoklastes*.[57] But Milton was obviously fighting against a trend. From the mid-1640s, the favorite "Turkish tyrant" of pamphlet writers was not Charles but Oliver Cromwell. Circumstances and common perceptions fell into place to allow the comparison: an upstart, violent Puritan general who killed a rightful monarch and then tyrannized the country politically and religiously. Striking here is the disjunction between polemic and reality. While his rule obviously depended upon the New Model Army and sometimes imposed itself harshly (as in Ireland), Cromwell either limited himself or had limits placed upon him. He consistently claimed to hold power only for the maintenance of good order during an emergency period. His personal religious convictions leaned noticeably toward toleration (within certain Protestant limits).[58] While a coordinated "smear campaign" was unlikely, the consistency with which pamphlet writers drew upon the image of "Turkish tyranny" to attack Cromwell is striking.

As early as 1643 *Mercurius Aulicus* compared Cromwell's destruction of Peterborough Cathedral with an impious Turkish attack on some Christian city.[59] Within two years the association was complete. Drawing upon the common story that Muhammad had received his revelation not from God's Holy Spirit but from that mock dove, a pigeon,[60] one writer cast Cromwell as a new impostor-prophet who similiarly—and in typically hypocritical Puritan fashion—claimed a direct word from God: "This *Cromwell* is never so valorous, as when he is making Speeches for the Association, which neverthelesse he doth somwhat ominously, with his necke awry, holding up his eare, as if he expected *Mahomets Pidgeon* to come, and prompt him."[61] By 1648 Cromwell was Muhammad's "Bastard sonne."[62]

As early as 1649, one of Cromwell's supporters recognized the force and power of this polemic: "And that the Common Souldiers may be the more exasperated and desperate, [Cromwell's enemies] tell them that *their Chiefe Commanders are new Tyrants, Turkish Janisaries, men that walke by no rule or principles, either of honestie or conscience, subverters of Lawes and Liberties,* [practitioners of the worst] *villany, slavery, that can be imagined, even tyranny at the hight.*"[63] It increasingly did little good to protest against these attacks, for the practical decisions that Cromwell made as a military ruler under troubled conditions proved ready material for those who would make him a "Turkish tyrant." The de facto martial law made him a sultan. A 19 December 1648 sheet entitled *The Tyranny of Tyrannies* attacked Cromwell and his son-in-law Richard Ireton in the aftermath of Pride's Purge: "These are to signify to all free-born English men, that the new Turkish *Tyrants, Cromwell* and *Ireton,* at a *Council of War,* have already privately condemned to death Sir William Waller and Major General [Richard] Browne, Members of Parliament, free men of *England,* men that have faithfully fought the battles of their country in order to their country's peace, not their own tyranny and dominion over the people."[64] Those arrested voiced the same refrain of "Turkish tyranny."[65] Shortly thereafter *Mercurius Pragmaticus* asserted that "by the assistance of his *Janizaries* [Cromwell] is become as absolute as the *Grand Signior.*"[66]

Although the reimposition of censorship eventually limited such attacks under the Protectorate, the motif of "Turkish tyranny" reappeared after the Stuart Restoration. Use of the stereotype represented pent-up frustrations, but more important, it signaled a continuation of royalist polemic to discredit the republic and to help rebuild Stuart legitimacy. The figure of the "Turkish tyrant" clearly continued to mean something to a popular audience. In 1660, one Colonel Baker lampooned Cromwell's prominent nose as "the Carbuncle that was left, / At Median to light *Mahomet.* / Thy Nose as great an Impostor was, / As many mischiefs brought to pass."[67]

James Heath's notorious *Flagellum* describes Cromwell as inhumanely sending his volunteers "to blunt the Weapons of the Kings generous Cavalry," just as the Turk uses his horsemen, the *sipahis*.[68] According to Heath, the death of the Earl of Essex in 1646 meant there was "not an Officer left in the Army that did not acknowledge *Cromwell's* Sultanship."[69] Cromwell did not date "his Empire and Sultanship," however, until after the war against the Scots in 1650–51.[70]

This Restoration polemic took special aim at the military rule that had brought about and followed the regicide. Cromwell himself remained an object of attack, but the pamphlet writers generalized their message to suggest that Turkish-style rule by the Army had destroyed the country. The New Model Army now appeared regularly as a standing force of "janizaries" and "mamluks," these latter the slave-rulers of Egypt.[71] Army actions at Worcester in 1651 had been particularly grievous; as at Peterborough, the soldiers once in town "according to their Order fell a plundering the Town in a most barbarous manner, as if Turks were again a *Sacking of Constantinople,* and giving no quarter to any they found in the Streets."[72] *Learne of a Turk* (1660) was especially direct in critiquing the Army's "Turkish tyranny." Having recorded a bloody janizary mutiny upon the death of the Sultan Achmet I in 1617, the tract then drew out theological, moral, and political lessons for Restoration England.[73] The political lessons were four:

> First, how dangerous a thing it is for any supream power to stand in need of a constant standing Army. . . .
> Secondly, what a dangerous thing it is for the Civil Power to permit the souldiers and Officers of the Army to hold their Counsels and Conventicles. . . .
> Thirdly, how much better it is to be under the worst of Monarchies, then at the courtesie of a mutinied Army. . . .
> Fourthly, that the common souldier, having been debauched by their [*sic*] own Officers, may at last prove honest, and delivering their *misleaders* to Justice, may return to their duty and obedience.[74]

The Turk provides a heuristic analogue for all the ills of the preceding two decades—a standing army led by a cabal of ambitious officers. But the "common souldier" at last fulfills his duty to support his king.

Given such judgments, strong polemic against the major-generals as the fulfillment of "Turkish tyranny" stands out. Established in 1655 after rumblings of royalist rebellion, the rule of the major-generals came under especially harsh attack.[75] As late as 1682, *Arbi-*

trary Government still called their creation a "Usurpation . . . the most Barbarous and Arbitrary as ever was heard of."[76] The pamphlet exclaims: "See now what was become of the Liberties of *English* men, when [Cromwell] following the Example of the *Grand Seignior,* set over the Land a company of *Bashaws* [pashas], with the same power, under the new title of *Major-Generals.*"[77] The Puritan pashas had "prohibited all Horse-races, Cock-fighting, Bull-baiting," as much to limit "Concourse of People" as to stop ungodliness.[78] They took livings from churchmen, "unless they would work with their hands, so that many were ready to starve, for they were prohibited any Cure, or to be Chaplains to any, or to keep School."[79] Earlier Heath had charged that the pashas' "Barbarous Cruelty and Severity" both "suffocated the true Religion" and "did warm and foster the viperous brood of Sects and Heresies into monstrous luxuriances."[80] The Puritans' "Turkish tyranny" had the expected consequences: cruel limitations on traditional freedoms and true faith and a consequent promotion of heresy.

Indeed, as was the case with janizaries, the sultan Cromwell could not control the major-generals and the Army. Thus "Grand Signieur and his Bashaws," a poem in the 1660 *Dregs of Drollery,* retrospectively depicted Cromwell as threatened by his own forces:

> Grand *Signieur Cromwell* now himself bewails,
> For spreading so fair's grander *Bashaws* sailes;
> For now, for want of *Ballast,* every day,
> Each their great Masters threates to over-sway.
> Yea so farre are they now with him to bring,
> In no wise will they hear of's being King.[81]

The writer goes on to exhort the European kings to action, urging them to "Come forth, for God's sake, all you Christian Kings, / And clip this great *Turks*, with his *Bashaws* wings." Only thus can they "settle an exile brother on his Throne."[82] By 1660, of course, when the poem appeared in print, reflections upon Cromwellian tyranny and ambition served to underscore the validity and order of the newly restored monarchy.

By 1660, it was clear that divine providence had worked through the preceding troubles to bring about the restoration of true order. *Learne of a Turk* gives four theological observations to match its political observations. First, God rules over earthly rulers with "absolute and uncontroulable Soveraignty." Nonetheless (second), God uses "the Passions, and lusts, and furies of men" to complete his wise and holy plan; in this case the bloody janizaries fulfilled God's decree. Third, God's justice will revenge the blood of wicked rulers, let alone that of his elect. It had done so with the defeat of the Army. And finally, God "stilleth the raging of the sea, and the tumults of the people" after all their "greatest rage and fury."[83] The writer's point is clear: with the return of the Stuarts, divine justice has avenged the king's murder, and divine providence has bridled the passions that had killed a king.

The anonymous poet of *Dregs of Drollery* used the accidental collapse of a staircase at Bridewell during the Protectorate to put an edge to this view of divine justice. In this account, the "*Janisaryes* to their grand *Signieur* [i.e., Cromwell] come / To visite, as to visite *Mecha's Tombe*." There they gather on the staircase to hear the "Visier," probably Hugh Peters.[84] The stairs collapse; in the rubble "heads are broak, and arms, and legs, and thighs; / But necks kept for a *Tiburn* sacrifice":

> And now may y' see what 'tis to make your King,
> From th' same room to pass to his suffering;
> And take this for the First-fruits of your doom,
> For Crowning thus your King with Martyrdom.[85]

The excesses and godlessness of Cromwell and his associates stand in contrast to the righteous ways of the royal martyr.

Seventeenth-century Englishmen had clear and definite views about the Turkish Other. Whereas polemical literature of the early 1640s cast the Stuarts as isolated sultans controlled by their janizary minions, literature circulating before, during, and after the Protectorate cast the "godly" Cromwell and his followers as the truly "Turkish tyrants." Puritan rule had so embodied the arbitrary power, violence, false religion, and inverted anarchy of the "Turkish tyranny" that royalist attacks deployed the comparison regularly, despite the best efforts of writers such as Milton to argue the contrary.

"Tyranny of the Godly" as "Turkish Tyranny"

But beyond the political and religious import of Turks for seventeenth-century Englishmen and women, why did the Turk image work in royalist polemic?[86] What does the usage suggest about the conflict and interplay between royalist and nonroyalist opinions, and between Puritan and non-Puritan ideals?

It is important first to emphasize the popular character and protean qualities of "Turkish tyranny." First, in contrast to the learned classical references so common in seventeenth-century political discourse, the stereotype of the Turk surfaces in the pamphlets here and there without obvious order or reason.[87] The image is often a "toss-away" lodged in the midst of some broader argument. But whether ephemeral or sustained, the image is set within the moment. It builds from the common stereotype of the violent, apostate Turk. It is a serviceable image that could communicate a broad spectrum of related meanings to a popular audience.

Second, as George Sandys's frontispiece suggests, the image of the Turk *could* fit with contemporary humanism. The frontispiece's classical symbols range from the Sibyl to figures for the classical virtues of truth and constancy. The entire assembly rests within a classical temple. All the captions are in Latin. When polemicists appealed to the Turk and the classics at the same time, the effect was either to subvert tyranny or to elaborate on its character. The frontispiece subverts (Turkish) tyranny by setting it beside the light and strength of true civilization: Christianized Greco-Roman culture. In contrast, while James Heath's *Flagellum* provides some choice examples of Cromwell and his followers as Turks, the work juxtaposes these images with classical references to Sejanus.[88]

A third aspect of this flexible usage appears when one remembers that the Turk image served within a constellation of similar images. The reputation of Cromwell and the Puritans for arbitrary harshness made the "Norman" and his yoke also common. Their duplicity encouraged comparison to the "Machiavel." And their self-serving legalism made them "Jews" long before Cromwell's policy of allowing Jews into England confirmed the Protector's actual interests. Within royalist polemic, all these "Others" embodied the effects of corrupt faith and the attitudes about government and society that flowed from it.[89] Of course the great "Other" for Puritanism had always been popery. The tie mentioned above between Turkism and popery was primarily important as a way of linking the two stereotyped "Others" whom Protestants most feared. Thus by calling on one figure, a writer called on its fellows. By calling Cromwell and the Puritans "Turkish tyrants," polemicists painted them with all the negative features also associated with Normans, Machiavels, Jews, and Catholics.

Finally, because Islam (fortuitously) did not separate mosque and state, the image of the Turk communicated well in an England that did not separate religion and politics. The Turk represented the legalistic, "atheistic" aspects of Puritanism. Similarly the image pointed to the violent, arbitrary violations associated with the Protector and the Army. These characteristics sometimes met at the semantic watershed that separated yet joined Puritan faith and Cromwellian politics, as when the major-generals' implementation of Puritan-inspired policies (e.g., the suppression of cockfighting and bullbaiting) yielded charges of "Turkish tyranny."

Thus the image of the Turk proved useful in polemic not only because it resonated with many contemporaries in a world of slave raids and renegades, of domestic rebellion and regicide, but also because it could convey many meanings in multiple contexts, for a popular or elite audience.[90] The Personal Rule of Charles I created conditions that fostered charges of "Turkish tyranny." Puritan supporters of Parliament argued that rule by the godly—based on a reasonable, persuasive gospel—would give true political and spiritual freedom: "the strength of the *Gospels* adversaries lies not in the *goodnesse* of their *cause*, but in the *ignorance* of peoples *minds* and meere *mistakes* thence arising. What is *Paganisme*, *Mahumetanisme*, *Popery* but a Rapsody and heape of grosse mistakes raised in the darke?"[91] Then conditions changed, and Cromwell and his Puritan supporters found themselves labeled as Turks. Especially after the Restoration they stood in stark contrast to good government and true religion. And when Puritan writers such as Milton continued to label *their* enemies as Turks, the obvious irony served to forward the royalist cause. Those who had sought to use the "Turkish mirror" found themselves gazing into its unforgiving frame, cast in popular stereotype as arbitrary, violent, hypocritical, and—most damning—as perverse followers of a false, legalistic religion. Charles II and his royalist supporters could stand as the opposite, as representatives of proper order in church and state.

Milton's famous allusions to the Turk in *Paradise Lost* suggest a denouement to this struggle. The poem is in many ways an extended consideration of Christian liberty and its place in public life, produced as Milton reflected on his career and on the Stuart Restoration.[92] God's providential monarchy is one in which men were created "sufficient to have stood, though free to fall."[93] Along with liberty go virtue and a strength of will only nurtured under a sense of responsibility. Milton favored republican government in this life because he thought it most fully embodied true Christian freedom. His prime opponent was not monarchy per se, however, but any form of tyranny by individual or group.[94] Satan represented such tyranny, and Milton regularly cast Satan in the Turk's image. Satan is the "great Sultan" of the gathering horde of demons in hell, and their meeting is a "dark *Divan*," the sultan's council. Satan's assembled forces are like janizaries, with "orient Colors waving."[95]

Milton's readers would have been highly sensitive to the allusions and would have recognized both Charles I and Cromwell, especially the latter, given the polemic of the 1650s.[96]

Paradise Lost, then, may represent Milton's direct response to the shift of polemical usage.[97] In Satan as a "Turkish tyrant" Milton represented the character of a tyranny he strongly opposed, be it in a king or in a republican. His readers would have seen in Satan and his followers the cringing servility imposed through "Turkish" control of political and religious life. They associated "Turkish" servility with violence and duplicity (Muslim raiders and renegades), with ignorance and false faith (Islam). Against this "Turkish tyranny," Milton set an all-powerful, all-knowing God whose ways (unlike the Turk's) allow justification because they are reasonable. Milton's God is quasi-deistic; he rules above all things in transcendent glory and light. Milton explains that true humanity, true love, and true communion with God depend on Adam's free will and subsequent responsibility for his sin. But God provides salvation through Christ. Milton's answer to the complex question of Christian liberty closely resembles Henry Marsh's in his description of "Turkish tyranny": that true faith means true liberty, and that true liberty is the only means to true faith. Milton's response also looks very much like Sandys's frontispiece, with Christ destroying the "Turkish tyranny," perhaps not immediately, but in his own good time.

CONCLUSION

In 1672 an equestrian statue of Charles II appeared on public display. Trampled under the king's mount was a Turk.[98] Given that Charles never literally encountered the Turks in battle, this victorious representation only makes sense in light of contemporary charges of "Turkish tyranny" against the king's enemies. It meant the victory of tradition over violent novelty, reasonable faith over Puritan enthusiasm, monarchy over regicide, the legitimate son of a martyr over the usurping sultan-Protector. Polemicists had successfully used the image of the Turk to stigmatize revolutionary behavior and sentiments, to identify these with the dreaded eastern tyrant and his false religion, and to spread these views by building on a popular stereotype. Of course, from the broad perspective of European cultural evolution, they had done even more. They had pointed to what later generations would consider the victory of modern civilization over barbarism. Collective soul-searching over political and religious identity was common in the world of new science and of embryonic nation-states during the seventeenth century; the period witnessed the definitive transition from medieval to modern. Perceptions of external difference—the "Other"—had a significant part in this soul-searching. The Turk evoked fear: fear that Christian faith in particular—not just the temporal regimes of Christendom—might fall to violence or ignorance or legalism. In the fallout of sixteenth-century Reformation and seventeenth-century revolution—the internal breakdown of Christendom as an ideal and its slow replacement with a humanist-inspired "Europe"—the Turk represented false faith, social barbarism, and violence.[99] When Cromwell and the Puritans were represented as Turks or Muslims, they became the ultimate treacherous outsiders, tyrannous over mind and body, threatening the norms of civilized behavior, even jeopardizing a newly evolving civilization based on true religion, humanist ideals, and reasonableness—a fearful prospect. True Protestantism absorbed apocalyptic and predestinarian hopes while repudiating the excesses of Puritan idealism as alien to good Englishmen. To call Cromwell and other Puritans Turks was to isolate them from this national ideal, to make them pariahs, supporters of a failed vision. Hope now lay with a political and religious moderation that would soon become the comfortable latitudinarianism and secularism of the expanding eighteenth century.[100]

NOTES

1. John Milton, *Observations upon the Articles of Peace with the Irish Rebels*, in *Complete Prose Works of John Milton*, ed. Don M. Wolfe et al. (New Haven: Yale University Press, 1953–82) 3: 312.
2. Ibid., 312–13.
3. Ibid., 313.
4. Nabil Matar's recent comprehensive study summarizes the general situation well: "[Islam and the Turkish Empire] served to clarify, support and vindicate Christian positions in the camps of the Nonconformists and the anti-Nonconformists, the Anglicans and the anti-Anglicans and the anti-Catholics," *Islam in Britain, 1558-1685* (Cambridge: Cambridge University Press, 1998), 106.
5. John Morrill, *The Nature of the English Revolution* (London and New York: Longman, 1993), 1–68.
6. Samuel C. Chew, *The Crescent and the Rose: Islam and England during the Renaissance* (New York: Oxford University Press, 1937); Franklin L. Baumer, "England, the Turk, and the Common Corps of Christendom," *American Historical Review* 50 (October 1944): 26–48. Following Norman Daniel's magisterial *Islam and the West: The Making of an Image* (Edinburgh: Edinburgh University Press, 1960; rev. ed., Oxford: Oneworld Publications, 1993) and Edward Said's *Orientalism* (New York: Pantheon Books, 1978), historians and literary scholars have increasingly studied the Muslim/Turkish "Other" to understand underlying Euro-

pean attitudes toward religious, ethnic, and cultural difference and the ways these attitudes molded self-perceptions at times of great social, political, and cultural change. See also Brandon H. Beck, *From the Rising of the Sun: English Images of the Ottoman Empire to 1715,* American University Studies, ser. 9, vol. 20 (New York: Peter Lang, 1987); David R. Blanks, "Western Views of Islam in the Premodern Period: A Brief History of Past Approaches," in *Western Views of Islam in Medieval and Early Modern Europe: Perception of Other,* ed. David R. Blanks and Michael Frassetto (New York: St. Martin's Press, 1999), 11–53; Bernard Lewis, *Islam and the West* (New York: Oxford University Press, 1993), 72–84; Nabil Matar, " 'Turning Turk': Conversion to Islam in English Renaissance Thought," *Durham University Journal* 86 (January 1994): 33–41; Lucette Valensi, *The Birth of the Despot: Venice and the Sublime Porte,* trans. Arthur Denner (Ithaca, N.Y.: Cornell University Press, 1993); Daniel J. Vitkus, "Early Modern Orientalism: Representations of Islam in Sixteenth- and Seventeenth-Century Europe," in *Western Views of Islam,* 207–30; Charles Woodhead, " 'The Present Terrour of the World'? Contemporary Views of the Ottoman Empire, c. 1600," *History* 72 (February 1987): 20–37; and M. E. Yapp, "Europe in the Turkish Mirror," *Past and Present* 137 (November 1992): 134–56.

7. Matar, *Islam in Britain,* 185.

8. Ibid., 4–11. Cf. *Newes from Sally of a Strange Delivery of Foure English Captives from the Slavery of the Turkes* (London, 1642).

9. Arthur L. Horniker, "William Harborne and the Beginning of Anglo-Turkish Diplomatic and Commercial Relations," *Journal of Modern History* 14 (September 1942): 289–316; S. A. Skilliter, "The Organization of the First English Embassy in Istanbul in 1583," *Asian Affairs* 10 (1979): 159–65; and idem, *William Harborne and the Trade with Turkey, 1578-1582: A Documentary Study of the First Anglo-Ottoman Relations* (London: Oxford University Press, 1977).

10. Matar, *Islam in Britain,* 10.

11. Daniel Goffman, *Britons in the Ottoman Empire, 1642-1660* (Seattle and London: University of Washington Press, 1998), 54, 108.

12. Matar, *Islam in Britain,* 25–49.

13. Ibid., 52–63; Daniel J. Vitkus, ed., *Three Turk Plays from Early Modern England: "Selimus," "A Christian Turned Turk," and "The Renegado"* (New York: Columbia University Press, 2000).

14. Matar, *Islam in Britain,* 63–71. Margo Todd has used the apostasy and formal reconversion of a renegade English sailor to explore the relationships between Laudian and Puritan responses ("A Captive's Story: Puritans, Pirates, and the Drama of Reconciliation," *The Seventeenth Century* 12 [Spring 1997]: 37–56).

15. Matar, *Islam in Britain.*

16. T. B., *The Saints Inheritance After the Day of Judgement* (London, 1643), 15; Joseph Mede, *The Key of the Revelation, searched and demonstrated out of the Naturall and proper Characters* of the *Visions* (London, 1643), 113. On the linkage of pope and Turk, see Anthony Milton, *Catholic and Reformed: The Roman and Protestant Churches in English Protestant Thought, 1600-1640* (Cambridge: Cambridge University Press, 1995), 114–16. On the Turk in seventeenth-century millenarianism generally, see Christopher Hill, *Antichrist in Seventeenth-Century England* (London: Oxford University Press, 1971), 26, 47, 82, 96, 181–82, and Paul Christianson, *Reformers and Babylon: English Apocalyptic Visions from the Reformation to the Eve of the Civil War* (Toronto: University of Toronto Press, 1978), 64, 104–5, 126. See also Peter Lake, "Anti-popery: The Structure of a Prejudice," in *Conflict in Early Stuart England: Studies in*

Religion and Politics, 1603-1642, ed. Richard Cust and Ann Hughes (London: Longman, 1989), 72–106.

17. *A Diurnal of Sea Designes, which is as strange as true* (London, 1642), 3–4.

18. Matar, *Islam in Britain,* 106–7.

19. Quoted in Woodhead, "'The Present Terrour,'" 20.

20. Beck, *From the Rising of the Sun,* 29–65.

21. E.g., Alexander Ross, *Pansebeia, or A View of all Religions in the World,* 2d ed. (London, 1655), 162–79.

22. Daniel, *Islam and the West;* Malcolm Barber, "How the West Saw Medieval Islam," *History Today* 47 (May 1997): 44–50.

23. Jerome Friedman, *The Battle of the Frogs and Fairford's Flies: Miracles and the Pulp Press during the English Revolution* (New York: St. Martin's Press, 1993), 144. On popular perceptions, see also Joad Raymond, ed., *Making the News: An Anthology of the Newsbooks of Revolutionary England, 1641-1660* (New York: St. Martin's Press, 1993), 270–72. See also Vitkus, "Early Modern Orientalism," 207–30.

24. William Bates, "The Divinity of the Christian Religion Proved by the Evidence of Reason, and Divine Revelation," in *The Whole Works of the Rev. W. Bates, D.D.,* ed. W. Farmer (London, 1815; reprint, Harrisonburg, Va.: Sprinkle Publications, 1990), 1:114–15.

25. Ibid., 115.

26. Ibid.

27. George Sandys, *Sandys Travells: Containing an History of the Original and Present State of the Turkish Empire,* 6th ed. (London, 1670).

28. See below for the significance of this juxtaposition of "Turkish tyranny" and classical references.

29. Henry Marsh, *A New Survey of the Turkish Empire and Government,* 2d ed. (London, 1663).

30. Ibid., 47.

31. Beck, *From the Rising of the Sun,* 62.

32. Marsh, *A New Survey,* 65–74.

33. Ibid., 75–93.

34. Ibid., 83.

35. Ibid., 85.

36. Ibid., 84.

37. For examples in addition to the ones cited below, see Stevie Davies, *Images of Kingship in "Paradise Lost": Milton's Politics and Christian Liberty* (Columbia, Mo.: University of Missouri Press, 1983), 51–52, 60.

38. *The Rebels' Turkish Tyranny, in their March, December 14, 1641* (London, 1641).

39. *A Brief Discourse upon Tyrants and Tyranny* (N.p., 1642), 2.

40. *Certain Considerations upon the Duties Both of Prince and People* (London, 1642), n.p. See also *Brief Discourse,* 3.

41. *Certain Considerations,* n.p.

42. *Equitable and Necessary Considerations and Resolutions for Association of Arms throughout the Counties of the Kingdom of England and Principality of Wales* (London, 1642), n.p.

43. *A Discourse upon the Questions in Debate between the King and Parliament* (Oxford, 1642), 13.

44. Davies, *Images of Kingship,* 60.

45. Jacques Davy du Perron, *Luther's Alcoran,* trans. N.N.P. (N.p., 1642), 3.

46. There are sections entitled "Of the conjunction of the Turkes, and some temporall Christian States, against Catholike Princes" and "The Reasons of the friendshippe betweene the Turke, and some Lutheran States" (ibid., 94–102), but these do not transplant the political concerns of the English scene.

47. Ibid., 27.

48. Ibid., 89.

49. John Doughty, *The Kings Cause Rationally, briefly, and plainly debated, as it stands De facto* (Oxford, 1644), 43–44.

50. James Howell, *Dendrologia: Dodona's Grove, or the Vocall Forrest,* 3d ed. (Cambridge, 1645), 66.

51. Ibid, 67–68.

52. *Relations and Observations, Historical and Politic, upon the Parliament, begun Anno Domini 1640* (N.p., 1648), 29–30.

53. *The Downfal of Dagon, or, Certain Signes of the Sudden and Unavoidable Ruine of this Parliament and Army* (London, 1652), 1.

54. *A Description of the Grand Signor's Seraglio, or Turkish Emperour's Court* (London, 1650), 187–88.

55. *A Winter Dream* (N.p., 1648), 15.

56. Griffith Williams, *Jura Majestatis: The Rights of Kings Both in Church and State* (Oxford, 1644), 213.

57. "So farr Turkish Vassals enjoy as much liberty under *Mahomet* and the Grand Signor: the other we neither yet have enjoyd under [the king], nor were ever like to doe under the Tyranny of a negative voice, which he claimes above the unanimous consent and power of a whole Nation virtually in the Parlament" (John Milton, *Eikonoklastes,* in *The Complete Prose Works of John Milton,* 3: 575).

58. Helpful here is Austin Woolrych's description and reassessment of conditions under the Protector ("The Cromwellian Protectorate: A Military Dictatorship?" *History* 75 [June 1990]: 207–31). He concludes: "[W]hat there was of the dictatorial in Cromwell's rule—and there was such an element, often though it has been overstated—stemmed not so much from its military origins or the participation of army officers in civil government as from his constant commitment to the interest of the people of God, and his conviction that suppressing vice and encouraging virtue constituted 'the very end of magistracy.'"

59. *Mercurius Aulicus, Communicating the Intelligence and Affaires of the Court, to the Rest of the Kingdome* (1643), 218.

60. According to a popular belief mentioned in a summary attack on twenty-nine London sects, Muhammad "taught a pigeon to pecke a pease from forth his eare, bearing the ignorant in hand that the *Holy Ghost* brought him newes from Heaven" (*A Discovery of Twenty-nine Sects Here in London* [London, 1641]).

61. John Cleveland, *The Character of a London-Diurnall,* 3d ed. (N.p., 1647), 5–6.

62. *The Second Part of the Westminster Monster* (N.p., 1648).

63. *The Discoverer,* part one (London, 1649), 19. Parliamentarians had used similar polemical tactics during the civil wars: "[S]o their cause may be advanced by it, the best of them care not, if all the Churches in England were converted into synagogues for Jewes, or Mosques for Mahomet, nay their height of joy it would be, if all our Churches were turned . . . into Prisons, so Puritans and Roundheads fill'd them" (*One Argument More Against the Cavaliers, Taken from their Violation of Churches* [London, 1643], 5–6).

64. *The Tyranny of Tyrannies* (N.p., 1648).

65. David Underdown, *Pride's Purge: Politics in the Puritan Revolution* (Oxford: Clarendon Press, 1971), 163. Waller was to spend three years in prison, Browne five (ibid., 162–63, 195; *Dictionary of National Biography*, s.v. "Waller, William" and "Browne, Richard.")

66. *Mercurius Pragmaticus*, num. 17 (1649).

67. Colonel Baker, *The Blazing-Star, or Nolls Nose Newly Revived, and taken out of his Tomb* (London, 1660), 3–4.

68. James Heath, *Flagellum, or, The Life and Death, Birth and Burial of Oliver Cromwell, the Late Usurper*, 2d ed. (London, 1663), 22.

69. Ibid., 43.

70. Ibid., 87.

71. Ibid., 121, 150, 167. See also William Baron, *Regicides No Saints nor Martyrs* (London, 1700), 17, 32, 38.

72. Heath, *Flagellum*, 118.

73. *Learne of a Turk, or Instructions and Advise sent from the Turkish Army at Constantinople, to the English Army at London* (London, 1660).

74. Ibid., 22.

75. Woolrych, "The Cromwellian Protectorate," 219–23, argues that "so far from acting like the satraps and bashaws to whom republicans and royalists likened them, they mostly tried hard to operate within the bounds of the law" (221).

76. *Arbitrary Government*, 119–20.

77. Ibid., 120. For a response see *A Modest Vindication of Oliver Cromwell from the Unjust Accusations of Lieutenant-General Ludlow in His Memoirs* (London, 1698), 63–64.

78. *Arbitrary Government*, 121.

79. Ibid., 120.

80. Heath, *Flagellum*, 173–74.

81. "Grand Signieur and his Bashaws," in *Dregs of Drollery, or Old Poetry in its Ragges: A Full Cry of Hell-Hounds Unkennelled to Go a King-Catching* (London, 1660), 17. These things happen under generally bad conditions in England: "Meantime, whilst we in *Coffee* daily health, / To make good w' have a *Turkish* Common-wealth; / And with our *Turkish* manners now we see, / This *Turkish Phtheseude* so well to agree." According to Matar, seventeenth-century public opinion frequently viewed coffee "as an 'infidel' berry and . . . the secret weapon of the Muslims" to seduce Englishmen both religiously and culturally (*Islam in Britain*, 114).

82. "Grand Signieur and his Bashaws," in *Dregs of Drollery*, 17.

83. *Learne of a Turk*, 21–22.

84. Royalist polemic frequently linked the infamous Peters with "Turkish tyranny." In *The Famous Tragedy of King Charles I* (London, 1649), Cromwell gleefully promises Peters that "We two (like *Mahomet* and his pliant *Monk*) will Frame an *English Alcoran*, which shall be written with the self same Pencil, great *Draco* grav'd his Laws" (6). John Arnway claims that Peters would "seduce [Englishmen] into the way . . . of the *Alcoran*, by indulgence of *Poligamy*" (*The Tablet, or Moderation of Charles the I, Martyr, with an Alarm to the Subjects of England*, 2d ed. [The Hague, 1649], 81–82). John Gauden thought Peters a "Western Mahomet and new Antichrist" in his "*Jugling* and *Sophistry*" over breaking his allegiance to Charles I (*Cromwell's Bloody Slaughter-house* [London, 1660], 64).

85. "Upon the fall of the Stair of the Banquetting-house," in *Dregs of Drollery*, 18.

86. For a recent study of satire on Cromwell more generally, see Laura Lunger

Knoppers, *Constructing Cromwell: Ceremony, Portrait, and Print, 1645-1661* (Cambridge: Cambridge University Press, 2000).

87. J. G. A. Pocock's *The Machiavellian Moment: Florentine Political Thought and the Atlantic Republican Tradition* (Princeton: Princeton University Press, 1975) has inspired a generation of historians to explore the relations between Christian humanism and the spread of republicanism. One of the most discussed classical references is Tacitus's description of the early Roman Empire and its significance for early modern thought about republicanism, reason of state, and Stoicism. Tacitean images and ideas provided a venue for systematic and sustained debate about the character and causes of tyranny (among other things) and thus present a striking comparison and contrast with the popular, sporadic use of the Turk image. See Pocock, *The Machiavellian Moment*, 351–52; Richard Tuck, *Philosophy and Government, 1572-1651* (Cambridge: Cambridge University Press, 1993), 39–45, 104–19; and Markku Peltonen, *Classical Humanism and Republicanism in English Political Thought, 1570-1640* (Cambridge: Cambridge University Press, 1995), 124–36.

88. Knoppers, *Constructing Cromwell*, 188–91.

89. Richard Pointer's essay in this volume suggests how intercultural dialogue could take a less aggressive and accusatory form. The differences between English views of Indians and of Turks were in part a matter of history, political context, and polemical goals. See also Nabil Matar's *Turks, Moors, and Englishmen in the Age of Discovery* (New York: Columbia University Press, 1999).

90. Charles Taylor's notion of "webs of [moral] interlocution" (*Sources of the Self: The Making of Modern Identity* [Cambridge: Harvard University Press, 1989], 38) helps explain how the protean image of the Turk could work as it did. According to Taylor, definitions of terms may change, but these changes do not alter the fundamental dependence on "webs" of meaning. Thus the image of the Turk—an agreed-upon collection of "un-English" attitudes and practices—was nonetheless a disputed object within seventeenth-century "webs of [moral] interlocution."

91. Thomas Hill, *The Militant Church, Triumphant over the Dragon and His Angels* (London, 1643), 19.

92. E.g., Armand Himy, "*Paradise Lost* as a Republican 'Tractatus Theologico-Politicus,'" in *Milton and Republicanism*, ed. David Armitage, Armand Himy, and Quentin Skinner (Cambridge: Cambridge University Press, 1995), 118–34.

93. John Milton, *Paradise Lost*, 3.99, in *Complete Poems and Major Prose of John Milton*, ed. Merritt Hughes (Indianapolis: Odyssey Press, 1957).

94. Martin Dzelzainis, "Milton's Classical Republicanism," in *Milton and Republicanism*, 3–24.

95. John Milton, *Paradise Lost* 1.48, 546, 10.47. Stevie Davies, *Images of Kingship*, has analyzed these images at length, 51–88.

96. On Milton's Satan and Charles I, see Joan Bennett, "God, Satan, and King Charles: Milton's Royal Portraits," *PMLA* 92 (1977): 441–57. More recently, for Satan as part of a republican critique of Oliver Cromwell, see David Norbrook, *Writing the English Republic: Poetry, Rhetoric, and Politics, 1627-1660* (Cambridge: Cambridge University Press, 1999).

97. Christopher Hill, *The Experience of Defeat: Milton and Some Contemporaries* (New York: Viking, 1984), 297–328.

98. Christopher Hill, *Milton and the English Revolution* (New York: Viking Press, 1978), 220.

99. Yapp, "Europe in the Turkish Mirror," 138–48, 152–54.

100. For the continuing influence of the Turk image on social and political ideas, especially for British North America, see Robert J. Allison's *The Crescent Obscured: The United States and the Muslim World, 1776-1815* (Oxford: Clarendon Press, 1995), which argues that American views about Muslims influenced early republican national identity and political ideology, especially with regard to slavery, and Matar's *Turks, Moors, and Englishmen in the Age of Discovery*, which explores the relations between British attitudes toward Turks and those toward American Indians.

Part IV
Puritanism and Community

Assurance, Community, and the Puritan Self in the Antinomian Controversy, 1636–38

Timothy D. Hall

THE ANTINOMIAN CONTROVERSY OF 1636–38 LOOMS LARGE IN EVERY STAN-
dard account of the early years of American Puritanism. The explosion of conflict over the meaning of justification and assurance only six years after Massachusetts Bay colony's founding revealed the unexpected presence of deep religious, political, and social divisions. For a time the discontents, labeled "Antinomians" for their reputed belief that justification freed converts from the constraints of divine or man-made law, threatened the settlement's political stability. The Antinomians' identification of John Cotton as their spiritual leader cast a pall of suspicion over the colony's most distinguished divine and drew him into a series of disputes that exposed serious theological disagreement among Puritan spiritual leaders. The trial and banishment of Anne Hutchinson as an Antinomian ringleader endowed the controversy with mythic force in American literature and historiography. Since the nineteenth century, the Hutchinson affair has often served as a classic instance of the American Puritan antithesis between self and community, a tension portrayed as diminishing only as the recurrent self-assertiveness of discontents such as Hutchinson eroded a repressive orthodox hegemony.[1] Yet the documents of the seventeenth-century controversy, read in light of recent scholarship on Puritan conversion and devotional practice, suggest that a more nuanced understanding of the Puritan self within community may be in order.

The potent image of Anne Hutchinson's disorderly womanhood has often distracted attention from the contested doctrines of which the woman herself, social threat though she may have posed, stood in the final analysis as a symbol. At the heart of the controversy lay not any one personality, but an effort to define properly the nature of justification, assurance, new birth, the new creature, and the newborn self's relationship to the covenant community. These issues, debated since the Reformation, took on new urgency in the

197

effort to carve a godly commonwealth out of the New World wilderness. The surviving texts of the New England debate reveal the dynamism of a seventeenth-century intellectual movement characterized by a remarkable degree of theological give-and-take. They also reveal a concern to promote, rather than repress, the flourishing of the individual redeemed self within the context of a nurturing community.

The nature of the seventeenth-century Antinomian conception of the self in community has sparked considerable scholarly controversy in recent years. The "sainted Anne Hutchinson" of Nathaniel Hawthorne's writings holds wide currency among those who portray Hutchinson as the tragic proto-liberal heroine of a seventeenth-century morality play, a courageous individual woman standing alone against Massachusetts Bay's repressive, patriarchal civil and ecclesiastical order.[2] An influential historiographical variant of this account treats the Antinomians as an emergent class of entrepreneurial merchants and artisans seeking to break the constraints of a collectivistic precapitalist moral economy to enlarge the scope of individual rational economic choice.[3] In either version, Antinomians sought to release the individual self from repressive ideological constraints to make its own way in the world. Yet the literary historian Amy Schrager Lang has argued that this Whiggish interpretation betrays deficiencies in its treatment of Antinomian beliefs. The Hutchinsonians went far beyond their Puritan neighbors in their teachings on the self and individual choice by understanding conversion as self-annihilation. In Lang's view, Puritan ministers opposed this tenet because it undermined their efforts to harness the self to communal, public ends. "Only by arguing that the language of the self-in-Christ masks an impulse toward radical self-assertion," Lang has observed, "can we arrive at the modern view of antinomianism as a liberating doctrine."[4]

Similar controversy exists over the image of Puritanism as a repressive monolith aimed at ruthless subordination of the self to the good of the community. The historian Philip Greven, for example, argues that Puritan selves were systematically "misshaped" by repressive child-rearing practices.[5] The political theorist Barry Alan Shain portrays the whole of Reformed Protestantism as intensely anti-individualistic, seeking to suppress or overcome the self while ruthlessly subordinating its interests and desires to the good of the community.[6] Shain sees Puritan New England as the field on which the latent communalism of Reformed Protestantism was most fully developed, supporting his views with nearly three decades worth of social histories that have drawn an intensely communal picture of a Puritan social life that appeared to leave little room for individual expression.[7]

Other works on seventeenth-century American Puritan devotional practices, pastoral care, and popular religion offer glimpses of a more complex, dynamic movement in which some traditional constraints on the self may have been relaxed. Puritanism constituted a complex of theological ideas and religious impulses that expressed themselves in radical as well as conservative forms.[8] The Antinomian Controversy was only one in a series of efforts during New England's first decade and after to negotiate among conflicting understandings of doctrine and practice.[9] In subsequent decades, New England laypeople felt free to dissent from their pastors on a wide range of important issues.[10] Puritan social teaching may have enhanced women's sense of selfhood by elevating their importance in family and community life.[11] Puritan piety fostered a significant measure of self-expression, as studies such as Patricia Caldwell's *Puritan Conversion Narrative* have shown.[12] While converts commonly described the unconverted self as "vile," they also experienced a passionately personal, private communion with Christ in their conversion and devotional life.

Indeed, the historian John Martin has recently argued that the Calvinist theology underpinning Puritanism was deeply rooted in the Renaissance "discovery of the individual." John Calvin himself made a crucial contribution to this discovery, Martin has argued, by helping to invent a new concept of "sincerity." Sincerity, as used by Calvin and other Renaissance thinkers, ascribed a new legitimacy to the expression of individual emotion and advanced a new conception of the self as agent or author, someone "responsible for his or her actions and assertions." This new Renaissance self, bound by the ethic of sincerity to express its essential difference from other selves, found itself less able to establish consensus or a sense of community.[13] Martin's explication of Calvin's role in the Renaissance discovery of the individual self is suggestive for our understanding of the tensions expressed in the Antinomian Controversy that sprang up among Calvin's New England heirs. Yet Martin's pessimism concerning the individual self's capacity for entering into community may signal a persisting inadequacy in late modern and postmodern understandings of Puritan teachings concerning the self.

Set in this recent historiographical context, the Antinomian Controversy appears not as a pitched battle between seventeenth-century individualists against Puritan collectivists. Rather, it begins to come into focus as the climax of a series of negotiations over how to understand new possibilities of personal agency and responsibility opened for the self through the transforming experience of conversion. Ministers struggled to affirm and cultivate the interior depth of selves liberated from the guilt of the Law to commune with God while at the same time harnessing that powerful new life to community formation. Thanks to the work of Michael McGiffert, Charles Hambrick-Stowe, Charles Lloyd Cohen, and others, historians now recognize that New England ministers inherited John Calvin's passion for fostering a sincere religion of the heart along with his predestinarian theology.[14] Yet the literary historian Janice Knight has recently detected significant disagreements over what this heart religion entailed and how it should be promoted. Knight argues that the disagreements pitted a small group that she calls the "Spiritual Brethren," led by John Cotton and John Davenport, against a larger group of "Intellectual Fathers" led by Thomas Hooker and Thomas Shepard. Knight's particular way of characterizing the alliances may be open to challenge, but a ferment of theological discussion and debate certainly did arise in the 1630s over such issues as the use of ordinances, the nature of saving faith, assurance of salvation, and the place of sanctification in a convert's life.[15] Analysis of the debate over these and other issues can illuminate the Puritan negotiations over the meaning and place of the individual self in a godly society.

However much Puritan ministers may have disagreed on other matters, they did share a common view of the effects of saving grace on the self: grace transformed the self but did not annihilate it. Thomas Shepard, the pastor of the church at Cambridge, Massachusetts, trained his parishioners to "loathe themselves" as the Holy Spirit gave them grace to "see their own vileness."[16] Church members appear to have expected such a recognition on the part of candidates for admission, sometimes probing those who had not sufficiently expressed their sense of sinfulness until candidates told how they came to the point of self-loathing.[17] Although at odds with Thomas Shepard on other important points, John Cotton agreed that the elect must be "drawn out of themselves by a spirit of bondage, and unto Christ by a spirit of poverty."[18] The self to be loathed was the soul corrupted in all its faculties by depravity. In his sermon series on Matthew's parable of the ten virgins, preached as the Antinomian Controversy was heating up, Shepard analyzed the sinful self as possessing a darkened understanding, with affections turned inward to "selfe-love" rather than upward in love to the Lord, and a will turned toward pleasing itself rather than pleasing Christ.[19] Consistent with the Renaissance emphasis on differences among individual selves, however, this depraved self-absorption manifested itself in a variety of ways. In his treatise on conversion, *The Sincere Convert*, Shepard sketched out at least three different types of people who "content themselves with a certaine measure of holiness," and at least four types who "reject Christ."[20]

For Shepard, Cotton, and other New England ministers, the remedy for the sinful self was gracious transformation. In *The Sincere Convert*, Shepard declared that the human soul was ultimately stamped with one of two images: the "image of the Devil" or the "image of God." He assured readers that a convert's "understanding with open face beholding Christ, is turned into the Image and likeness of Christ."[21] Similarly, Cotton viewed conversion and its fruit in sanctification as "the new man created in us . . . after the image of Christ especially."[22] The unity of the New England ministers on this point may be seen in the Assembly of Churches' confutation of the Antinomians' first error, that "in the conversion of a sinner, which is saving and gracious, the faculties of the soule, and the workings therof, in things pertaining to God, are destroyed and made to cease." To this error the Assembly retorted that Scripture "speaketh of the faculties of the soule (as the understanding and the will) not as destroyed in conversion, but as changed."[23] The understanding was enlightened, the affections fired with love for Christ, and the will turned to pleasing Christ.

However unified the ministers may have been regarding the transformative effects of conversion on the self, they perceived divisions among themselves that impinged on their ability to individualize pastoral care, adapting it to the differing needs of parishioners who came to them for spiritual comfort. They also perceived differences in their understanding of, and their ability to shape, the horizontal, communal dimension of the self's transformation. In the mid-1630s those differences appeared to divide John Cotton and John Wheelwright from most other New England ministers. Cotton's views on faith, assurance, and sanctification appeared to Shepard and Hooker to undermine both the individual and social dimensions of grace and pastoral care. The lay dissent welling up from Cotton's Boston congregation in 1636 made clarification and resolution of these matters imperative.

The controversial issue of whether saving faith was active or passive, whether the self exercised any agency in the process of justification, held important implications for both the individual and society. Peter Bulkeley, the pastor of the church in Concord, Massachusetts, expressed a concern for individual agency in faith that was consonant with the Renaissance insistence that responsible human actions should flow from heartfelt dispositions. Bulkeley protested that John Cotton's view of faith as wholly passive was inimical to any possibility of affectionate relationship between human beings and God, for union with Christ and the soul must involve "a mutuall giving and taking each other." To deny such agency implied "a mere taking on Gods part, noe givinge," and logically entailed the unthinkable possibility that the "spirit of God" might "be united . . . to a Reprobate" whose heart was set against God.[24] Cotton was as concerned as Bulkeley and other New England ministers to promote heartfelt union or "living faith" between the soul and Christ. Yet he worried that to concede the possibility of active faith prior to "union with Christ" would betray the Reformed theology of the human will as bound by sin. "I dare not acknowledge any *liberum Arbitrius* [free judgment] to close with Christ," Cotton declared, "till *Arbitrius* be liberated."[25]

Cotton went to great lengths in his exchange with Bulkeley and in later debates to show how his view of faith as passive could preserve the notion of responsibility so central to the Renaissance understanding of the self without compromising the Reformed emphasis on the bondage of the will. The soul's initial faith in Christ constituted an "actuall Receyving" even though it was not "active"; it was a "Habit of Faith" that operated by "emptying the soule of all confidence in it self and in the Creature, and so leaving and constituting the soule as an empty vessell, empty of its owne worth, and goodnesse, but full of Christ."[26] Cotton marshalled quotations from Augustine and Calvin to demonstrate that his view of faith stood squarely in the center of the great tradition of Reformed orthodoxy and did not invalidate the self's authorship of or responsibility for its acts. "It will be said we are therefore acted upon, and you then act well when you are acted upon by one that is good," Cotton quotes Augustine via Calvin, continuing: "Nay, you act and are acted upon, and you then act well when you are acted upon by one that is good. The Spirit of God who actuates you is your helper in acting, and bears the name of helper, because you, too, do something."[27] Grace did not obliterate the self's capacity for responsible action in Cotton's view: "The act of beleeving is an act of our owne, though given of grace."[28] The Spirit did not simply possess the believer as a channel of divine action as Antinomians were alleged to believe, but acted upon the believer to act. Furthermore, saving faith made possible the relational "giving and taking" so prized by Bulkeley, producing in the believer an active striving "to receyve Christ for any helpe unto further measure of Grace."[29]

John Cotton's views on assurance further demonstrate his passion for promoting the "mutuall giving and taking" of union with Christ in an intensely personal relationship of dependence upon Christ. Cotton opposed the practice of other Massachusetts ministers who taught their parishioners to look for evidence of their election to salvation in "gracious works." It was not the Spirit's pleasure, he declared, "to breathe the comfort or Assurance of our Justification in works; lest any flesh should rejoyce in itself, before it have learned to fetch all his rejoycing and consolation from Christ."[30] To be sure, Cotton's concern arose in part out of his determination to preserve the absolute purity of the Reformed understanding of grace. To concede that believers might receive assurance from the good works produced by true conversion would "derogate from grace." The *sine qua non* of Protestantism, in Cotton's view, was that assurance of justification by the witness of the Spirit "goeth before works, and doth not follow after."[31] Furthermore, ministers who argued from apparently gracious works to offer assurance to "weak Christians" drew dangerously close to the error of the sixteenth-century Jesuit theologian Robert Bellarmine, who pled "that Justification by works doth not derogate from Justification by Grace."[32]

For Cotton, the Reformed understanding of grace prevented potential converts from stopping short of full repentance, full forgiveness, and a full measure of Christ's consolation through the witness of the Spirit, where they might "find comfort, and satisfying to their hearts desire . . . by coming unto Christ, and drinking a more full draught of his Spirit; as Christ directeth thirsty soules to doe."[33] A mere "thirsting for Christ," though it might evidence the Spirit's work in an individual soul, could also suggest that the person had not yet received the Christ who could slake that thirst. John Wheelwright, Cotton's colleague at Boston, similarly held that a person who took assurance from thirsting alone risked dying of thirst: "When the Lord is pleased to convert any soule to him, he revealeth not to him some worke, and from that worke, carieth him to Christ, but there is nothing revealed but Christ, when Christ is lifted up, he draweth all to him, that belongeth to the election of grace; if men thinke to be saved, because they see some worke of sanctification in them, as hungring and thirsting and the like: if they be saved, they are saved without the Gospell. No, no, this is a covenant of works."[34] No attempt to deduce one's "safe Estate" from good works could satisfy the soul, whose "further need of Christ" remained until assured by the "witness of the Spirit."[35] True converts could never rest content with the indirect evidence of grace in gracious works and longed for an intense personal encounter with

Christ, "the kisses of Christs mouth, not for a single kisse, but for kisse upon kisse."[36]

Wheelwright's intemperate decision to fan the flames of controversy by expounding these views in his fast-day sermon of 19 January 1637 soon got him banished from Massachusetts Bay as an Antinomian. His sermon constituted a public slur on the well-known teaching of most Bay Colony ministers that "thirst for Christ" and other "gracious works" *could* evidence salvation, and Wheelwright refused to retract or modify his statements when called to account. Cotton too, respected though he was, still found himself on thin ice in the early days of 1637, for his rigorous view that assurance must come by the witness of the Spirit prior to any gracious work held disturbing implications for the pastoral care of individual souls as well as for the communal goals of the godly commonwealth. The ministers' delicate negotiations with Cotton over assurance and sanctification, coupled with their determined prosecution of less moderate figures such as Wheelwright, reveal an effort to frame a view of the self that remained true to Calvin's individualism while adapting it to the requirements of life in New England's "closed corporate communities."[37]

Consistent with the Renaissance recognition of distinctions among individuals, one strand of the ministers' exchanges with John Cotton on assurance focused on the implications of Cotton's views for the differing pastoral needs of their parishioners. If, as Cotton believed, a convert could recognize sanctification as genuine only after receiving assurance of justification, then that person "shall evidence by sanctification only that which was evident before; and thus upon point is no more evidence than a Candle in the Sun."[38] The ministers did not dispute Cotton's claim that such assurance was possible for "the strong" among their parishioners. Yet in their view "the Epistle of John and many other Scriptures . . . hold forth evidence of Sanctification" to accommodate "babes in Christ and such as believe and know not that they do believe."[39] Indeed, a denial of such individual distinctions among true believers might logically lead to the exclusion from church membership of converts such as Nicholas Wyeth and Isabel Jackson, whose respective "want of assurance" and oscillation between spiritual comfort and uncertainty did not prevent Thomas Shepard from admitting either to membership in his Cambridge congregation.[40] The Assembly of Churches condemned the notion that those who saw "any grace of God in themselves, before they have the assurance of Gods love sealed to them are not be received as members of Churches."[41] A minister's ability to point to sanctification as an evidence of assurance would permit him to nurture a "weak Christian" toward fuller assurance, even when that person "cannot prove how he came to his Vocation."[42]

Shepard's record of over fifty church relations exemplifies the Puritan ministry's concern to accommodate the gospel to the needs of particular saints. While all converts were expected to recount their passage through certain standard stages of the "morphology of conversion" and could expect to be questioned if an element of that passage was absent or unclear, the narratives also display a sense of freedom to come to those stages in a variety of ways.[43] The ministers sought to make available a wide range of practical "arguments" for assurance from the saints' "own Spiritual miseries and infirmities" as well as "from the graces of Christ in them. . . . and of these not some sorts only, but all sorts."[44] As David D. Hall has shown, this recognition of a need for sensitivity to the variety of individual needs among parishioners became an important feature of a rich tradition of Puritan pastoral care.[45]

Yet a danger lurked in the matter of how a convert gained assurance of salvation, the most intimate personal concern a pastor could expect to treat. While ministers sought to accommodate the individual needs of potential converts for assurance, they also followed John Calvin in seeking clear boundaries to individual self-expression in the Scriptures "rightly interpreted." Cotton's belief that assurance could come by the "witness of the Spirit" apart from any evidence of gracious work struck them as straying perilously close to, if not actually transgressing, the bounds of scriptural authority. As Bay Colony dissension over assurance was beginning to heat up, Thomas Shepard questioned Cotton closely on whether "this revelation of the spirit" that Cotton advocated for assurance "is a thing beyond and above the woord, and whether 'tis safe to say; because the spirit is not seperated from the woord but in it and is ever according to it."[46] Cotton eventually satisfied the ministers that he too wished to uphold the twofold witness of the Spirit and the Word, balancing the need to remain under scriptural authority with the recognition that "the word without the Spirit of God breathing in it is a dead letter and unable to beget faith."[47]

The ministers remained suspicious, however, that those who attended private meetings in Anne Hutchinson's home did set the witness of the Spirit "beyond and above the woord," and Hutchinson herself dramatically confirmed their suspicions at her trial by claiming to hear the voice of God "by an immediate revelation."[48] Hutchinson's accusers did not share the quibble of later historians that her views concerning self-annihilation were technically not individualistic. To Puritan authorities such claims clearly masked a radical self-assertiveness, licensing the individual to burst asunder all bounds of communal restraint. Governor John Winthrop declared that such "bottomless revelations, as either came without any word, or without the sense of the word . . . for they being above reason and Scripture, they are not subject to control."[49] The history of the sixteenth-century Anabaptist disturbances at Munster had taught Puritans how "professions of new revelations" apart from the Word could lead to "manifold grievous heresies and grosse schismes," usurpation of ecclesiastical and state authority to the point of "proclaiming a Commission . . . from heaven to kill not only all the Magistrates, but also all the wicked people of the whole earth."[50]

To most New England ministers, the use of sanctification as a legitimate "evidence of assurance" provided the antidote to such unrestrained individualism, and their successful defense of this use of sanctification enabled them to adapt Calvinist individualism to the communal demands of life in Puritan Massachusetts. Sanctification was not only an effective means of offering pastoral comfort to "weak Christians" by leading them to greater assurance; it also made assurance a very effective instrument of communal control by enabling pastors to raise questions concerning the spiritual state of supposed saints who fell into sin. It was not the Lord's "usual course with his people," the ministers admonished Cotton, to maintain assurance when the "frame of a man's Spirit and course is grown much degenerate," for the Lord "carr[ies] on all parts of his work both of Faith and holiness in some nearer Symmetry and proportion."[51] The symmetry of the relationship between assurance and sanctification provided an essential link between the inner experience of grace, which the New England ministry universally strove to foster, and the public, social dimensions of that experience. Confutation 20 of the Assembly of Churches "Catalog of Errors" asserted that "Gods people under a Covenant of grace" who fell into "some hainous sinnes, (as Murther, Incest, &c.)" might well find themselves "exercised with sweete doubtings and questions." Such exercises would bring a true saint to repentance, by which he would resume "his claime of his right in God by vertue of his Covenant."[52] Here the connection between sanctification and assurance enabled ministers to join pastoral concern for the "frame" of the individual saint's spirit with a social concern to contain the saint's behavior within acceptable social bounds.

By challenging the connection between sanctification and assurance, the Hutchinsonians had threatened New England Puritans' effort to forge communities in which individual saints could covenant together to nurture one another toward an intense enjoyment of "Christ's familiar love," both collectively as a gathered church and individually as "Christian souls."[53] The challenge extended beyond the disruption of New England's covenanted social order to strike at the ministry's humanist effort to promote the individual flourishing of sincere converts. The ministry and magistrates dealt with the Antinomian social threat by banishing Anne Hutchinson and John Wheelwright. The ministry met the theological challenge by reasserting and strengthening the link between sanctification and assurance. In so doing they secured assurance as an important means of incorporating a Calvinist, Renaissance individualism within New England's communal social order for over a hundred years.

NOTES

1. For a perceptive analysis of Anne Hutchinson's role in the shaping of American identity see Amy Schrager Lang, *Prophetic Women: Anne Hutchinson and the Problem of Dissent in the Literature of New England* (Berkeley and Los Angeles: University of California Press, 1987).

2. Nathaniel Hawthorne, *The Scarlet Letter* (New York: Rinehart and Company, 1947), 45; Hawthorne, "Mrs. Hutchinson," in *Tales, Sketches and Other Papers* (Boston: Houghton, Mifflin and Company, 1883), 217–26; Ben Barker-Benfield, "Anne Hutchinson and the Puritan Attitude toward Women," *Feminist Studies* 1 (1972): 55–78; Lyle Koehler, "The Case of the Feminine Jezebels: Anne Hutchinson and Female Agitation during the Years of Antinomian Turmoil, 1636–1640," *William and Mary Quarterly*, 3d ser., 31 (1974): 55–78. For a more recent example, see Amanda Porterfield, "The Triumph of Spirituality over Religion: Anne Hutchinson and American Culture," Wyoming Web Lecture on Religion, University of Wyoming, Laramie, Wyoming, 1 May 1998.

3. Bernard Bailyn, *The New England Merchants in the Seventeenth Century* (New York: Harper and Row, 1964), 39–44; Darren Staloff, *The Making of an American Thinking Class: Intellectuals and Intelligentsia in Puritan Massachusetts* (New York: Oxford University Press, 1998), 40–72.

4. Amy Schrager Lang, "Antinomianism and the 'Americanization' of Doctrine," *New England Quarterly* 54 (1981): 241; *idem, Prophetic Women*, 8–9.

5. Philip Greven, "The Self Shaped and Misshaped: *The Protestant Temperament* Reconsidered," in *Through a Glass Darkly: Reflections on Personal Identity in Early America*, ed. Ronald Hoffman, Mechal Sobel, and Fredrika J. Teute (Chapel Hill, N.C.: University of North Carolina Press, 1997), 348–54.

6. Barry Alan Shain, *The Myth of American Individualism: The Protestant Origins of American Political Thought* (Princeton: Princeton University Press, 1994), 100–9.

7. See, for example, Philip Greven, *Four Generations: Population, Land, and Family in Colonial Andover, Massachusetts* (Ithaca, N.Y.: Cornell University Press, 1970); Kenneth Lockridge, *A New England Town: The First Hundred Years,* expanded ed. (New York: W. W. Norton, 1985); David Grayson Allen, *In En-*

glish Ways: The Movement of Societies and the Transferral of English Local Law and Custom to Massachusetts Bay in the Seventeenth Century (Chapel Hill, N.C.: University of North Carolina Press, 1981).

8. See Philip Gura, *A Glimpse of Sion's Glory: Puritan Radicalism in New England, 1620-1660* (Middletown, Conn.: Wesleyan University Press, 1984).

9. See Stephen Foster, *The Long Argument: English Puritanism and the Shaping of New England Culture, 1570-1700* (Chapel Hill, N.C.: University of North Carolina Press, 1991); Janice Knight, *Orthodoxies in Massachusetts: Re-reading American Puritanism* (Cambridge: Harvard University Press, 1994).

10. See David D. Hall, *Worlds of Wonder, Days of Judgment: Popular Religious Belief in Early New England* (New York: Knopf, 1989), 21–70.

11. Amanda Porterfield, *Female Piety in Puritan New England: The Emergence of Religious Humanism* (New York: Oxford University Press, 1992), 80–115.

12. Patricia Caldwell, *The Puritan Conversion Narrative: The Beginnings of American Expression* (Cambridge: Cambridge University Press, 1983).

13. John Martin, "Inventing Sincerity, Refashioning Prudence: The Discovery of the Individual in Renaissance Europe," *American Historical Review* 102 (1997): 1309–42.

14. Michael McGiffert, ed., *God's Plot: Puritan Spirituality in Thomas Shepard's Cambridge*, rev. ed. (Amherst, Mass.: University of Massachusetts Press, 1994); Charles L. Cohen, *God's Caress: The Psychology of Puritan Religious Experience* (New York: Oxford University Press, 1986); Charles E. Hambrick-Stowe, *Practice of Piety: Puritan Devotional Disciplines in Seventeenth-Century New England* (Chapel Hill, N.C.: University of North Carolina Press, 1982).

15. David D. Hall, "Narrating Puritanism," in *New Directions in American Religious History*, ed. Harry S. Stout and D. G. Hart (New York: Oxford University Press, 1997), 51–75; Knight, *Orthodoxies in Massachusetts*.

16. Thomas Shepard, *The Parable of the Ten Virgins Opened and Applied: Being the Substance of Divers Sermons on Matth. 25. 1-13* (London: J. Hayes, 1660), 2:216.

17. McGiffert, *God's Plot*, 159.

18. John Cotton, *A Sermon Preached by the Reverend Mr. John Cotton Deliver'd at Salem, 1636,* in *John Cotton on the Churches of New England*, ed. Larzer Ziff (Cambridge: Harvard University Press, 1968), 57.

19. Shepard, *Parable of the Ten Virgins*, 2:216–17.

20. Thomas Shepard, *The Sincere Convert: Discovering the Paucity of True Beleevers and the Great Difficulty of Saving Conversion* (London: T. P. and M. S., 1641), 34–37, 113–15; Martin, "Inventing Sincerity," 1333.

21. Shepard, *Sincere Convert*, 40.

22. John Cotton, "Mr. Cotton's Rejoynder," in *The Antinomian Controversy, 1636-1638: A Documentary History*, 2d ed., ed. David D. Hall (Durham, N.C.: Duke University Press, 1990), 104.

23. Winthrop, "A Short Story of the rise, reign, and ruine of the Antinomians, Familists, and Libertines," in *Antinomian Controversy*, 219.

24. Hall, ed., "Peter Bulkeley and John Cotton: On Union with Christ," in *Antinomian Controversy*, 36.

25. Ibid., 40.

26. Ibid., 37, 40.

27. "Mr. Cotton's Rejoynder," in *Antinomian Controversy*, 145. The quotation is from John Calvin, *Institutes of the Christian Religion*, 2 vols., trans. Ford Lewis Battles (Philadelphia: Westminster Press, 1960).

28. Hall, ed., "A Conference Mr. John Cotton Held at Boston with the Elders of New England," in *Antinomian Controversy*, 195.

29. Hall, ed., "Peter Bulkeley and John Cotton," in *Antinomian Controversy*, 37.

30. Cotton, "Cotton's Rejoynder," in *Antinomian Controversy*, 109.

31. "A Conference at Boston," in *Antinomian Controversy*, 189.

32. Cotton, "Cotton's Rejoynder," in *Antinomian Controversy*, 97.

33. "A Conference at Boston," in *Antinomian Controversy*, 187.

34. John Wheelwright, "A Fast-Day Sermon," in *Antinomian Controversy*, 161.

35. John Cotton, "Sixteene Questions of Serious and Necessary Consequence," in *Antinomian Controversy*, 58; compare Cotton, "Cotton's Rejoynder," in *Antinomian Controversy*, 149.

36. John Cotton, *A Brief Exposition with Practical Observations upon the whole Book of Canticles* (London: T. R. and E. M. for Ralph Smith, 1655; reprint, New York: Arno Press, 1972), 4.

37. See Lockridge, *New England Town*, 3–23.

38. Hall, ed., "The Elders Reply," in *Antinomian Controversy*, 67.

39. Ibid., 68.

40. McGiffert, *God's Plot*, 204, 215.

41. Winthrop, "Short Story," in *Antinomian Controversy*, 227.

42. "Elders Reply," in *Antinomian Controversy*, 69.

43. McGiffert, *God's Plot*, 149–225, *passim*.

44. "Elders Reply," in *Antinomian Controversy*, 76.

45. David D. Hall, *The Faithful Shepherd: A History of the New England Ministry in the Seventeenth Century* (New York: W. W. Norton, 1974), 48–71.

46. "Letters between Thomas Shepard and John Cotton," in *Antinomian Controversy*, 26.

47. Cotton, "Cotton's Rejoynder," *Antinomian Controversy*, 149.

48. Hall, ed., "The Examination of Mrs. Anne Hutchinson at the Court at Newtown," in *Antinomian Controversy*, 337.

49. Winthrop, "Short Story," in *Antinomian Controversy*, 274.

50. Robert Baillie, *Anabaptism, the True Fountaine of Independency, Antinomy, Brownisme, Familisme, and the most of the other Errours, which for the time do trouble the Church of England, Unsealed* (London: M. F., 1646), 16, 32; compare Winthrop, "Short Story," in *Antinomian Controversy*, 275.

51. "Elders Reply," in *Antinomian Controversy*, 66.

52. Winthrop, "Short Story," in *Antinomian Controversy*, 224.

53. Cotton, *Whole Book of Canticles*, 2.

Staging a Puritan Saint: Cotton Mather's
Magnalia Christi Americana
Stephen Woolsey

> Cotton Mather died when I was a boy. The books
> He read, all day, all night and all the nights,
> Had got him nowhere. There was always the doubt,
> That made him preach the louder, long for a church
> In which his voice could roll its cadences,
> After the sermon, to quiet that mouse in the wall.
> —Wallace Stevens, "The Blue Buildings in the Summer Air"

THE OPENING LINES OF WALLACE STEVENS'S POEM "THE BLUE BUILDINGS IN the Summer Air" point playfully—and a bit mischievously—to Cotton Mather's serious dilemma as one of American Puritanism's most vocal representatives.[1] On the one hand, Mather made it his mission both in speech and in writing to announce the success of the Puritan enterprise in the new world, reminding listeners and readers alike that the vitality of this transplanted community of believers demonstrated God's approval of their efforts. As John Higginson puts it in his introductory "Attestation" to Mather's immense epic-drama of the Church in New England, *Magnalia Christi Americana; or, The Ecclesiastical History of New-England*: "It hath been deservedly esteemed one of the great and wonderful works of God in this last age, that the Lord stirred up the spirits of so many thousands of his servants, to leave the *pleasant land* of England . . . and to transport themselves, and families, over the *ocean sea*, into a *desert land* in America. . . . And that the Lord was pleased to grant such a gracious *presence* of his with them, and such a *blessing* upon their undertakings, that within a few years a *wilderness* was subdued before them, and so many Colonies planted, Towns erected, and Churches settled, wherein the true and living God in Christ Jesus is worshipped and served."[2]

On the other hand, the end of the seventeenth century—the century that witnessed the birth of the Puritan experiment in America—

brought internal and external crises that must have nagged at Mather's consciousness and shaken his confidence to the core, like Wallace Stevens's church mouse gnawing endlessly in the wall. First, Mather struggled with the fear that in severing its ties with the larger church community, especially in England, American Puritanism had unwittingly rendered itself insignificant and marginal, invisible to the church in England and the rest of Europe. Out of sight was out of mind for the purposes of ongoing reformation and evangelism.[3] Moreover, according to Kenneth Silverman, Mather's Boston, the heart of Puritan New England, was morally corrupt and "culturally stagnant."[4] Finally, wars among members of various European alliances over competing political, territorial, and colonial claims threatened to engulf New England as well.[5] Thus, at the very moment Mather may have felt most disheartened about the absence of American Puritanism from the world stage, he faced the real possibility that circumstances and events would pull Puritan New England, apparently in disarray and possibly faltering, into a drama of power scripted by players hostile or at least indifferent to the cause of reformation and revival.

Mather's response was characteristically aggressive, though it took an unexpected form. Determined to "fight fire with fire" as he had done so often before both in his writing and his preaching, Mather wrote his grand history, the *Magnalia Christi Americana*, to offer readers an intentionally dramatic picture of the New England Church playing an active role on the world stage.[6] Perhaps it had seemed to those left behind at the time of the Great Migration that Puritans had behaved like prima donnas, storming off the stage in a self-righteous huff. Along with his much shorter and more polemical *Lapis e Monte Excisus*, the *Magnalia* was Mather's declaration that Puritan New England "desired to be . . . a part of international Protestantism," an active member of the worldwide community of faith; New World Puritanism was ready "to devote its best energies to fighting its way in the marketplace and to being implemented at the seats of power" around the globe.[7] Ritchie Kendall suggests that "displaced drama"—"theater of the soul" that dispenses with the public, physical stage—was characteristic of early Puritanism.[8] Several hundred years later Mather was ready to take the whole world for his stage.

The terms in which Mather framed his untiring efforts to market his work confirm that he hoped for an international audience appropriate to this new international role for New England and its leading advocate. In his diary Mather records his gratitude to God for the one immediate audience he can be sure of—his congregation.[9] But the diary also records his hope for an international audience, first for the *Magnalia* and later for the *Lapis*.[10] As he writes in July of 1693, "because I foresaw an inexpressible Deal, of Service, like to bee thereby done for the *Church* of God, not only here, but abroad in *Europe*, especially at the approaching *Reformation*, I formed a Design, to endeavour, THE CHURCH-HISTORY OF THIS COUN-TREY."[11]

A diary entry written almost five years later records Mather's "Supplications" for this work, especially for divine "Direction" about "the Time and Way of . . . sending it into *Europe*."[12] Another two and a half years passed before Mather could note in his diary a prayer for the manuscript of the *Magnalia*, often delayed but finally completed and on its way to an English publisher: "that my *Church-History* now upon the Waters, may be praeserved [*sic*], prospered, published, accepted and serviceable among the Churches of the Lord."[13] Thus through his written works, especially the *Magnalia* and the *Lapis*, the man who addressed his New England congregation each week from the pulpit sent his voice out across the ocean, hoping to address the world at large.[14] In the process Mather was signaling New England Puritanism's desire both to rejoin the international community of faith—suggesting in fact that the separation had never been anything other than a geographical one—and to play a more active role in the ongoing story of world-wide Protestantism.[15]

The unexpected and even surprising thing is that Mather conceived the story he tells in the *Magnalia* in overtly dramatic terms, and that he was clearly concerned with the literary and dramatic representation of Puritans and Puritanism as he began its composition.[16] "It was the common reproach of old cast upon Christians, 'That they were all poor, weak, unlearned men,'" Mather writes, adding that "the sort of men sometime called *Puritans,* in the English nation have been reproached with the same character." Indeed, he continues, "the terms of an *ass,* and a *fool*" have been applied casually to those who deserve honor, not contempt (1: 233). As Mather makes clear, however, one of his primary purposes in the *Magnalia* is to counter the stereotypical Puritan hypocrite of text and stage with the heroic stories of hundreds of real men and women who left England with an earnest intention to "enlarg[e] the *dominion*" both of their earthly and their heavenly kings (1: 52) and "to express and pursue the Protestant Reformation" (1: 86). Mather goes about creating his countertext in a remarkable way. While it is commonly supposed that hostility to the theater and Puritanism were virtually synonymous even in his day, Mather calls the old negative Puritan stereotypes into question, deliberately employing the language of acting and drama as he recasts New England's story, making it one element in the great drama of global Reformation.[17]

William Prynne is probably the Puritan most closely associated with the scathing, indignant rejection of theater presumed to be typical of the movement.[18] As he puts the matter in his caustic *Histrio-Mastix, The Players Scourge or Actors Tragaedie*: "A just man cannot endure hypocrisie, but all the acts of Players is dissimulation, and the proper name of Player . . . is hypocrite. . . . For what else is *hypocrisie* in the proper signification of the word, but the acting of anothers part or person on the Stage: or what else is an hypocrite, in his true etymologie, but a Stage-player, or one who acts anothers part."[19] With these harsh words Prynne locates the heart of the widely assumed Puritan ambivalence or hostility toward the theater.[20] Certainly Prynne was one of the Puritan movement's fiercest critics of the theater, but he was not alone in his condemnation.[21] Patrick Collinson suggests that many Puritans shared Prynne's "instinctive" or "subliminal" revulsion against drama as a tissue of seductive lies, and against actors as lying agents of that seduction, especially when plays blurred the lines of sexual identity, adding the "transvestite lie implicit in the acting of female parts by boys" to the larger "dramatic fiction."[22] According to Eric Linklater, those disciples of Ben Jonson who called themselves the Sons of Ben "knew very well what a Puritan was," and Prynne must have seemed to them the very embodiment of the Puritan at his worst: "a gloomy fellow who saw sin in pleasure, virtue in none but himself, merit in tears, and punishment for everything except his own hypocrisy."[23] They gleefully reflected that perception in their poetic and dramatic representations of religious zealots.[24]

But both Prynne and the Sons of Ben viewed the world from a perspective—essentially limited to the *English* stage and *English* Puritanism—that was much too narrow for Mather's purposes.[25] If Mather's appropriation of theatrical similes and metaphors to endorse an internationalist view of the church's work is surprising, even more so perhaps is one possible source or inspiration for that means of representing God's work in the world and humanity's role in the grand drama of redemption: the reformer John Calvin.[26] Again and again in his *Institutes of the Christian Religion* and his commentaries on biblical texts, Calvin describes this world as the vast theater in which God continually reveals himself and his purposes. Writing on the doctrine of divine sovereignty, for example, Calvin laments the human tendency to view the manifold examples of "fatherly kindness" expressed in "heavenly providence" as mere "chance occurrences." All but those who are blessed with "rare and singular wisdom" are so "immersed in their own errors" that they are "struck blind in such a *dazzling theater*" of divine goodness. Nor is the problem too much subtlety on God's part, for "however much the glory of God shines forth, scarcely one man in a hundred is a true *spectator* of it."[27] A few pages later Calvin offers an alternative to the old image of the created universe as a book in which humankind may read the story of a benevolent creator. The universe is a grand *theater*, the reformer suggests, and wise and faithful Christians would do well to pay careful attention both to the written word of Scripture and to the drama unfolding around them. In this "glorious" play of salvation history, God's word and his works together help believers understand both the divine purposes God is acting out before their very eyes and God's call for active human involvement in those purposes: "[t]herefore, however fitting it may be for man seriously to turn his eyes to contemplate God's works, since he has been placed in this most glorious theater to be a spectator of them, it is fitting that he prick up his ears to the Word, the better to profit."[28]

Whether his echo of Calvin's universal theater image is intentional, Mather's point of view clearly has more in common with the reformer's than it does with William Prynne's.[29] Despite this fact, dominant readings of the *Magnalia* have explored the work in a narrowly American cultural context, ignoring or shortchanging Mather's insistently international frame of reference, his staging of the work, and his transformation of the stereotypical stage Puritan.[30] Rather than fixating on America, Mather wanted to show his readers "the intersection of [New England's] little story with the big story" of worldwide "Evangelical Reformation" (*Magnalia* 1: 26).[31] He was determined in the process to restore to the Puritan story what years of suspicion, misunderstanding, and provincialism had written out or distorted, opposing the hypocritical and canting Puritans of the English stage with the lives and history of pious and godly counterparts.[32]

In his "dramatic" prose text, Mather rejects contemporary assumptions about comedy and brings his representations more nearly in line with Aristotelean rhetorical modes, especially of tragedy and epic. Aristotle declares that audiences should respond to properly written comedy with a kind of benign ridicule as they watch the foolish actions of characters who are unpleasant or even disgusting, but not deeply or intentionally evil. As Aristotle writes in *On Poetry and Style,* comedy is "an imitation of men who are inferior but not altogether vicious. The ludicrous is a species of ugliness; it is a sort of flaw and ugliness which is not painful or injurious."[33] Seventeenth-century English comedy from Jonson to the Restoration often departs from this principle, especially in its representation of Puritans, typically depicted as corrupt, cynical, vicious characters whose moral flaws are indeed painful and injurious to themselves and to those around them.[34] The stage Puritans of this era are usually oblivious to the damage they do, however, because their hypocritical, narrow-minded self-righteousness makes them morally obtuse.[35] In short, while comedy in the Aristotelean mode confronts the audience with the ugliness even of mild wickedness and foolishness, comic representations of Puritans on the English stage often assume the willingness of the audience to laugh at religious bigotry and affectation, or even deliberate, heartless evil.

The Puritans whom Mather represents in the *Magnalia* would seem to have more in common with Aristotle's tragic heroes, who, according to Bonamy Dobree, are "personages better than the ordinary man . . . reaching for the absolute, trying to establish something definite in opposition to the unsatisfactory compromises of life."[36] As they strive mightily to achieve moral equilibrium and understanding, these tragic "personages" reflect Aristotle's principle that "tragedy . . . is the imitation of a good action."[37] In turn, as members of the audience are emotionally engaged in watching the tragic action unfold, they finally experience a catharsis that restores them to spiritual and moral balance.[38] Although Mather is obviously writing a prose work and not the tragic drama in verse that Aristotle had in mind, we can see from the very beginning of the *Magnalia* his intention to "stage" a story that makes moral demands on its audience. On the opening page of the General Introduction, Mather tells his readers that he will "first introduce the *Actors,* that have in . . . exemplary manner served [the New England] colonies; and give Remarkable Occurrences, in the exemplary LIVES of many Magistrates, and of more Ministers, who so lived as to leave unto Posterity *examples* worthy of everlasting remembrance" (1: 25). Mather means to write dramatic history with the moral force of classical tragedy.

Of course one can only go so far with this connection. Aristotle's tragic hero is certainly not deliberately evil, but neither is he a moral paragon; he is a noble man of a middling moral stature whose character is fatally compromised by a tragic flaw that ultimately brings him to disaster.[39] Mather, by contrast, endows many of his heroes with the near-perfection of sainthood, and their actions with an epic grandeur. In fact, if Mather's work shares some characteristics with classical tragedy, in other ways the *Magnalia* reads like a prose epic in the Aristotelean mode. Like tragedy, epic is "an imitation in verse of what is morally worthy," though the time frame of tragedy is limited while "the time of an epic is unlimited."[40] Moreover, the epic's narrative line transcends the experience of any one heroic mortal, incorporating multiple "reversals, recognitions, and scenes of suffering"—an apt description of the great story that the *Magnalia* recounts.[41]

The narrative line of the *Magnalia* shares one other striking similarity with Aristotelean tragedy. Aristotle declares that in a tragic plot "the change of fortune should not be from misfortune to prosperity but, on the contrary, from prosperity to misfortune" as a result of some basic moral flaw in the hero, precisely the plot that Mather fears is being acted out by the New England Puritan community.[42] For all of his determination to remind the New England Puritans of their glorious heritage, Mather seems far from sure that their New World experiment will reach a glorious conclusion. In fact, as he began writing the *Magnalia* almost forty-five years after John Winthrop's death, Mather set out to reconstruct Winthrop's life and interpret his significance for what he feared might be the last generation of New England Puritans. As Mather puts it in the General Introduction to the *Magnalia,* it may well be that "*all* [is] *done,* that New-England was planted for" and Puritan New England may soon pass away (1: 27). Mather's vocation as historian and biographer is to tell the stories that will be what he calls "our 'acts and monuments'" (1: 32), to set up verbal memorial stones (1: 26) to those who have gone before.[43] Yet Mather offers this drama of holy action not only to stimulate the believer's memory, but also to recall godly exemplars who will provide "the whole world with vertuous objects of emulation" (1: 25).

The *Magnalia*'s literary flaws are evident to almost any reader. Worthington Ford calls the book "a storehouse of ill-compiled and ill-digested matter,"[44] and Thomas Wertenbaker describes it as a "hodge-podge of history and biography."[45] Still, the power of the work cannot be denied. The passionate intensity of the *Magnalia* reflects Mather's own deep commitment to a Puritan vision that he both celebrates as a living reality and mourns as a fading triumph, and for the receptive reader even Mather's densely allusive style and self-conscious erudition never quite obscure the remarkable story he is telling.[46] Such a statement implies that the book's power is accidental; I believe, however, that something intentional is going on. To see this clearly, we must consider Mather's life of Winthrop in the full context of the *Magnalia,* rather than following the lead of Bercovitch and others in focusing more narrowly on the biography and the issue of American identity.

First, in the *Magnalia,* Mather reworks and transforms the power of theater—the dramatic force of represented gesture, speech, and action—understanding, as Paula Backscheider puts it, that "access to and control of representation is power," especially in the writing of history.[47] In some sense writers *make* the truth of "the world and experience as they present and interpret it" for the reader.[48] Given the breadth and depth of his reading, Cotton Mather must have been aware of the ways in which Puritans and Puritanism were mocked on the English stage.[49] In his use of dramatic techniques Mather is, with nice historical irony, appropriating on behalf of Puritans strategies often used against them, bending those strategies to his own purposes by reversing the representational polarity. Moreover, he counters the artifice of the English stage and its ridicule of Puritans with accounts of real men and women acting out their parts in a noble international story, taking European cities, English villages, and New England forests alike as their stage. The *Magnalia* is a vast theater of words, a stage upon which Mather recasts the Puritan story in New England not as a sorry tale of self-exile by a band of hapless entrepreneur-zealots, but as a triumphant adventure "made of Memorable Occurrences, and amazing Judgments and Mercies befalling many particular persons" (1:25). These faithful heroes have "given great examples of the methods and measures wherein an Evangelical Reformation is to be prosecuted" (1:26). The actors in this great play, Mather emphasizes, are neither small-minded nor self-serving; they are "Protestants that highly honored and affected the Church of England," and "petition[ed] to be a *part* of it," but because they dared to call for its reformation they were forced to give up their homes and comforts for "the desarts of America" (1:26).

Mather reminds his readers that the New England Puritans are not the first band of evangelist-exiles to set sail for the New World. Book 1, entitled "Antiquities; or, A Field Prepared for Considerable Things to Be Acted Thereupon," begins with a brief introduction that recounts the story of "a noble and learned knight called Villagagnon," who was commissioned by "that admirable hero and martyr, of the Protestant religion, Gasper Coligni" to lead a group to the Americas for the "propagation" of the Reformed faith (1:39).[50] Villagagnon guided his followers to Brazil, seeking "quiet seats, for the retreat of a people harrassed already with deadly persecutions, and threatened with yet more calamities" (1:39). The spiritual needs of the colonists were met by pastors sent directly from Geneva by "the blessed Calvin"; these pastors "soon set up an evangelical church order, in those corners of the earth where God in our Lord Jesus Christ had never before been called upon" (1:39, 40). By implication, the international evangelistic commitments of these Protestant forerunners of the Puritans should remind the New Englanders that all the world is the proper stage for Christian action.

But the Coligny story is also a cautionary tale. Mather observes that "it was not long before some unhappy controversies arose among them"; but that was only the beginning of their troubles. When three of the group's ministers were "murthered by their apostate Governour," the other ministers returned to Europe. So far as can be determined the remaining colonists were "entirely lost," Mather writes, "either in paganism or disaster," and "that horrible *massacre*" when a "hundred thousand of their brethren were soon after butchered at home" completed the catastrophe.[51] Mather's summary of the whole episode should call the New England colonists to a thoughtful consideration of their own analogous situation. "So has there been utterly *lost* in a little time," says Mather solemnly, "a *country intended for a receptacle of Protestant Churches* on the American Strand" (1:40).

Mather suggests that the dramatic ramifications of this precedent are clear: "'Tis now time for me to tell my reader that in our *age* there has been another essay made not by French, but by English PROTESTANTS, to fill a certain country in America with *Reformed Churches*" (1:40). Noting that New England Protestants are not much different from the Huguenot forerunners, "nothing in *doctrine,* little in *discipline,* different from that of Geneva" (1:40), Mather implicitly asks his contemporaries what script *they* will follow. Will they repeat the mistakes of the Brazilian Huguenots, replaying that disaster on another American strand, or will they strive to play out faithfully their part in the triumphant epic drama of God's work around the world?

The author of the *Magnalia* further emphasizes his international perspective by eschewing particular labels or perspectives. He would not be a schismatic, disturbing the peace of church or nation.[52] Mather protests that he has "endeavoured, with all good conscience, to decline . . . writing merely for a party" (1:29), choosing instead to offer his work to all Christians of clear conscience in a "Catholick spirit of communion" (1:35).[53] Indeed, as we have seen, Mather insists repeatedly that it is not merely New England's story that we see reenacted in the pages of the *Magnalia*; rather, it is the newest act or scene in the story of the Reformation, and thus he represents New England as a living branch still fully connected to the worldwide family tree of the church universal. As he rehearses the more recent roles of Bradford, Winthrop, and others, in effect he is also rehearsing the roles of their glorious forebears—Wycliffe, Foxe, Cranmer, Bucer, Baxter, and all of those who played a part in the *"first* Age" of the English Reformation, "the *golden* Age." Mather adds that replaying this drama can change one's life, bringing a microcosmic Reformation to each participant, for revisiting that age of gold "will make a man a Protestant, and, I may add, a Puritan" (1:27).

Mather was also conscious of the dramatic power of architecture and symbol. He suggests in the General Introduction that the church historian is "like the builder of the temple" (1:30), and as a temple builder Mather adorns his work with appropriate and dramatically potent symbols. He answers stage depictions of Puritan ignorance with the image of New England's settlements as "golden Candlesticks" shining in "this 'outer darkness'" (1:27). He answers the stereotype of crude Puritan physicality and gluttony with an image of the *Magnalia* (and of his proposed but never completed *Biblia Americana)* as intellectual and spiritual banquet tables laden with "soul-feasting thoughts" (1:33). And in "Nehemias Americanus" he answers the caricature of the craven and cowardly Puritan with the image of Winthrop as an American Daniel, whose "courage made him *dare to do right,* and fitted him to stand among the lions that have sometimes been the supporters of the throne" (1:119). Winthrop was also the steady hand on the helm, steering the people of New England faithfully; despite some political storms and one major mutiny, Mather declares, "the people would not . . . entrust the helm of the weather-beaten bark in any other hands but Mr. Winthrop's until he died" (1:128). These images make it clear that Winthrop was no grasping, strident, low-born, self-righteous Puritan; rather, he played out his part in "the noble design" of American settlement "with the constant liberality and hospitality of a gentleman" (1:119).

Even the circumstances of the *Magnalia*'s publication are striking and significant, a sort of mythic metaphor of transatlantic pilgrimage that its author must have anticipated.[54] Mather states that he composed the "main body" of his work "by the stolen hour or two in the day," over a two- or three-year period (1:32). According to Kenneth Silverman, however, the busy minister began to work on the *Magnalia* in late 1693 and did not ship the manuscript to London for publication until June 1700.[55] Another two years passed before the printed book repeated the transatlantic crossing made

many years before by William Bradford, John Winthrop, and some
of the other colonial fathers whose lives it recounts and celebrates.
The completed *Magnalia* came back to its author on Thursday, 29
October 1702, and Mather set "apart the next day for thanksgiving,
praising God for 'His watchful and gracious Providence over the
Work, and for the Harvest of so many Prayers, and Cares, and
Tears, and Resignations, as I had employ'd upon it.'"[56] Mather declares that the "first planting" came to New England when "multi-
tudes of pious, peaceable Protestants were driven" from "the *best
Island* of the universe" to "a wilderness, in the ends of the earth"
(1:26). Thus it is appropriate that the book that tells this story
should reenact that journey. Moreover, its author's prayers, cares,
tears, and resignations echo God's own travail in the establishment
of his church in the wilderness. That is the clear implication of the
Latin motto printed on the title page of the first volume, translated
"So Mighty was the Work to Found Christ's Empire Here."[57]

Many critics have noted the implicit drama—or melodrama—of
the well-known first line of the General Introduction: "I write the
wonders of the Christian Religion, *flying* the depravations of Europe, to the American Strand" (1:25). Few have commented on the
theatrical images that follow as Mather outlines his plan for the
whole work. He will tell New England's story by preparing "a
Field"—the stage for that story—and then relating "the *Considerable Matters* which have been acted thereupon" (1:25). Figures of
speech taken from drama and representations of dramatic gestures
both by Mather as narrator and by the subjects of his biographical
and historical sketches recur throughout the first books of the *Magnalia,* from the subtitle to the volume, entitled *Antiquities: A Field
Prepared for Considerable Things to be Acted Thereupon* (1:39),
to the culminating dramatic scene of Winthrop's death, which is a
sort of Puritan *Art of Holy Dying.* Though Winthrop's "grand cli-
macterial" may strike the modern reader as a bit anticlimactic,
since Mather tells us that Winthrop began to fret about "the approaches of his dissolution" while that event was "yet seven years
off" (1:130), there is a certain dramatic power in this depiction of
"the *old serpent* . . . nibbling" at the old Puritan's "*heel*" as his life
draws to its close, and of the saint "buffeted with the disconsolate
thoughts of black and sore *desertions*" (1:130). The triumphant
conclusion to this scene comes as Winthrop "thus lay ripening for
heaven" (1:130); the prayer and fasting of "the elders . . . and the
whole church" prevailed, and "it was not long before [the] clouds
were dispelled, and he enjoyed in his holy soul the great consola-
tions of God!" (1:130).

This deathbed battle with spiritual anxiety breaks with classical dramatic convention, since benevolent providential intervention (human and divine) and not fate-driven conflict shapes the story. Of course it also breaks with conventional English stage representations of the Puritan, in which plot complications are often powered by the religious bigot's greed, affectation, gluttony, and barely disguised lust. In fact, Mather frames the drama of Winthrop's life in terms of tender domestic nurture and family as community. "Nehemias Americanus" opens with a paean to a man who is not just the "founder" of New England but also its "father" (1:118). Near the story's end Mather quotes "the venerable" John Cotton's plea for prayer on behalf of the old dying saint who "is to us as a friend, a brother, a mother . . . parent-like distributing his goods to brethren and neighbors . . . and *gently* bearing our infirmities" (1:130, 131). For Mather, Winthrop embodies the saintliness of human service in the family of God, and not the holy self-obliteration that Bercovitch emphasizes.[58]

Familial imagery elsewhere in the *Magnalia*—especially maternal and sibling—not only underscores Mather's international outlook and his commitment to the Church Universal but also serves as a counter to the notorious lechery of stereotypical stage Puritans. The picture is both vividly physical and poignant as Mather identifies the Church of England as the spiritual mother from whom Bradford, Winthrop, and the other Puritan settlers of New England were eventually driven against their will: "Notwithstanding the trouble they had undergone for desiring to see the Church of England *reformed* of several things, which they thought its *deformities,* yet they now called the Church of England their *dear mother*; acknowledging that such *hope* and *part* as they had obtained in the *common salvation* they had *sucked from her breasts*" (1:74).[59] Nonetheless, Mather suggests, some good has come of this apparently tragic drama of family separation within the church. The Plymouth Plantation helped to prepare the way for the other, later New England colonies, "her *younger sisters*" (1:64). Best of all, New England's estrangement from the motherland is merely spatial, not spiritual; the mutual "tenderest affections" of mother and daughters are represented and preserved in the names of dozens of New England towns that "have their *name-sakes* in England . . . the *happy Island*" (1:89). Moreover, New England bears the name of her mother England as "the most *resembling daughter* to the chief lady of the European world" (1:45) and must hope for a mother's nurture and protection as she plays her part in God's great drama of salvation, at the end of which heaven's king will have *the utmost parts of the earth for his possession* (1:46).

While he offers his *Magnalia* as a history of New England's first seventy years, Mather never lets the reader forget that it is an ecclesiastical history, a record of God's great work through his church in America, which the author dedicates to Christ, "King of Heaven," "Head," "Prince, and Law-Giver" of all "Churches which [he] hast purchased with [his] own blood" (1:37). Thus, if the *Magnalia* focuses the reader's attention on New England's story, it also decenters New England with its constant reminders that this is just one chapter in God's grand scheme of Reformation and redemption. As Mather declares early in the first book: "The *Church* of God must no longer be wrapped up in Strabo's cloak; *Geography* must now find work for a *Christiano-graphy* in regions far beyond the bounds wherein the *Church* of God had, through all former ages, been circumscribed. . . . the *Church* of our Lord Jesus Christ, well compared unto a ship, is now *victoriously* sailing round the *globe* after Sir Francis Drake's renowned ship, called, *The Victory*" (1:42, 43).

Nor are native peoples left out of Mather's international perspective on the New England Church. Of course, the record of New England Puritan dealings with the local American Indian tribes is full of blood and trouble, but Mather argues that the church's covenants of mutual Christian aid and comfort must include the native population as well; he notes with approval the early ritual of covenant between Plymouth and Salem whereby both groups promise neither to "[slight] *our sister churches*" nor to "[lay] *a stumbling-block before any, no, not the Indians, whose good we desire to promote*" (1:71). New England's white settlers must always remember the larger narrative in which their story may only be a short chapter.[60]

In fact, as already noted, Mather surprises the reader of the General Introduction by acknowledging that in God's scheme of things New England may prove to be a minor episode that fades into oblivion.[61] When all is said and done—and perhaps sooner rather than later—the New England plantation may *come to nothing* (1:27). Yet this broader scope increases rather than decreases the importance of the historical and biographical record. Even if New England is finally a detour on the road to worldwide Reformation, Mather suggests, the lives and events chronicled in the *Magnalia* will endure as "small Memorials that may be serviceable to the designs of Reformation" elsewhere (1:26). Thus the authorial imperative:

"whether New-England may *live* any where else or no, it must *live* in our History!" (1:27).

Mather anticipates the skepticism of some readers and tries to disarm his critics, first by freely acknowledging the flaws of his work and then by calling the reader to an interpretation as generous and as universal as his own stated purposes. He concedes, for instance, that the *Magnalia* could and should be more polished and coherent. He notes his hope, though, that by divine grace the reader will see not just a patchwork history's "fault of inaccuracy or inadvertency," but also the "rhapsody" of this great story of God's work in New England, "made up (like the paper whereon 'tis written) with many little rags" (1:34), pieced together with all the passionate improvisational intensity that this mixed musical-literary image evokes. Greek tragedy brings sacred myth and drama together in an unrelenting rhapsody of emotional extremes; Mather uses the language and imagery of drama to create rhapsodic history, fragments of a much larger mythic story of Puritan origins and Reformation ideals. His role as historian is to tell a story that preserves "the memory of the *great things done for* us *by our God,*" that it "may be impartially handed unto posterity" (1:40). Thus, this old story may engage new stories still to be lived and written by the generations to come.

Yet we know from history that most of Mather's readers did not recognize as their own the drama, the myth, or the story that he fashioned from the facts of Winthrop's life and the larger Puritan experience that contained it. Francis J. Bremer observes that "though religious revivalism would [temporarily] rekindle elements of the Puritan tradition," the seventeenth century would give way to "a new, non-Puritan century."[62] Why did Cotton Mather's dramatic, mythic re-creation of their story fail to recall Puritans to a golden past?

Paula Backscheider offers one explanation from the realm of politics, arguing that the power of any spectacle or representation depends upon the willingness of the audience to embrace its structuring metaphors and symbols, or at least to "negotiate" their acceptance with those constructing the representation.[63] If the metaphors and symbols—or the larger myth—do not conform to "people's lived experience," or do not "contain their hopes and confirm the indigenous zeitgeist," the audience will either reject or re-form these "structures that give meaning and shape to experience."[64] It seems evident that the spirit of golden age Puritanism and of the Church Universal evoked by Mather in "Nehemias Americanus" and in the *Magnalia* as a whole was at odds with the early-eighteenth-century American zeitgeist.

The related issue of audience looms large here as well. Francis J. Bremer notes not only the increasing religious and political diversity of the American colonies in the late seventeenth and early eighteenth centuries, but also the shifting religious and political tides in England and on the Continent following the Glorious Revolution.[65] In the last pages of the *Magnalia* Mather calls upon his generation to act in the present and thus to play a part in the epic of salvation, past, present, and future. If we will attend not just to "*our selves* at home" but also to "the *church* abroad," Mather says, we will find that "there is a REVOLUTION and a REFORMATION at the very door, which will be vastly more wonderful than any of the deliverances yet seen by the church of God from the beginning of the world" (2:653). Most of the people he intended to inspire, however, had their minds on other things. One gets the feeling that Mather's dramatic myth of Puritan forefathers, origins, and ideals never really found a coherent audience on this side of the Atlantic, and that it seemed entirely irrelevant on the other side.[66]

On the other hand, one also gets the feeling that, despite the urgency of the *Magnalia*'s call to remember and Mather's emphasis on the grand international evangelistic vision, he understood the limits of human aspiration and effort. Again Robert Middlekauff reminds us of the humbling perspective that astronomy imposed on Mather: "One could not help thinking of the earth in this vast sea of stars and space. The fixed stars took on a size 'vastly greater' than 'this poor Lump of Clay.' Their number defied the power of the mind to count—they are 'like the *Sand* of the sea, innumerable.' In these pluralities 'this Globe is but as a Pins point, if compared with the mighty *Universe*. Never did any man yet make a tolerable guess at its Dimensions: but were we among the *Stars,* we would utterly lose sight of the earth, although it be above twenty six thousand *Italian* miles in the compass of it.'"[67] The time-bound drama of human action and divine grace, humanity and God in dialogue, is contained by the unimaginably grand epic of divine creation and purpose, and the part played by each individual, and each age, is comparatively small.

And yet in a sense Cotton Mather did finally fulfill his purpose in writing the *Magnalia Christi Americana*. It is, Mather says, an "Ebenezer" or "*stone of help,*" but with a difference. We cannot know whether anything was written on the original Ebenezer of the Old Testament book of 1 Samuel, Mather says (1:90), but *his* Ebenezer, the *Magnalia,* is a monument consisting entirely of words.

These words can bring the past to life in the reader's imagination, as Mather's Puritan actors walk again the "field which the Lord has blessed" (1:86). Thus his stories become "durable tokens" (1:92) meant to remind the people of New England that their collective lives have been shaped by divine grace. Kenneth Silverman offers some proof of Mather's success when he reports that Thomas Prince, one of Mather's eulogists, extolled him " 'for the noble Care He has taken to preserve the *Memory* of the great and excellent Fathers of these religious Plantations, that was just a sinking into Oblivion.' "[68]

Taken as a whole, then, the *Magnalia Christi Americana* is just as much a reminder to New England Puritans that they still belong on the international stage as it is a call to remember the fathers and mothers who initiated their particular New World enterprise. New England is, Mather tells his readers, just part of the "American corner of the world" (1:86), which means that the errand into the wilderness is just a part of the Reformation errand into the whole world (1:41). This late Puritan writer uses dramatic techniques as well as history and biography to rehabilitate Puritan ideals, restaging New England's history to show his readers men and women who were not hypocrites, nor canting zealots, nor mere victims of satire, but serious actors in the drama of redemption.

NOTES

1. Wallace Stevens, "The Blue Buildings in the Summer Air," in *The Collected Poems of Wallace Stevens* (New York: Alfred A. Knopf, 1961), 216, lines 1–6.

2. John Higginson, "An Attestation to This Church-History of New-England," in *Magnalia Christi Americana; or, The Ecclesiastical History of New-England,* (1852; reprint, New York: Russell and Russell, 1967), 1:13. All subsequent quotations from the *Magnalia* are taken from this edition and noted parenthetically in the text.

3. Kenneth Silverman states that Mather "obsessively wanted to put America on the cultural map" and "to restore American Puritanism to the mainstream of European culture," introduction to *Selected Letters of Cotton Mather* (Baton Rouge, La.: Louisiana State University Press, 1971), xvi.

4. Silverman, introduction to *Selected Letters of Cotton Mather*, xv.

5. In his diary for April 1701, Mather writes of the war that is "breaking forth in *Europe*," noting his fear that "the French Oppressor [may] fall foul upon us" and "before we do so much as hear of a *War* proclaimed, utterly swallow us up" (*Diary of Cotton Mather*, ed. Worthington Chauncey Ford, MHSC 7th ser. (1911–12; reprint, New York: Frederick Ungar Publishing Co., 1957), 1:397 ff.

6. Silverman, introduction to *Selected Letters of Cotton Mather*, xv.

7. Ibid., xvi. According to Silverman, *Lapis* "is a brief work, containing only twenty-six pages, thirteen of Latin and thirteen of facing English translation. The

spirit of the work derives from the growing ecumenism in Mather. . . . In the *Lapis* he attempted to reduce Reformed Christianity to fourteen maxims on which all Reformed Christians could agree," as "gems refined from the mountain of doctrine" (*Selected Letters of Cotton Mather*, 194).

8. Ritchie Kendall, *The Drama of Dissent: The Radical Poetics of Nonconformity, 1380-1590* (Chapel Hill, N.C.: University of North Carolina Press, 1986), 140. Kendall explains further: "Although the reformers tended to excoriate representational drama, they nonetheless labored tirelessly to transform their own world of letters into a theater of the soul. . . . to dramatize the soul's awakening to its idealized self through a ritualistic encounter with its spiritual adversaries" (prologue to *The Drama of Dissent*, 8).

9. "I gave thanks unto the Lord. . . . For His granting mee continually to dispense His Truths, unto as *great Auditories* in my own Congregation, as one Man can well speak to, and calling mee to Dispensations ever [*sic*] now and then, upon the most *solemn Occasions*, that the Countrey could have afforded" (*Diary of Cotton Mather,* 1:228).

10. As the years passed, Mather apparently believed that this hope was realized, at least to some extent. In a letter written on 27 January 1719, he comments on the "various reception" the *Magnalia* was then receiving in the British Isles and Ireland: "decried . . . in London," but "[i]n several other parts of England, and much more in Scotland and in Ireland, it is cried up; yea, hyperbolically spoken of, and has its desired operation" (Mather to Robert Hackshaw, 27 January 1719, *Selected Letters of Cotton Mather*, 272, 273). In an earlier letter dated 6 August 1716, Mather commends both the *Magnalia* and the *Lapis* to pietist congregations in Lower Saxony (Mather to Anthony William Boehm, 6 August 1716, *Diary of Cotton Mather,* 2:411) and urges his correspondent to put the *Lapis* in the hands of the French reformed churches—"if it be possible, gett [*sic*] the Instrument into France" (ibid., 413). Finally, in his diary for February 1716–1717, he resolves to "[d]irect the, *Lapis e Monte Excisus*, to *Geneva*. It may be a seasonable Action, and attended with marvellous Consequences" (ibid., 437).

11. *Diary of Cotton Mather,* 1:166.

12. Ibid.,1:247.

13. Ibid., 1:358.

14. Mather often notes with a kind of urgency his desire to broadcast his messages throughout the world via the written word. In a letter discussing the *Lapis* with a correspondent in Saxony in 1715, for example, he writes: "A small spark, will sett [sic] fire to a mighty Train, when it is already prepared. . . . My request therefore is, that you would please, to disperse these little Engines of Piety, as fast and as far as you can. . . ." He pleads with this friend to distribute copies of the little volume in Prussia, the East Indies, and France, adding, "yea, excuse me, if I say, procure them to be translated into as many Languages as you can" (Mather to Anthony William Boehm, 2 December 1715, *Diary of Cotton Mather, Vol.* 2:333). Mather's motives for seeking this international platform might well be debated, but certainly he pursued a transoceanic voice tirelessly.

15. According to Kristen Poole, sixteenth- and seventeenth-century Puritans were regularly represented as "sectarians" who turned "the body of Christ into a grotesque figure," a monster made up of incongruous parts (*Radical Religion from Shakespeare to Milton: Figures of Nonconformity in Early Modern England* [Cambridge: Cambridge University Press, 2000], 3ff). Mather wants very much to demonstrate that the Puritan Church in New England is part of the Church Universal, and not a monstrous, separated upstart.

16. Poole's great interest in *Radical Religion from Shakespeare to Milton* is the "history of representation" (14), and she notes that rather than "label[ing] a particular type of person," "Puritan" as a term "most often signified social elements that *resisted* categorization." Poole adds that the way contemporaries represented Puritans reflects "the anxieties" and "uneasy fascination" of the age "with certain cultural figures that indicate the disorder of things" (4, 5), suggesting the magnitude of the representational challenge Mather faced.

17. D. N. Deluna writes felicitously of the *Magnalia* as a literary record of the Puritans' "innovative internationalist project" of New World settlement and evangelism, in "Cotton Mather Published Abroad," *Early American Literature* 26 (1991): 147. Joseph Wood Krutch offers a more stereotypical summary of Puritans' supposed narrowness and provincialism, especially with regard to the theater, in *Comedy and Conscience after the Restoration* (New York: Columbia University Press, 1949), 91.

18. According to Martin Butler, when "the possibility of establishing a godly reformed stage" was raised, Prynne rejected it, albeit conceding that plays might be read for "recreation sake" or if they had "godly purposes." The problem for Prynne, Butler argues, was public performance (*Theatre and Crisis, 1632-1642* [Cambridge: Cambridge University Press, 1984], 98).

19. Quoted in Ian Donaldson, *The World Upside-Down: Comedy from Jonson to Fielding* (Oxford: Clarendon Press, 1970), 66.

20. Intriguingly, Butler suggests that the most interesting drama of the 1630s reflected what might be called a Puritan (or "opposition") stance or "feeling" (*Theatre and Crisis*, 4).

21. Alfred Harbage, *Cavalier Drama: An Historical and Critical Supplement to the Study of the Elizabethan and Restoration Stage* (New York: Russell and Russell, 1964), 14, 16.

22. Patrick Collinson, *The Birthpangs of Protestant England: Religious and Cultural Change in the Sixteenth* and *Seventeenth Centuries* (New York: St. Martin's Press, 1988), 112. For an alternative reading of this whole question, see Walter Cohen, *Drama of a Nation: Public Theater in Renaissance England and Spain* (Ithaca, N.Y.: Cornell University Press, 1985). See also David M. Bevington, *Tudor Drama and Politics: A Critical Approach to Topical Meaning* (Cambridge: Harvard University Press, 1968), esp. 294–98. Bevington argues for a tenuous accommodation between Puritanism and popular culture, but Cohen comments that Bevington "perhaps overemphasizes the fragility of this consensus" (191 n. 15).

23. Eric Linklater, *Ben Jonson and King James: Biography and Portrait* (London: Jonathan Cape, 1931), 273.

24. See Kristen Poole on Falstaff's association with the Lollards as an archetypal example, in *Radical Religion from Shakespeare to Milton*, 41, 44.

25. Of course there is some irony in Mather's intentions here. Kristen Poole notes that during the Martin Marprelate episode the anti-Martinists unintentionally kept Puritan representations and issues at center stage (*Radical Religion*, 28, 29). In a sense Mather had to move things in the opposite direction. With their Great Migration, American Puritans had apparently walked off the stage completely, leaving Mather the task either of recentering the stage or trying to prove that the New England church had never actually made an exit.

26. While it would probably be difficult to prove Mather's direct debt to Calvin for this trope, the evidence of his general indebtedness to Calvin is strong. See Richard F. Lovelace, *The American Pietism of Cotton Mather: Origins of Ameri-*

can Evangelicalism (Grand Rapids, Mich.: Christian University Press, 1979), 57, and Perry Miller, *The New England Mind: The Seventeenth Century,* 2d ed. (Cambridge: Harvard University Press, 1954), 92.

27. John Calvin, *Institutes of the Christian Religion,* trans. Ford Lewis Battles (Philadelphia: Westminster Press, 1960), 1:60, 61. My emphases in the quoted phrases.

28. Calvin, *Institutes,* 1:72.

29. Martin Butler's dramatic description of John Foxe's "astonishingly influential *Acts and Monuments*" suggests another possible inspiration or model for Mather (*Theatre and Crisis,* 87).

30. In *The Puritan Origins of the American Self* (New Haven and London: Yale University Press, 1975), for instance, Sacvan Bercovitch argues that Mather's life of Winthrop in the *Magnalia* is an ur-text and an interpretive key to understanding "the complexity, the intricacy, the coherence, and the abiding significance of the American Puritan vision" (preface, ix). Perry Miller connects Mather's ritual guilt and confession with "the problem of [American] identity" ("Errand into the Wilderness," in *Errand into the Wilderness* [Cambridge: Harvard University Press, 1956], 9ff).

31. Parker J. Palmer, "The Grace of Great Things," a talk presented at the Coalition of Christian Colleges and Universities National Forum, spring 1998. Palmer was not speaking about New England Puritanism; the editorial brackets indicate my appropriation of a phrase he used in a very different context.

32. Mather rejects New England's separatist identity, whether that identity is self-assumed or imposed, trying instead to make the case that New World Puritans are part of Christ's "one coterminous body," to use Kristen Poole's phrase. See her discussion of the representational implications of separatism and "semi-separatism" within "the coterminous body" of church and state (*Radical Religion,* 68, 69).

33. Aristotle, *On Poetry and Style,* trans. and ed. G. M. A. Grube (Indianapolis: Bobbs-Merrill, 1958), 10.

34. See, for example, Jonson's *The Alchemist* (1610) and *Bartholomew Fair* (1614), in *The Complete Plays of Ben Jonson,* ed. G. A. Wilkes, 4 vols. (Oxford: Clarendon Press, 1981–82), and William Wycherley's *Love in a Wood* (1671/72), in *The Complete Plays of William Wycherley,* ed. Gerald Weales, Stuart Editions (New York: New York University Press, 1967). In *Love in a Wood* the stage Puritan, Alderman Gripe, is described in the dramatis personae as "a seemingly precise, but a covetous, lechereous, old Usurer of the City" (9).

35. On the Restoration stage's jaded moral sense see Krutch, *Comedy and Conscience,* 1.

36. Bonamy Dobree, *Restoration Tragedy, 1660–1720* (Oxford: Clarendon Press, 1929), 21, 22.

37. Aristotle, *On Poetry and Style,* 12.

38. Ibid. See also note 2 on 12, and the introduction, xv–xvii.

39. Ibid., 24.

40. Ibid., 11. Certainly in the last pages of the *Magnalia,* Mather emphasizes that he writes not just for the present generation, but also for the future, especially for the children and youth in whose day many of the Reformation's promises will finally be fulfilled. See *Magnalia,* 2:653, 657.

41. Aristotle, *On Poetry and Style,* 50.

42. Ibid., 24.

43. Sacvan Bercovitch notes that in this passage Mather takes "Foxe's great

church history . . . as precedent for the *Magnalia*" (*The Puritan Origins of the American Self*, 72).

44. Preface to *Diary of Cotton Mather*, 1:xvi.

45. Thomas J. Wertenbaker, *The Puritan Oligarchy: The Founding of American Civilization* (New York: Charles Scribner's Sons, 1947), 90.

46. In the "General Introduction" to the *Magnalia,* 31, Mather calls his profusely scattered allusions and figures of speech "embellishments" and "choice *flowers*," adding that "As a little salt seasons food, and increases its relish, so a spice of antiquity heightens the charm of style."

47. Paula Backscheider, *Spectacular Politics: Theatrical Power and Mass Culture in Early Modern England* (Baltimore and London: The Johns Hopkins University Press, 1993), 67.

48. Ibid., 69.

49. Admittedly, the evidence for this supposition is mostly circumstantial. See Samuel Eliot Morison, *The Intellectual Life of Colonial New England* (Ithaca, N.Y.: Cornell University Press, 1956), 150, 273, and Roger Thompson, "The Puritans and Prurience: Aspects of the Restoration Book Trade," in *Contrast and Connection: Bicentennial Essays in Anglo-American History*, ed. H. C. Allen and Roger Thompson (Athens, Ohio: Ohio University Press, 1976), 49 ff.

50. The aristocratic Caspard de Coligny (1519–72), "Admiral of France" and "titular King of Navarre," was a Huguenot convert and then leader. See Kenneth Scott Latourette, *A History of Christianity* (New York: Harper and Row, 1953), 767. According to *Compton's Encyclopedia,* "Coligny sent three unsuccessful colonies to the New World—the first in 1552 to Brazil; the second in 1562 to South Carolina, where they settled Port Royal; and the third in 1564 to Florida, where the promising settlement of Fort Caroline was established on the St. John's River. The Fort Caroline settlers were all killed by a Spanish expedition in 1565," s.v. Coligny, Caspard de, 1987 ed., 546, 547.

51. The August 1572 Massacre of St. Bartholomew in Paris. Latourette, *History of Christianity*, 767.

52. Division and sectarianism within the church were matters of concern to Mather. In a letter written to Anthony William Boehm, for example, Mather reveals his dismay with rigid and ignorant British "Dissenters," who were suspicious of his work: "I expect no distinguishing Favour from any distinguished party of Christians. And, the Dissenters in London have particularly treated me . . . as I have ever expected, from men of their narrow Spirits; and among whom, I wish, learning were more esteemed and exemplified" (Mather to Anthony William Boehm, 6 August 1716, *Diary of Cotton Mather,* 413).

53. A sentiment Mather echoes several times in letters and diary entries. In the letter to Boehm mentioned in the preceding note, for instance, Mather refers to his hopes for the completion of a massive project entitled *Biblia Americana*, suggesting that he needs the help of catholic-minded Christians of varied theological traditions to bring the work to fruition: "If this work ever see the Light, I expect it will be from the Countenance and Contribution, of men of our *Universal Religion*; who will every way appear more and more in the several Forms of Christianity" Mather to Anthony William Boehm, 6 August 1716, *Diary of Cotton Mather,* 2:413.

54. For a helpful overview of Cotton Mather's experience with English publishers, printers, booksellers, and book exporters, see Deluna's "Cotton Mather Published Abroad."

55. *Selected Letters of Cotton Mather*, 58.

56. *Diary of Cotton Mather,* 1:445.

57. Mather's obvious debt to Virgil's *Aeneid* for this motto reminds us that if seventeenth-century dramatic strategies inform the *Magnalia,* so too does the classical epic tradition. Clearly Mather the author is aware of and ready to employ elements of several literary modes.

58. Bercovitch, *The Puritan Origins of the American Self*, 13, 14.

59. Compare this tender mother and child imagery with the "transvestite lie implicit in the acting of female parts by boys" to which Collinson refers in *The Birthpangs of Protestant England,* 112.

60. Robert Middlekauff points to Mather's interest in astronomy as evincing his consciousness that all human endeavors—even those driven by Reformation zeal—are dwarfed by the grandeur of the divine scheme of things, in *The Mathers: Three Generations of Puritan Intellectuals, 1596-1728* (New York: Oxford University Press, 1971), 282.

61. Compare Calvin's depiction of the human capacity to forget quickly a moving spectacle or a great truth apprehended; he uses the image of fast-fading applause in a theater soon after the show is over: "In the end, like applause in the theater for some pleasing spectacle, it evaporates" (*Institutes of the Christian Religion,* 1:714).

62. Francis J. Bremer, *The Puritan Experiment: New England Society from Bradford to Edwards*, rev. ed. (Hanover and London: University Press of New England, 1995), 224.

63. Backscheider, *Spectacular Politics*, 64.

64. Ibid., 35, 65, 64.

65. Bremer, *The Puritan Experiment*, 209 ff.

66. Compare Ritchie Kendall's description of the actual audience for "the Puritan program of reform" in Thomas Cartwright's day; though ostensibly addressing "not only . . . the faithful but . . . the nation at large," Puritan pastors found themselves speaking only to " 'a church within a Church,' a small body of true believers set in the midst of a nominally Protestant society" (*The Drama of Dissent*, 150, 151).

67. Middlekauff, *The Mathers*, 282. Quote is from Mather, *The Wonderful Works of God Commemorated* (Boston: S. Green, 1690).

68. Kenneth Silverman, *The Life and Times of Cotton Mather* (New York: Harper and Row, 1984), 424.

Bibliography

Allen, David Grayson. *In English Ways: The Movement of Societies and the Transferral of English Local Law and Custom to Massachusetts Bay in the Seventeenth Century*. Chapel Hill, N.C.: University of North Carolina Press, 1981.

Allen, William. "A faithful Memorial of that remarkable meeting of many Officers of the Army, at Windsor Castle in 1648." In *Somers Tracts,* 6: 498–504. London, 1811.

Allison, Robert. *The Crescent Obscured: The United States and the Muslim World, 1776-1815*. Oxford: Clarendon Press, 1995.

apRoberts, Ruth. *Arnold and God*. Berkeley and Los Angeles: University of California Press, 1983.

Arbitrary Government. 1682.

Aristotle. *On Poetry and Style*. Translated and edited by G. M. A. Grube. Indianapolis: Bobbs-Merrill, 1958.

Arnold, Matthew. *The Complete Prose Works of Matthew Arnold*. Edited by R. H. Super. 11 vols. Ann Arbor, Mich.: University of Michigan Press, 1960–71.

———. *Culture and Anarchy*. Edited by J. Dover Wilson. Cambridge: Cambridge University Press, 1969.

———. *Letters of Matthew Arnold, 1848-88*. Edited by George W. E. Russell. 2 vols. New York: Macmillan, 1896.

———. *Matthew Arnold, Prose Writings: The Critical Heritage*. Edited by Carl Dawson and John Pfordresher. London: Routledge and Kegan Paul, 1979.

———. *The Poetry and Criticism of Matthew Arnold*. Edited by A. Dwight Culler. Boston: Houghton Mifflin, 1961.

———. *St. Paul and Protestantism*. In *Matthew Arnold: Dissent and Dogma*. Edited by R. H. Super. 1870. Reprint, Ann Arbor, Mich.: University of Michigan Press, 1968.

Arnold, Thomas. "The Oxford Malignants and Dr. Hampden." *Edinburgh Review* 63 (April 1836): 225–39.

Arnway, John. *The Tablet, or Moderation of Charles the I, Martyr, with an Alarm to the Subjects of England*. 2d ed. The Hague, 1649.

Ashton Church Devon. Exeter: Ashton PCC, 1984, 1993.

Aubrey, John. *Brief Lives*. Edited by Oliver Lawson Dick. London: Secker and Warburg, 1960.

Axtell, James. *After Columbus: Essays in the Ethnohistory of Colonial America*. New York: Oxford University Press, 1988.

———. *Beyond 1492: Encounters in Colonial North America*. New York: Oxford University Press, 1992.

———. *The Invasion Within: The Contest of Cultures in Colonial North America*. New York: Oxford University Press, 1985.

B. T. *The Saints Inheritance After the Day of Judgement*. London, 1643.

Backscheider, Paula. *Spectacular Politics: Theatrical Power and Mass Culture in Early Modern England*. Baltimore and London: The Johns Hopkins University Press, 1993.

Baillie, Robert. *Anabaptism, the True Fountaine of Independency, Antinomy, Brownisme, Familisme, and the most of the other Errours, which for the time do trouble the Church of England, Unsealed*. London: M. F., 1646.

Bailyn, Bernard. *The New England Merchants in the Seventeenth Century*. New York: Harper and Row, 1964.

Baker, Colonel. *The Blazing-Star, or Nolls Nose Newly Revived, and taken out of his Tomb*. London, 1660.

Ball, Thomas. *The Life of the Renowned Doctor Preston*. Edited by E. W. Harcourt. Oxford and London, 1885.

Ball, William. *A Caveat for Subjects, Moderating the Observator*. London, 1642.

Barber, Malcolm. "How the West Saw Medieval Islam." *History Today* 47 (May 1997): 44–50.

Barker-Benfield, Ben. "Anne Hutchinson and the Puritan Attitude toward Women." *Feminist Studies* 1 (1972): 55–78.

Barlow, William. *The Summe and Substance of the Conference, which, it pleased his Exceelent Majestie to have with the Lords, Bishops, and other of his Clergie (at which the most of the Lordes of the Councell were present) in his Majesties Privy-Chamber, at Hampton Court, January 14, 1603*. London, 1604.

Baron, William. *Regicides No Saints nor Martyrs*. London, 1700.

Baskerville, S. K. "Puritans, Revisionists, and the English Revolution." *Huntington Library Quarterly* 61, no. 2 (2001): 151–71.

Bastwick, John. *The Confession*. London, 1641.

Bates, William. *The Whole Works of the Rev. W. Bates, D.D.* Edited by W. Farmer. 4 vols. London, 1815. Reprint, Harrisonburg, Va.: Sprinkle Publications, 1990.

Baumer, Franklin L. "England, the Turk, and the Common Corps of Christendom." *American Historical Review* 50 (October 1944): 26–48.

Baxter, Richard. *The Autobiography of Richard Baxter*. Edited by N. H. Keeble. London: Rowan and Littlefield, 1974.

———. *Reliquiae Baxterianae*. London: printed for T. Parkhurst, J. Robinson, F. Lawrence, and F. Dunton, 1696.

Baylie, Robert. *Satan the Leader in chief to all who resist the Reparation of Sion*. London, 1643.

Beck, Brandon H. *From the Rising of the Sun: English Images of the Ottoman Empire to 1715*. American University Studies, ser. 9, vol. 20. New York: Peter Lang, 1987.

Bennett, Joan. "God, Satan, and King Charles: Milton's Royal Portraits." *PMLA* 92 (1977): 441–57.

Bercovitch, Sacvan. *The American Jeremiad*. Madison: University of Wisconsin Press, 1978.

————. *The Puritan Origins of the American Self*. New Haven and London: Yale University Press, 1975.

Bevington, David M. *Tudor Drama and Politics: A Critical Approach to Topical Meaning*. Cambridge: Harvard University Press, 1968.

Birch, Thomas. *The Court and Times of Charles I*. London: Henry Colburn, 1849.

Birdsall, Virginia Ogden. *Wild Civility: The English Comic Spirit on the Restoration Stage*. Bloomington, Ind., and London: Indiana University Press, 1970.

Blanks, David R. "Western Views of Islam in the Premodern Period: A Brief History of Past Approaches." In *Western Views of Islam in Medieval and Early Modern Europe: Perception of Other,* edited by David R. Blanks and Michael Frassetto, 11–53. New York: St. Martin's Press, 1999.

Bodleian Library, Sancroft MS 18.

Bodleian Library, Tanner MS 72.

Bondos-Greene, Stephen. "The End of an Era: Cambridge Puritanism and the Christ's College Election of 1609." *The Historical Journal* 25, no. 1 (1982): 197–208.

Bossy, John. "Some Elementary Forms of Durkheim." *Past and Present* 95 (1982): 3–18.

Bowden, Henry W., and James P. Ronda. Introduction to *John Eliot's Indian Dialogues: A Study in Cultural Interaction*, edited by Henry W. Bowden and James P. Ronda, 3–45. Westport, Conn.: Greenwood Press, 1980.

Bozeman, Theodore Dwight. *To Live Ancient Lives: The Primitivist Dimension in Puritanism*. Chapel Hill, N.C.: University of North Carolina Press, 1988.

————. "The Puritans' 'Errand into the Wilderness' Reconsidered." *New England Quarterly* 59 (1986): 231–51.

Bradshaw's Ghost: A Poem. London, 1660.

Bragdon, Kathleen J. *Native Peoples of Southern New England, 1500-1650*. Norman, Okla.: University of Oklahoma Press, 1996.

Bremer, Francis J. *Congregational Communion: Clerical Friendship in the Anglo-American Puritan Community, 1610-1692*. Boston: Northeastern University Press, 1994.

————. *The Puritan Experiment: New England Society from Bradford to Edwards*. Rev. ed. Hanover, N.H., and London: University Press of New England, 1995.

————, ed. *Puritanism: Transatlantic Perspectives on a Seventeenth-Century Anglo-American Faith*. Boston: Massachusetts Historical Society, 1993.

A Brief Discourse on Tyrants and Tyranny. N.p. 1642.

British Library, Harleian MS 3783.

British Library, Harleian MS 7091.

Brockett, Allan. *Nonconformity in Exeter 1650-1875*. Manchester: Manchester University Press, 1962.

Bulkeley, Peter, and John Cotton. "Peter Bulkeley and John Cotton: On Union with Christ." In *The Antinomian Controversy, 1631-1638: A Documentary History*. 2d ed. Edited by David D. Hall, 34–42. Durham, N.C.: Duke University Press, 1990.

Bunyan, John. *Grace Abounding to the Chief of Sinners*. Edited by Roger Sharrock. Oxford: Clarendon Press, 1962.

————. *Seasonable Counsel* and *A Discourse upon the Pharisee and the Publicane*. Edited by Owen C. Watkins. Oxford: Clarendon Press, 1988.

Burke, Peter. *Popular Culture in Early Modern Europe*. London: T. Smith, 1978.

————. "Tacitism." In *Tacitus*, edited by T. A. Dorey, 149–71. New York: Basic Books, 1969.

Burroughes, Jeremiah. *A Gracious Spirit a Choyce and Pretious Spirit*. London, 1638.

Butler, Martin. *Theatre and Crisis, 1632-1642*. Cambridge: Cambridge University Press, 1984.

Butler, Samuel. *Hudibras*. Edited by John Wilders. Oxford: Clarendon Press, 1967

Butts, Francis. "The Myth of Perry Miller." *The American Historical Review* 87, no. 3 (1982): 665–94.

Calamy, Edward. *England's Looking Glass, Presented in a Sermon Preached before the Honourable House of Commons*. London, 1642.

————. *The Nonconformist's Memorial: Ministers Ejected or Silenced in Devonshire*. Samuel Palmer, n.d.

Caldwell, Patricia. *The Puritan Conversion Narrative: The Beginnings of American Expression*. Cambridge: Cambridge University Press, 1983.

Calendar of State Papers, Domestic Series, 1649-50. Edited by Mary Anne Everett Green. London: Longman and Co., 1875.

Calloway, Colin. *New Worlds for All: Indians, Europeans, and the Remaking of Early America*. Baltimore: The Johns Hopkins University Press, 1997.

Calvin, John. *Institutes of the Christian Religion*. 2 vols. Translated by Ford Lewis Battles. Philadelphia: Westminster Press, 1960.

Cambridge University Library, Additional MS 22.

Cambridge University Library, Com. Ct. III.

Cambridge University Library, MS CUR 6.1.

Cambridge University Library, MS Mm 1.46.

Cambridge University Library, MS Mm 2.23, 25.

Cambridge University Library, MSS Vice Chancellors Court I.

Cambridge University Library, MSS Vice Chancellors Court III.24, 26, 27.

Carlyle, Thomas. *Letters and Speeches of Oliver Cromwell with Elucidations by Thomas Carlyle*. Edited by S. C. Lomas. 3 vols. London: Methuen and Co., 1904.

————. *On Heroes and Hero-Worship*. 1841. Reprint, London: Chapman and Hall, 1897.

Case, Thomas. *Spirituall Whordome Discovered in a Sermon Preach'd before the Honourable House of Commons*. London, 1647.

Cave, Alfred A. *The Pequot War*. Amherst, Mass.: University of Massachusetts Press, 1996.

Certain Considerations upon the Duties Both of Prince and People. London, 1642.

Chew, Samuel C. *The Crescent and the Rose: Islam and England during the Renaissance*. New York: Oxford University Press, 1937.

Cheynell, Francis. *The Rise, Growth, and Danger of Socinianisme*. London, 1643.

Christianson, Paul. *Reformers and Babylon: English Apocalyptic Visions from the Reformation to the Eve of the Civil War*. Toronto: University of Toronto Press, 1978.

Chudleigh, Mary Lee. *The Poems and Prose of Mary, Lady Chudleigh*. Edited by Margaret J. M. Ezell. New York: Oxford University Press, 1993.

Clarke, Samuel. *The Lives of Sundry Eminent Persons in this Later Age*. London, 1683.

Cleveland, John. *The Character of a London-Diurnall*. 3d ed. N.p., 1647.

Cliffe, J. T. *The Puritan Gentry Besieged 1650-1700*. London and New York: Routledge, 1993.

Cogley, Richard W. *John Eliot's Mission to the Indians before King Philip's War*. Cambridge: Harvard University Press, 1999.

Cohen, Charles L. "Conversion among Puritans and Amerindians: A Theological and Cultural Perspective." In *Puritanism: Transatlantic Perspectives on a Seventeenth-Century Anglo-American Faith*, edited by Francis J. Bremer, 233–56. Boston: Massachusetts Historical Society, 1993.

———. *God's Caress: The Psychology of Puritan Religious Experience*. New York: Oxford University Press, 1986.

———. "The Post-Puritan Paradigm of Early American Religious History." *William and Mary Quarterly*, 3d ser., 54 (1997): 695–722.

Cohen, Walter. *Drama of a Nation: Public Theater in Renaissance England and Spain*. Ithaca, N.Y.: Cornell University Press, 1985.

Coleridge, Samuel Taylor. *Literary Remains*. Edited by H. N. Coleridge. London: William Pickering, 1838.

Colie, Rosalie L. *Light and Enlightenment: A Study of the Cambridge Platonists and the Dutch Arminians*. Cambridge: Cambridge University Press, 1957.

Collinson, Patrick. "Ben Jonson's *Bartholomew Fair*: The Theatre Constructs Puritanism." In *The Theatrical City: Culture, Theatre and Politics in London, 1576-1649*, edited by David L. Smith, Richard Strier, and David Bevington, 157–69. Cambridge: Cambridge University Press, 1995.

———. *The Birthpangs of Protestant England: Religious and Cultural Change in the Sixteenth and Seventeenth Centuries*. New York: St. Martin's Press, 1988.

———. "The Cohabitation of the Faithful with the Unfaithful." In *From Persecution to Toleration: The Glorious Revolution and Religion in England*, edited by Ole Peter Grell, Jonathan I. Israel, and Nicholas Tyacke, 51–76. Oxford: Clarendon Press, 1991.

———. "A Comment: Concerning the Name Puritan." *Journal of Ecclesiastical History* 31 (1980): 483–88.

———. "Ecclesiastical Vitriol: Religious Satire in the 1590s and the Invention of Puritanism." In *The Reign of Elizabeth I: Court and Culture in the Last Decade*, edited by John Guy, 150–70. Cambridge: Cambridge University Press, 1995.

———. "Elizabethan and Jacobean Puritanism as Forms of Popular Religious Culture." In *The Culture of English Puritanism, 1560-1700*, edited by Christopher Durston and Jacqueline Eales, 32–57. Basingstoke: Macmillan, 1996.

———. *The Elizabethan Puritan Movement*. Berkeley and Los Angeles: University of California Press, 1967.

———. *Godly People: Essays on English Protestantism and Puritanism*. London: Hambledon Press, 1983.

———. *The Puritan Character: Polemics and Polarities in Early Seventeenth Century English Culture*. Los Angeles: William Andrews Clark Memorial Library, 1989.

———. *The Religion of Protestants: The Church in English Society, 1559-1625*. Oxford: Clarendon Press, 1982.

"A Conference Mr. John Cotton Held at Boston with the Elders of New England." In *The Antinomian Controversy, 1631-1638: A Documentary History*. 2d ed. Edited by David D. Hall, 173–98. Durham, N.C.: Duke University Press, 1990.

Cooke, John. *Monarchy No creature of Gods making*. [Waterford, 1651].

Cooper, C. H. *Annals of Cambridge*. Edited by J. W. Cooper. 5 vols. Cambridge: Cambridge University Press, 1908.

Corbett, Richard. *The Poems of Richard Corbett*. Edited by J. A. W. Bennett and H. R. Trevor-Roper. Oxford: Clarendon Press, 1955.

Cosin, John. *The Correspondence of John Cosin, D.D.* Publications of the Surtees Society, vol. 52. London, 1869.

———. *The Works of the Right Reverend Father in God, John Cosin, Lord Bishop of Durham*. Edited by John Henry Parker. 6 vols. Oxford, 1843–55.

Cotton, John. *A Brief Exposition with Practical Observations upon the whole Book of Canticles*. London: T. R. and E. M. for Ralph Smith, 1655. Reprint, New York: Arno Press, 1972.

———. "Mr. Cotton's Rejoynder." In *The Antinomian Controversy, 1636-1638: A Documentary History*. 2d ed. Edited by David D. Hall, 78–151. Durham, N.C.: Duke University Press, 1990.

———. *A Sermon Preached by the Reverend Mr. John Cotton Deliver'd at Salem, 1636*. In *John Cotton on the Churches of New England*. Edited by Larzer Ziff. Cambridge: Harvard University Press, 1968.

———. "Sixteene Questions of Serious and Necessary Consequence." In *The Antinomian Controversy, 1631-1638: A Documentary History*. 2d ed. Edited by David D. Hall, 43–59. Durham, N.C.: Duke University Press, 1990.

Cragg, G. R. *From Puritanism to the Age of Reason: A Study of Changes in Religious Thought within the Church of England 1660 to 1700*. Cambridge: Cambridge University Press, 1966.

Cressy, David. *Bonfires and Bells: National Memory and the Protestant Calendar in Elizabethan and Stuart England*. Berkeley and Los Angeles: University of California Press, 1989.

———. *Coming Over: Migration and Communication between England and New England in the Seventeenth Century*. Cambridge: Cambridge University Press, 1987.

———. "Conflict, Consensus, and the Willingness to Wink: The Erosion of Community in Charles I's England." *Huntington Library Quarterly* 61.2 (2000): 131–50.

Cromwell, Oliver. *Letters and Speeches of Oliver Cromwell, with Elucidations by Thomas Carlyle*. Edited by S. C. Lomas. 3 vols. London: Methuen and Co. , 1904.

———. *The Writings and Speeches of Oliver Cromwell*. 4 vols. Edited by Wilbur Cortez Abbott. Cambridge: Harvard University Press, 1937–47.

Cunningham, Valentine. *Everywhere Spoken Against: Dissent in the Victorian Novel*. Oxford: Clarendon Press, 1975.

Curteis, George Herbert. *Dissent, in its Relation to the Church of England*. The 1871 Bampton Lectures. London and New York: Macmillan, 1872.

Cust, Richard, and Ann Hughes, eds. *Conflict in Early Stuart England: Studies in Religion and Politics, 1603-1642*. London and New York: Longman, 1989.

Dale, R. W. "Mr. Arnold and the Nonconformists." *The Contemporary Review* 14 (July 1870), 540–71.

Daniel, Norman. *Islam and the West: The Making of an Image*. Edinburgh: Edinburgh University Press, 1960. Rev. ed., Oxford: Oneworld Publications, 1993.

Davie, Donald. *A Gathered Church: The Literature of the English Dissenting Interest, 1700-1930*. New York: Oxford University Press, 1978.

Davies, Julian. *The Caroline Captivity of the Church: Charles I and the Remoulding of Anglicanism, 1625-1641*. Oxford: Clarendon Press, 1992.

Davies, Stevie. *Images of Kingship in "Paradise Lost": Milton's Politics and Christian Liberty*. Columbia, Mo.: University of Missouri Press, 1983.

Davis, J. C. "Religion and the Struggle for Liberty in the English Revolution." *Historical Journal* 35 (1992): 507–30.

A Declaration on their just Resentment of the Horrid Murther perpetrated on the body of Isaac Dorislaus. London, 1649.

Defoe, Daniel. *King William's Affection to the Church of England Examined*. 5th ed. London, 1703.

Delbanco, Andrew. "The Puritan Errand Re-Viewed." *Journal of American Studies* 18 (1984): 343–60.

Deluna, D. N. "Cotton Mather Published Abroad." *Early American Literature* 26 (1991): 145–72.

Dennis, John. *The Advancement and Reformation of Poetry*. London: Rich. Parker, 1701.

Dering, Edward. *Four Speeches Made by Sir Edward Dering in the High Court of Parliament*. London, 1641.

A Description of the Grand Signor's Seraglio, or Turkish Emperour's Court. London, 1650.

Dewhurst, Kenneth. *Dr. Thomas Sydenham, 1624-1689: His Life and Original Writings*. Berkeley and Los Angeles: University of California Press, 1966.

Dillingham, William. *Laurence Chaderton, D.D.*. Translated by E.S. Shuckburgh. Cambridge: Macmillan and Bowes, 1884.

A Discourse upon the Questions in Debate between the King and Parliament. Oxford, 1642.

The Discoverer. Part one. London, 1649.

A Discovery of Twenty-nine Sects Here in London. London, 1641.

A Diurnal of Sea Designes, which is as strange as true. London, 1642.

Dobree, Bonamy. *Restoration Tragedy, 1660-1720*. Oxford: Clarendon Press, 1929.

Donaldson, Ian. *The World Upside-Down: Comedy from Jonson to Fielding*. Oxford: Clarendon Press, 1970.

238 BIBLIOGRAPHY

Donne, John. *Sermons*. Edited by G. R. Potter and E. M. Simpson. 10 vols. Berkeley and Los Angeles: University of California Press, 1953–62.

Doughty, John. *The Kings Cause Rationally, briefly, and plainly debated, as it stands De facto*. Oxford, 1644.

The Downfal of Dagon, or, Certain Signes of the Sudden and Unavoidable Ruine of this Parliament and Army. London, 1652.

Dregs of Drollery, or Old Poetry in its Ragges: A Full Cry of Hell-Hounds Unkennelled to Go a King-Catching. London, 1660.

Dunton, John. *The Visions of the Soul, Before it Came into the Body*. London: printed for John Dunton, at the Raven in the Poultry, 1692.

Durston, Christopher. "Puritan Rule and the Failure of Cultural Revolution, 1645–1660." In *The Culture of English Puritanism, 1560-1700*, edited by Christopher Durston and Jacqueline Eales, 210–33. Basingstoke: Macmillan, 1996.

Durston, Christopher, and Jacqueline Eales. "Introduction: The Puritan Ethos, 1560–1700." In *The Culture of English Puritanism, 1560-1700*, edited by Christopher Durston and Jacqueline Eales, 1–31. Basingstoke: Macmillan, 1996.

———, eds. *The Culture of English Puritanism, 1560-1700*. Basingstoke: Macmillan, 1996.

Dzelzainis, Martin. "Milton's Classical Republicanism." In *Milton and Republicanism*, edited by David Armitage, Armand Himy, and Quentin Skinner, 3–24. Cambridge: Cambridge University Press, 1995.

Eales, Jacqueline. "A Road to Revolution: The Continuity of Puritanism, 1559–1642." In *The Culture of English Puritanism, 1560-1700*, edited by Christopher Durston and Jacqueline Eales, 184–209. Basingstoke: Macmillan, 1996.

Earle, John. *Microcosmographie*. Facsimile ed. Leeds, England: Scolar Press, 1966.

Edwards, Thomas. *Gangraena: or a Catalogue and Discovery of many Errours, Heresies, Blasphemies and pernicious Practices of the Sectaries of this Time*. London, 1646.

"The Elders Reply." In *The Antinomian Controversy, 1631-1638: A Documentary History*. 2d ed. Edited by David D. Hall, 60–77. Durham, N.C.: Duke University Press, 1990.

Eliot, George. *Felix Holt*. Vol. 3 of *The Novels of George Eliot*. New York: Harper and Brothers, 1866.

Eliot, John. *The Dying Speeches of Several Indians*. Cambridge, [1685?].

[———]. *A Further Account of the Progress of the Gospel amongst the Indians in New England*. London: John Macock, 1660.

———. *A Late and Further Manifestation of the Progress of the Gospel amongst the Indians in New-England*. London: M.S., 1655.

———. "Letters of Rev. John Eliot of Roxbury, to Hon. Robert Boyle." Massachusetts Historical Society, *Collections*, 1st ser., 3 (1794).

Eliot, John, and Thomas Mayhew. "Tears of Repentance: Or, a further Narrative of the Progress of the Gospel amongst the Indians in New England." 1653. Reprinted in Massachusetts Historical Society, *Collections*, 3d ser., 4 (1834): 197–260.

Emmanuel College Archives, COL 9.1. "William Bennet's Book, Containing Anecdotes Relative to the College, or to Persons Connected with It." 2 vols.

Equitable and Necessary Considerations and Resolutions for Association of

Arms throughout the Counties of the Kingdom of England and Principality of Wales. London, 1642.

"The Examination of Mrs. Anne Hutchinson at the Court at Newtown." In *The Antinomian Controversy, 1631-1638: A Documentary History*. 2d ed. Edited by David D. Hall, 311–348. Durham, N.C.: Duke University Press, 1990.

Fairchild, Hoxie Neale. *Religious Trends in English Poetry, Volume 1: 1700-1740: Protestantism and the Cult of Sentiment*. New York: Columbia University Press, 1939.

The Famous Tragedy of King Charles I. As It Was Acted before White-Hall by the Fanatical Servants of Oliver Cromwell. London, 1649.

Ferrell, Lori Anne. *Government by Polemic: James I, the King's Preachers, and the Rhetorics of Conformity, 1603-1625*. Stanford, Calif.: Stanford University Press, 1998.

Fielding, J. "Opposition to the Personal Rule of Charles I: The Diary of Robert Woodford, 1637-1641." *Historical Journal* 31 (1988): 769–88.

Fiennes, Nathaniel. *Treason's Masterpiece*. London, 1680.

Fink, Zera. *The Classical Republicans*. 2d ed. Evanston, Ill.: Northwestern University Press, 1962.

Finlayson, Michael G. *Historians, Puritanism, and the English Revolution: The Religious Factor in English Politics before and after the Interregnum*. Toronto: University of Toronto Press, 1983.

Fletcher, Anthony. *The Outbreak of the English Civil War*. New York: New York University Press, 1981.

———. *Reform in the Provinces: The Government of Stuart England*. New Haven: Yale University Press, 1986.

Folger Library, MS X.d.483. Bennett Papers.

Ford, Worthington Chauncey. Preface to vol. 1 of *Diary of Cotton Mather*. 2 vols. New York: Frederick Ungar Publishing Co., 1911.

Foster, Stephen. *The Long Argument: English Puritanism and the Shaping of New England Culture, 1570-1700*. Chapel Hill, N.C.: University of North Carolina Press, 1991.

———. "New England and the Challenge of Heresy, 1630–1660: The Puritan Controversy in Transatlantic Perspective." *William and Mary Quarterly*, 3d ser., 38 (1981): 624–60.

———. *Notes from the Caroline Underground: Alexander Leighton, the Puritan Triumvirate, and the Laudian Reaction to Nonconformity*. Hamden, Conn.: Archon Books, 1978.

Foxe, John. *Acts and Monuments* (or *Book of Martyrs*). 1610.

Frei, Hans. *The Eclipse of Biblical Narrative: A Study in Eighteenth and Nineteenth Century Hermeneutics*. New Haven: Yale University Press, 1974.

Freud, Sigmund. *Civilization and Its Discontents*. Translated by Joan Riviere. London: Hogarth Press, 1930.

Friedman, Jerome. *The Battle of the Frogs and Fairford's Flies: Miracles and the Pulp Press during the English Revolution*. New York: St. Martin's Press, 1993.

Fuller, Thomas. *The Church History of Britain*. Vol. 4. Edited by J. S. Brewer. Oxford, 1845.

Games, Alison. *Migration and the Origins of the English Atlantic World*. Cambridge: Harvard University Press, 1999.

Gauden, John. *Cromwell's Bloody Slaughter-house*. London, 1660.

Giddens, Anthony. *Central Problems in Social Theory: Action, Structure, and Contradiction in Social Analysis*. Berkeley and Los Angeles: University of California Press, 1979.

Godbeer, Richard. *The Devil's Dominion: Magic and Religion in Early New England*. Cambridge: Cambridge University Press, 1992.

Goffman, Daniel. *Britons in the Ottoman Empire, 1642-1660*. Seattle and London: University of Washington Press, 1998.

Greaves, Richard L. *Deliver Us from Evil: The Radical Underground in Britain, 1660-1663*. New York: Oxford University Press, 1986.

Green, Jack P. *Pursuits of Happiness: The Social Development of Early Modern British Colonies and the Formation of American Culture*. Chapel Hill, N.C.: University of North Carolina Press, 1988.

Greenblatt, Stephen. *Marvelous Possessions: The Wonder of the New World*. Chicago: University of Chicago Press, 1991.

Greven, Philip. *Four Generations: Population, Land, and Family in Colonial Andover, Massachusetts*. Ithaca, N.Y.: Cornell University Press, 1970.

———. "The Self Shaped and Misshaped: *The Protestant Temperament* Reconsidered." In *Through a Glass Darkly: Reflections on Personal Identity in Early America*, edited by Ronald Hoffman, Mechal Sobel, and Fredrika J. Teute, 348–69. Chapel Hill, N.C.: University of North Carolina Press, 1997.

Grumet, Robert S. *Historic Contact: Indian People and Colonists in Today's Northeastern United States in the Sixteenth through Eighteenth Centuries*. Vol. 1, Contributions to Public Archeology. Norman, Okla.: University of Oklahoma Press, 1995.

Gura, Philip F. *A Glimpse of Sion's Glory: Puritan Radicalism in New England, 1620-1660*. Middleton, Conn.: Wesleyan University Press, 1984.

Hall, Basil. "Puritanism: the Problem of Definition." *Studies in Church History* 2 (1965): 283–96.

Hall, David D. *The Faithful Shepherd: A History of the New England Ministry in the Seventeenth Century*. New York: W. W. Norton, 1974.

———. "Narrating Puritanism." In *New Directions in American Religious History*, edited by Harry S. Stout and D. G. Hart, 51–75. New York: Oxford University Press, 1997.

———. "On Common Ground: The Coherence of American Puritan Studies." *William and Mary Quarterly*, 3d ser., 44 (1987): 193–229.

———. *Worlds of Wonder, Days of Judgment: Popular Religious Belief in Early New England*. New York: Knopf, 1989.

———, ed. *The Antinomian Controversy, 1636-1638: A Documentary History*. 2d ed. Durham, N.C.: Duke University Press, 1990.

Hall, Joseph. *The Works of the Right Reverend Joseph Hall*. 10 vols. Edited by Philip Wynter. Oxford: Clarendon Press, 1863.

Haller, William. *The Rise of Puritanism*. New York: Columbia University Press, 1938.

Hambrick-Stowe, Charles E. *The Practice of Piety: Puritan Devotional Disci-*

plines in Seventeenth-Century New England. Chapel Hill, N.C.: University of North Carolina Press, 1982.

Harbage, Alfred. *Cavalier Drama: An Historical and Critical Supplement to the Study of the Elizabethan and Restoration Stage*. New York: Russell and Russell, 1964.

Hawthorne, Nathaniel. "Mrs. Hutchinson." In *Tales, Sketches, and Other Papers*. Boston: Houghton, Mifflin, and Company, 1883.

———. *The Scarlet Letter*. New York: Rinehart and Company, 1947.

Heath, James. *Flagellum, or, the Life and Death, Birth and Burial of Oliver Cromwell, the Late Usurper*. 2d ed. London, 1663.

Heylyn, Peter. *Cyprianus Anglicus*. London, 1668.

Hill, Christopher. *Antichrist in Seventeenth-Century England*. London: Oxford University Press, 1971.

———. *The Experience of Defeat: Milton and Some Contemporaries*. New York: Viking, 1984.

———. *Milton and the English Revolution*. New York: Viking Press, 1978.

———. *Society and Puritanism in Pre-Revolutionary England*. 2d ed. New York: Schocken Books, 1967.

Hill, Thomas. *The Militant Church, Triumphant over the Dragon and His Angels*. London, 1643.

Himy, Armand. "*Paradise Lost* as a Republican 'Tractatus Theologico-Politicus.'" In *Milton and Republicanism*, edited by David Armitage, Armand Himy, and Quentin Skinner, 118–34. Cambridge: Cambridge University Press, 1995.

Hobbes, Thomas. *Behemoth, or The Long Parliament*. Edited by Ferdinand Tönnies. Chicago: University of Chicago Press, 1990.

Honan, Park. *Matthew Arnold: A Life*. Cambridge: Harvard University Press, 1983.

Hooker, Richard. *Of the Lawes of Ecclesiasticall Politie*. London, 1593.

Horniker, Arthur L. "William Harborne and the Beginning of Anglo-Turkish Diplomatic and Commercial Relations." *Journal of Modern History* 14 (September 1942): 289–316.

Howell, James. *Dendrologia: Dodona's Grove, or the Vocall Forrest*. 3d ed. Cambridge, 1645.

Howell, T. B., ed. *A Complete Collection of State Trials*. 33 vols. London, 1816–26.

Hoyle, David. "A Commons Investigation of Arminianism and Popery in Cambridge on the Eve of Civil War." *The Historical Journal* 29 (1986): 419–25.

Hoyles, John. *The Waning of the Renaissance, 1640-1687: Studies in the Poetry of Henry More, John Norris, and Isaac Watts*. The Hague: Nijhaff, 1971.

Hughes, Ann. "Anglo-American Puritanisms." *Journal of British Studies* 39, no. 1 (January 2000): 1–7.

———. *The Causes of the English Civil War*. New York: St. Martin's Press, 1991.

Hunt, William. *The Puritan Moment: The Coming of Revolution in an English County*. Cambridge: Harvard University Press, 1982.

Huntington Library, HM MS 371.

Hutton, Ronald. *The Rise and Fall of Merry England: The Ritual Year, 1400-1700*. New York: Oxford University Press, 1994.

Hutton, R. H. "Mr. Arnold on St. Paul and His Creed," *The Contemporary Review* 14 (June 1870), 329–41.

Hyde, H. Montgomery. *Oscar Wilde*. New York: Farrer, Straus, and Giroux, 1975.

Ibish, Joan Schenk. "Emmanuel College: The Founding Generation, with a Biographical Register of the Members of the College, 1584–1604." D. Phil. Thesis, Harvard University, 1985.

Ingram, Martin. *Church Courts, Sex, and Marriage in England, 1570-1640*. Cambridge: Cambridge University Press, 1987.

Jann, Rosemary. *The Art and Science of Victorian History*. Columbus, Ohio: Ohio State University Press, 1985.

Jeffrey, David Lyle. *People of the Book: Christian Identity and Literary Culture*. Grand Rapids, Mich.: Eerdmans, 1996.

Johnson, Eric S. "Uncas and the Politics of Contact." In *Northeastern Indian Lives, 1632-1816*, edited by Robert S. Grumet, 29–47. Amherst, Mass.: University of Massachusetts Press, 1996.

Johnson, Margery Ruth. "The Mayhew Mission to the Indians, 1643–1806." D. Phil Thesis, Clark University, 1966.

Jonson, Ben. *The Complete Plays of Ben Jonson*. Edited by G. A. Wilkes. 4 vols. Oxford: Clarendon Press, 1981–82.

Journall of the English Plantation at Plimoth. 1622. Reprint, Ann Arbor, Mich.: University Microfilms, 1966.

Kamensky, Jane. *Governing the Tongue: The Politics of Speech in Early New England*. New York: Oxford University Press, 1997.

Keeble, N. H. *The Literary Culture of Nonconformity*. Athens, Ga.: University of Georgia Press, 1987.

Kendall, Ritchie. *The Drama of Dissent: The Radical Poetics of Nonconformity, 1380-1590*. Chapel Hill, N.C.: University of North Carolina Press, 1986.

Kenyon, John. "Christopher Hill's Radical Left." Review of *The World Turned Upside Down*, by Christopher Hill. *The Spectator*, 8 July 1972, 54–55.

———. *The History Men: The Historical Profession in England since the Renaissance*. London: Weidenfeld and Nicolson, 1983.

Kingsley, Charles. *Charles Kingsley: His Letters and Memories of His Life*. 2 vols. Edited by [F. Kingsley]. London: Macmillan, 1894.

Knight, Janice. *Orthodoxies in Massachusetts: Rereading American Puritanism*. Cambridge: Harvard University Press, 1994.

Knights, Ben. *The Idea of the Clerisy in the Nineteenth Century*. London: Cambridge University Press, 1978.

Knoppers, Laura Lunger. *Constructing Cromwell: Ceremony, Portrait, and Print, 1645-1661*. Cambridge: Cambridge University Press, 2000.

Koehler, Lyle. "The Case of the Feminine Jezebels: Anne Hutchinson and Female Agitation during the Years of Antinomian Turmoil, 1636–1640." *William and Mary Quarterly*, 3d ser., 31 (1974): 55–78.

Krutch, Joseph Wood. *Comedy and Conscience after the Restoration*. New York: Columbia University Press, 1949.

Kupperman, Karen Ordahl. *Providence Island, 1630-1641: The Other Puritan Colony*. Cambridge: Cambridge University Press, 1993.

———. *Settling with the Indians: The Meeting of English and Indian Cultures in America, 1580-1640*. Totowa, N.J.: Rowman and Littlefield, 1980.

Lake, Peter. *Anglicans and Puritans? Presbyterianism and English Conformist Thought from Whitgift to Hooker*. London: Unwin Hyman, 1988.

———. "Anti-popery: The Structure of a Prejudice." In *Conflict in Early Stuart England: Studies in Religion and Politics, 1603-1642*, edited by Richard Cust and Ann Hughes, 72–106. London: Longman, 1989.

———. "'A Charitable Christian Hatred': The Godly and their Enemies in the 1630s." In *The Culture of English Puritanism, 1560-1700*, edited by Christopher Durston and Jacqueline Eales, 145–83. Basingstoke: Macmillan, 1996.

———. "Deeds against Nature: Cheap Print, Protestantism and Murder in Early Seventeenth Century England." In *Culture and Politics in Early Stuart England*, edited by Kevin Sharpe and Peter Lake, 257–84. Basingstoke: Macmillan, 1994.

———. "Defining Puritanism—Again?" In *Puritanism: Transatlantic Perspectives on a Seventeenth-Century Anglo-American Faith*, edited by Francis J. Bremer, 3–29. Boston: Massachusetts Historical Society, 1993.

———. "Laurence Chaderton and the Cambridge Moderate Puritan Tradition." D. Phil.Thesis, University of Cambridge, 1978.

———. *Moderate Puritans and the Elizabethan Church*. Cambridge: Cambridge University Press, 1982.

———. "William Bradshaw, Antichrist and the Community of the Godly." *Journal of Ecclesiastical History* 36, no. 4 (1985): 570–89.

Lake, Peter, and David Como. "'Orthodoxy and Its Discontents': Dispute Settlement and the Production of 'Consensus' in the London (Puritan) Underground." *Journal of British Studies* 39 (January 2000): 34–70.

Lamont, William. "Pamphleteering, the Protestant Consensus and the English Revolution." In *Freedom and the English Revolution: Essays in History and Literature*, edited by R. C. Richardson and G. M. Ridden, 72–92. Manchester: Manchester University Press, 1986.

Lang, Amy Schrager. "Antinomianism and the 'Americanization' of Doctrine." *New England Quarterly* 54 (1981): 225–42.

———. *Prophetic Women: Anne Hutchinson and the Problem of Dissent in the Literature of New England*. Berkeley and Los Angeles: University of California Press, 1987.

Lang, Timothy. *The Victorians and the Stuart Heritage: Interpretations of a Discordant Past*. Cambridge: Cambridge University Press, 1995.

Latourette, Kenneth Scott. *A History of Christianity*. New York: Harper and Row, 1953.

Laud, William. *The Works of the Most Reverend Father in God, William Laud, Sometime Lord Archbishop of Canterbury*. 7 vols. Oxford, 1847–60.

Learne of a Turk, or Instructions and Advise sent from the Turkish Army at Constantinople, to the English Army at London. London, 1660.

Lepore, Jill. *The Name of War: King Philip's War and the Origins of American Identity*. New York: Alfred A. Knopf, 1998.

Leslie, Henry. *A Full Confutation of the Covenant Lately Sworne and Subscribed by Many in Scotland; Delivered in a Speech at the Visitation of Downe and Conner*. London, 1639.

A Letter to a Dissenter in Exeter. London: printed for John Noon, 1719.

Lewis, Bernard. *Islam and the West*. New York: Oxford University Press, 1993.

Linklater, Eric. *Ben Jonson and King James: Biography and Portrait*. London: Jonathan Cape, 1931.

Lipsius, Justus. *Ad Annales Corn. Taciti liber commentarius*. Antwerp, 1581.

Lockridge, Kenneth. *A New England Town: The First Hundred Years*. Expanded ed. New York: W. W. Norton, 1985.

Lovejoy, David. *Religious Enthusiasm in the New World: Heresy to Revolution*. Cambridge: Harvard University Press, 1985.

Lovelace, Richard F. *The American Pietism of Cotton Mather: Origins of American Evangelicalism*. Grand Rapids, Mich.: Christian University Press, 1979.

Macaulay, Thomas. *The History of England from the Accession of James II*. 5 vols. London: Longman, Brown, Green, and Longmans, 1849–61.

Maccioni, P. Alessandra and Marco Mostert. "Isaac Dorislaus (1595–1649): The Career of a Dutch Scholar in England." *Transactions of the Cambridge Bibliographical Society* 8 (1984): 438–47.

Mainwaring, Roger. *Religion and Allegiance*. London, 1627.

Mandell, Daniel. " 'Standing by His Father': Thomas Waban of Natick, circa 1630–1722." In *Northeastern Indian Lives, 1632–1816*, edited by Robert S. Grumet, 166–92. Amherst, Mass.: University of Massachusetts Press, 1996.

Manningham, John. *The Diary of John Manningham of the Middle Temple, 1602–1603*. Edited by R. P. Sorlien. New Haven: Yale University Press, 1976.

Marsh, Henry. *A New Survey of the Turkish Empire and Government*. 2d ed. London, 1663.

Marshall, John. *John Locke: Resistance, Religion and Responsibility*. Cambridge: Cambridge University Press, 1994.

Marshall, Stephen. *Threnodia, or the Churches Lamentation for the Good Man his Losse*. London, 1644.

Martin, John. "Inventing Sincerity, Refashioning Prudence: The Discovery of the Individual in Renaissance Europe." *American Historical Review* 102 (1997): 1309–42.

Matar, Nabil. *Islam in Britain, 1558–1685*. Cambridge: Cambridge University Press, 1998.

———. *Turks, Moors, and Englishmen in the Age of Discovery*. New York: Columbia University Press, 1999.

———. " 'Turning Turk': Conversion to Islam in English Renaissance Thought." *Durham University Journal* 86 (January 1994): 33–41.

Mather, Cotton. *Diary of Cotton Mather*. Edited by Worthington Chauncey Ford. 2 vols. MHSC, 7th ser., 1911–12. Reprint, New York: Frederick Ungar Publishing Co., 1957.

———. *Magnalia Christi Americana, or, The Ecclesiastical History of New England*. 2 vols. 1852. Reprint, New York: Russell and Russell, 1967.

———. *Selected Letters of Cotton Mather*. Edited by Kenneth Silverman. Baton Rouge, La.: Louisiana State University Press, 1971.

———. *The Triumphs of the Reformed Religion: The Life of the Reverend John Eliot*. Boston: Benjamin Harris and John Allen, 1691.

———. *The Wonderful Works of God Commemorated*. Boston: S. Green, 1690.

Mather, Increase. *A Brief History of the War with the Indians in New-England*. Boston: John Foster, 1676.

———. "An Earnest Exhortation." In *So Dreadfull a Judgment: Puritan Responses to King Philip's War, 1676-1677*, edited by Richard Slotkin and James K. Folsom. Middletown, Conn.: Wesleyan University Press, 1978.

[Mather, Increase, Cotton Mather, and Nehemiah Walter]. *A Letter, about the Present State of Christianity, among the Christianized Indians of New-England*. Boston: Timothy Green, 1705.

Mayhew, Matthew. *A Brief Narrative of the Success which the Gospel hath had, among the Indians*. Boston: Bartholomew Green, 1694.

McGiffert, Michael, ed. *God's Plot: Puritan Spirituality in Thomas Shepard's Cambridge*. Rev. ed. Amherst, Mass.: University of Massachusetts Press, 1994.

Mede, Joseph. *The Key of the Revelation, searched and demonstrated out of the Naturall and proper Characters of the Visions*. London, 1643.

Mendle, Michael. *Henry Parker and the English Civil War*. Cambridge: Cambridge University Press, 1995.

Mercurius Aulicus, Communicating the Intelligence and Affaires of the Court, to the Rest of the Kingdome. 1643.

Mercurius Pragmaticus. 1649.

Meriton, George. *A Sermon of Nobilitie*. London, 1627.

Middlekauff, Robert. *The Mathers: Three Generations of Puritan Intellectuals, 1596-1728*. New York: Oxford University Press, 1971.

Miller, Perry. *Errand into the Wilderness*. Cambridge: Harvard University Press, 1956.

———. *The New England Mind: From Colony to Province*. Cambridge: Harvard University Press, 1953.

———. *The New England Mind: The Seventeenth Century*. 2d ed. Cambridge: Harvard University Press, 1954.

———. *Orthodoxy in Massachusetts, 1630-1650*. Cambridge: Harvard University Press, 1933.

Milton, Anthony. *Catholic and Reformed: The Roman and Protestant Churches in English Protestant Thought, 1600-1640*. Cambridge: Cambridge University Press, 1995.

Milton, John. *Complete Poems and Major Prose of John Milton*. Edited by Merritt Hughes. Indianapolis: Odyssey Press, 1957.

———. *Complete Prose Works of John Milton*. Edited by Don M. Wolfe et al. 8 vols. New Haven: Yale University Press, 1953–82.

Mocket, Thomas. *The Churches Troubles and Deliverance*. London, 1642.

A Modest Vindication of Oliver Cromwell from the Unjust Accusations of Lieutenant-General Ludlow in His Memoirs. London, 1698.

Moffitt, John F., and Santiago Sebastian. *O Brave New People: The European Invention of the American Indian*. Albuquerque, N.Mex.: University of New Mexico Press, 1996.

Montagu, Richard. *Appello Caesarem: A just appeale from two unjust informers*. 1625.

More, Henry. *The Complete Poems of Dr. Henry More, 1614-1687*. Edited by Alexander B. Grosart. St. George's Blackburn, Lancashire: Printed for private circulation, 1878.

———. *Democritus Platonissans, or An Essay upon the Infinity of Worlds*. London, 1647.

Morgan, Edmund S. *Visible Saints: The History of a Puritan Idea*. Ithaca, N.Y.: Cornell University Press, 1963.

Morgan, Irvonwy. *Prince Charles's Puritan Chaplain*. London: George Allen and Unwin, 1957.

Morgan, V. "Country, Court and Cambridge University, 1558–1640: A Study in the Evolution of a Political Culture." D. Phil. Thesis, University of East Anglia, England, 1983.

Morison, Samuel Eliot. *The Intellectual Life of Colonial New England*. Ithaca, N.Y.: Cornell University Press, 1956.

Morrill, John. "The Making of Oliver Cromwell." In *Oliver Cromwell and the English Revolution*, edited by John Morrill, 19–48. London and New York: Longman, 1990.

———. *The Nature of the English Revolution*. London and New York: Longman, 1993.

———. "Oliver Cromwell, the Regicide and the Sons of Zeruiah." In *The Trial and Execution of Charles I*, edited by J. Peacey. Basingstoke: Macmillan, 2001.

———. *The Revolt of the Provinces: Conservatives and Radicals in the English Civil War, 1630-1650*. London: Allen and Unwin, 1976.

———. "William Dowsing and the Administration of Iconoclasm in the Puritan Revolution." In *The Journal of William Dowsing*, edited by T. Cooper. Woodbridge: Boydell and Brewer, 2001.

———. "William Dowsing, the Bureaucratic Puritan." In *Public Duty and Private Conscience in Seventeenth-Century England: Essays Presented to G. E. Aylmer*, edited by John Morrill, Paul Slack, and Daniel Woolf, 173–203. Oxford: Clarendon Press, 1993.

Morris, Burnet. *The Burnet Morris Index, 1940-1990*. Exeter: Devon Library Services, 1990.

Morrison, Dane. *A Praying People: Massachusett Acculturation and the Failure of the Puritan Mission, 1600-1690*. New York: Peter Lang, 1995.

Morton, Thomas. *New English Canaan*. New York: Da Capo Press, 1969.

Mullinger, J. B. *The History of Cambridge University*. 3 vols. Cambridge: Cambridge University Press, 1873–1911.

Naeher, Robert James. "Dialogue in the Wilderness: John Eliot and the Indian Exploration of Puritanism as a Source of Meaning, Comfort, and Ethnic Survival." *New England Quarterly* 62 (1989): 346–68.

The Names of Orthodox Divines, presented by the Knights and burgesses . . . as fit persons to be consulted with by the Parliament, touching the Reformation of Church Government and Liturgie. London, 1642.

New College Oxford, MS 9502.

New England's First Fruits: with Divers other Special Matters Concerning that Country. 1643. Reprint, New York: Joseph Sabin, 1865.

Newes from Sally of a Strange Delivery of Foure English Captives from the Slavery of the Turkes. London, 1642.

Newlyn, Lucy. *"Paradise Lost" and the Romantic Reader*. Oxford: Clarendon Press, 1993.

Newman, John Henry. *Apologia Pro Vita Sua*. Edited by David J. DeLaura. 1865. Reprint, New York: Norton, 1968.

Nicolson, Marjorie Hope. *The Breaking of the Circle: Studies in the Effect of the "New Science" upon Seventeenth-Century Poetry*. Rev. ed. New York: Columbia University Press, 1960.

Norbrook, David. *Writing the English Republic: Poetry, Rhetoric, and Politics, 1627-1660*. Cambridge: Cambridge University Press, 1999.

Norris, John. "The Passion of the Virgin Mother: Beholding the Crucifixion of Her Divine Son." In *A Collection of Miscellanies*. Oxford: John Crofley, 1687.

Oldridge, Darren. *Religion and Society in Early Stuart England*. Aldershot: Ashgate, 1998.

Olive, Barbara. "A Puritan Subject's Panegyric to Queen Anne." *Studies in English Literature* 42 no. 3 (2002): 475–99.

Oliver, George. *Ecclesiastical Antiquities in Devon, Being Observations on Several Churches in Devonshire with Some Memoranda for the History of Cornwall*. Vol. 1. Exeter: W. C. Featherstone, 1840.

One Argument More Against the Cavaliers, Taken from their Violation of Churches. [London, 1643].

Owen, David. *Herod and Pilate Reconciled. Or, The Concord of Papist and Puritan . . . for the Coercion, Deposition, and Killing of Kings*. Cambridge, 1610.

Palmer, Parker J. "The Grace of Great Things." Coalition of Christian Colleges and Universities National Forum, spring 1998.

Park, Samuel. *A Discourse of Ecclesiastical Polity*. 1669.

Parker, Kenneth. *The English Sabbath: A Study of Doctrine and Discipline from the Reformation to the Civil War*. Cambridge: Cambridge University Press, 1988.

Parker, T. *De Politeia Ecclesiastica*. London, 1620.

Peacock, B., ed. *Army Lists of the Roundheads and Cavaliers*. 2d ed. London: Chatto and Windus, 1874.

Pearce, Roy Harvey. " 'The Ruines of Mankind': The Indian and the Puritan Mind." *Journal of the History of Ideas* 13 (1952): 200–17.

Peltonen, Markku. *Classical Humanism and Republicanism in English Political Thought, 1570-1640*. Cambridge: Cambridge University Press, 1995.

Perkins, William. *A Golden Chain*. In *The Workes of that Famous Minister of Christ in the University of Cambridge, Mister William Perkins*. Vol. 1. 1612.

———. *The Work of William Perkins*. Edited by Ian Breward. London, Sutton Courtenay, 1969.

Perron, Jacques Davy du. *Luther's Alcoran*. Translated by N.N.P. N.p., 1642.

Petkov, Kiril. "England and the Balkan Slavs, 1354–1583: An Outline of a Late-Medieval and Renaissance Image." *Slavonic and East European Review* 75 (January 1997): 86–117.

———. *Infidels, Turks, and Women: The South Slavs in the German Mind, ca. 1400-1600*. New York: Peter Lang, 1997.

Pfizenmaier, Thomas C. *The Trinitarian Theology of Dr. Samuel Clarke (1625-1729): Context, Sources and Controversy*. Leiden: Brill, 1997.

Pigman, G. W., III. "Versions of Imitation in the Renaissance." *Renaissance Quarterly* 33 (1980): 1–32.

Plum, Harry Grant. *Restoration Puritanism: A Study of the Growth of English Liberty*. Port Washington, N.Y.: Kennikat Press, 1943.

Pocock, J. G. A. *The Machiavellian Moment: Florentine Political Thought and the Atlantic Republican Tradition*. Princeton: Princeton University Press, 1975.

Pointer, Richard. "Selves and Others in Early New England: Refashioning American Puritan Studies." In *History and the Christian Historian*, edited by Ronald A. Wells, 149–58. Grand Rapids, Mich.: Eerdmans, 1998.

Poole, Kristen. *Radical Religion from Shakespeare to Milton: Figures of Nonconformity in Early Modern England*. Cambridge: Cambridge University Press, 2000.

———. "Saints Alive! Falstaff, Martin Marprelate, and the Staging of Puritanism." *Shakespeare Quarterly* 46 (1995): 47–75.

Porterfield, Amanda. *Female Piety in Puritan New England: The Emergence of Religious Humanism*. New York: Oxford University Press, 1992.

———. "The Triumph of Spirituality over Religion: Anne Hutchinson and American Culture." Wyoming Web Lecture on Religion, University of Wyoming, Laramie, Wyoming, 1 May 1998.

Powicke, F. W., ed. *Some Unpublished Correspondence of the Reverend Richard Baxter and the Reverend John Eliot, the Apostle of the American Indians, 1656-1682*. Manchester: Manchester University Press, 1931.

Prins, Harold E. L. "Chief Rawandagan, Alias Robin Hood: Native 'Lord of Misrule' in the Maine Wilderness." In *Northeastern Indian Lives, 1632-1816*, edited by Robert S. Grumet, 93–115. Amherst, Mass.: University of Massachusetts Press, 1996.

Proceedings in Parliament, 1626. Vol. 3: *House of Commons*. Edited by William B. Bidwell and Maija Jansson. New Haven: Yale University Press, 1992.

Proceedings of the Short Parliament of 1640. Edited by Esther Cope and Willson H. Coates. London: Royal Historical Society, 1977.

A Profound Discourse between the old Protector and the new Lord General, truly reported by Hugh Peters. London, 1660.

Prynne, William. *A Breviate of the Life of William Laud*. London, 1644.

———. *Canterburies Doome*. London, 1646.

———. *Lord Bishops None of the Lord's Bishops*. London, 1640.

Public Record Office, State Papers 16/86.

Raymond, Joad, ed. *Making the News: An Anthology of the Newsbooks of Revolutionary England, 1641-1660*. New York: St. Martin's Press, 1993.

Reardon, Bernard M. G. *Religious Thought in the Victorian Age: A Survey from Coleridge to Gore*. 1971. Reprint, London: Longman, 1980.

The Rebels' Turkish Tyranny, in their March, December 14, 1641. London, 1641.

Relations and Observations, Historical and Politic, upon the Parliament, begun Anno Domini 1640. N.p, 1648.

Reports and Transactions of the Devonshire Association for the Advancement of Science, Literature, and Art 34 (1902).

Richardson, R. C., and G. M. Ridden, eds. *Freedom and the English Revolution.* Manchester: Manchester University Press 1985.

Riesman, David. *Thomas Sydenham: Clinician.* New York: Paul B. Hoebner, 1926.

Robinson, Paul A. "Lost Opportunities: Miantonimi and the English in Seventeenth-Century Narragansett Country." In *Northeastern Indian Lives, 1632-1816,* edited by Robert S. Grumet, 13–28. Amherst, Mass.: University of Massachusetts Press, 1996.

Rogers, Richard and Samuel Ward. *Two Elizabethan Diaries.* Edited by Marshall M. Knappen. Chicago: University of Chicago Press, 1978.

Rolph, Rebecca Seward. "Emmanuel College, Cambridge, and the Puritan Movements of Old and New England." D. Phil. Thesis, University of Southern California, 1979.

Ronda, James P. "Generations of Faith: The Christian Indians of Martha's Vineyard." *William and Mary Quarterly,* 3d ser., 38 (1981): 369–94.

———. "'We Are Well As We Are': An Indian Critique of Seventeenth-Century Christian Missions." *William and Mary Quarterly,* 3d. ser., 34 (1977): 66–82.

Ross, Alexander. *Pansebeia, or A View of all Religions in the World.* 2d ed. London, 1655.

Rudyerd, Benjamin. *The Speeches.* London, 1641.

Russell, Conrad, ed. *The Origins of the English Civil War.* New York: Barnes and Noble, 1973.

———. *Parliaments and English Politics, 1621-1629.* Oxford: Clarendon Press, 1979.

Sadler, S. L. "Dowsing's Arguments with the Fellows of Pembroke." In *The Journal of William Dowsing,* edited by T. Cooper. Woodbridge: Boydell and Brewer, 2001.

Said, Edward W. *Orientalism.* New York: Pantheon Books, 1978.

Salisbury, Neal. "Squanto: Last of the Patuxets." In *Struggle and Survival in Colonial America,* edited by David G. Sweet and Gary B. Nash, 228–46. Berkeley and Los Angeles: University of California Press, 1981.

Samuel. Raphael. "The Discovery of Puritanism, 1820–1914: A Preliminary Sketch." In *Revival and Religion since 1700: Essays for John Walsh,* edited by Jane Garnett and Colin Matthew, 201–47. London: Hambledon, 1993.

Sandys, George. *Sandys Travells: Containing an History of the Original and Present State of the Turkish Empire.* 6th ed. London, 1670.

Seaver, Paul. *Wallington's World: A Puritan Artisan in Seventeenth-Century London.* Stanford, Calif.: Stanford University Press, 1985.

The Second Part of the Westminster Monster. N.p., 1648.

Shain, Barry Alan. *The Myth of American Individualism: The Protestant Origins of American Political Thought.* Princeton: Princeton University Press, 1994.

Shakespeare, William. *The Riverside Shakespeare.* Edited by G. Blakemore Evans. Boston: Houghton Mifflin, 1974.

Sharpe, Kevin. "The Foundation of the Chairs of History at Oxford and Cambridge: An Episode in Jacobean Politics." *History of Universities* 2 (1982): 127–52.

———. *The Personal Rule of Charles I.* New Haven: Yale University Press, 1992.

————. *Politics and Ideas in Early Stuart England*. London and New York: Pinter, 1989.

Shepard, Thomas. *The Clear Sunshine of the Gospel Breaking Forth upon the Indians in New-England*. London, 1648. New York: Joseph Sabin, 1865.

[————]. *The Day-Breaking if not the Sun-Rising of the Gospell with the Indians in New-England*. Reprint, London, 1647. New York: Joseph Sabin, 1865.

————. *The Parable of the Ten Virgins Opened and Applied: Being the Substance of Divers Sermons on Matth. 25.1-13*. London: J. Hayes, 1660.

————. *The Sincere Convert: Discovering the Paucity of True Beleevers and the great Difficulty of Saving Conversion*. London: T. P. and M. S., 1641.

Shephard, Thomas, and John Cotton. "Letters between Thomas Shephard and John Cotton." In *The Antinomian Controversy, 1631-1638: A Documentary History*. 2d ed. Edited by David D. Hall, 24–33. Durham, N.C.: Duke University Press, 1990.

Shirley, James. "The Bird in a Cage" (1633). In *Three Centuries of Drama: English, 1516-1641*. New York: Readex Microprint, 1954.

Shuckburgh, E. S. *Emmanuel College*. London: F. E. Robinson and Co., 1904.

Silverman, Kenneth. Introduction to *Selected Letters of Cotton Mather*. Baton Rouge, La.: Louisiana State University Press, 1971.

————. *The Life and Times of Cotton Mather*. New York: Harper and Row, 1984.

Simmons, William. "Cultural Bias in the New England Puritans' Perceptions of Indians." *William and Mary Quarterly*, 3d ser., 38 (1981): 56–72.

Skilliter, S. A. "The Organization of the First English Embassy in Istanbul in 1583." *Asian Affairs* 10 (1979): 159–65.

————. *William Harborne and the Trade with Turkey, 1578-1582: A Documentary Study of the First Anglo-Ottoman Relations*. London: Oxford University Press, 1977.

Skinner, Quentin. *The Foundations of Modern Political Thought*. 2 vols. Cambridge: Cambridge University Press, 1978.

Slotkin, Richard, and James K. Folsom. *So Dreadfull a Judgment: Puritan Responses to King Philip's War, 1676-1677*. Middletown, Conn.: Wesleyan University Press, 1978.

Sommerville, C. John. "Interpreting Seventeenth-Century English Religion as Movements." *Church History* 69, no. 4 (December 2000): 749–69.

Southey, Robert. *The Pilgrim's Progress, with a Life of John Bunyan*. London: John Murray, 1830.

Spufford, Margaret. "Puritanism and Social Control." In *Order and Disorder in Early Modern England*, edited by Anthony Fletcher and John Stevenson, 41–57. Cambridge: Cambridge University Press, 1985.

Spurr, John. *English Puritanism, 1603-1689*. New York: St. Martin's Press, 1998.

————. "From Puritanism to Dissent, 1660–1700." In *The Culture of English Puritanism, 1560-1700*, edited by Christopher Durston and Jacqueline Eales, 234–65. Basingstoke: Macmillan, 1996.

————. *The Restoration Church in England, 1646-1689*. New Haven: Yale University Press, 1991.

Stachniewski, John. *The Persecutory Imagination: English Puritanism and the Literature of Religious Despair*. Oxford: Clarendon Press, 1991.

Staloff, Darren. *The Making of an American Thinking Class: Intellectuals and Intelligentsia in Puritan Massachusetts*. New York: Oxford University Press, 1998.

Steele, Ian K. "Exploding Colonial American History: Amerindian, Atlantic, and Global Perspectives." *Reviews in American History* 26, no. 1 (1998): 70–95

Stephens, Leslie. *English Thought of the Eighteenth Century*. 2 vols. 3d ed. New York: Peter Smith, 1949.

Stevens, Wallace. *The Collected Poems of Wallace Stevens*. New York: Alfred A. Knopf, 1961.

Stoyle, Mark. *Loyalty and Locality: Popular Allegiance in Devon during the English Civil War*. Exeter: University of Exeter Press, 1994.

Stubbings, Frank, trans. and ed. *The Statutes of Sir Walter Mildmay . . . for the government of Emmanuel College founded by him*. Cambridge: Cambridge University Press, 1983.

Sydenham, Thomas. *The Whole Works of that Excellent Practical Physician, Dr. Thomas Sydenham*. 4th ed., trans. John Pechey. London, 1705.

Tate, Nahum. "The Blessed Virgin's Expostulation." In *Miscellanea Sacra, or, Poems on Divine & Moral Subjects*. 2d ed. London: Hen[ry] Playford, 1698.

Taylor, Charles. *Sources of the Self: The Making of Modern Identity*. Cambridge: Harvard University Press, 1989.

Thomas, Elizabeth. *Pylades and Corinna*. Vol. 1. London, 1731–3.

Thomas, G. E. "Puritans, Indians, and the Concept of Race." *New England Quarterly* 48 (1975): 3–27.

Thomas, Keith. *Religion and the Decline of Magic: Studies in Popular Beliefs in Sixteenth and Seventeenth Century England*. New York: Oxford University Press, 1971.

Thompson, Roger. "The Puritans and Prurience: Aspects of the Restoration Book Trade." In *Contrast and Connection: Bicentennial Essays in Anglo-American History*, edited by H. C. Allen and Roger Thompson, 36–65. Athens, Ohio: Ohio University Press, 1976.

Todd, Margo. "'An Act of Discretion': Evangelical Conformity and the Puritan Dons." *Albion* 18, no. 4 (1986): 581–99.

———. "A Captive's Story: Puritans, Pirates, and the Drama of Reconciliation." *The Seventeenth Century* 12 (spring 1997): 37–56.

———. *Christian Humanism and the Puritan Social Order*. Cambridge: Cambridge University Press, 1987.

Trevor-Roper, H. R. *Archbishop Laud, 1573-1645*. Hamden, Conn.: Archon Books, 1962.

———. "Laudianism and Political Power." In *Catholics, Anglicans, and Puritans: Seventeenth-Century Essays*, 40–119. Chicago: University of Chicago Press, 1988.

Tricomi, Albert H. *Anticourt Drama in England, 1603-1642*. Charlottesville, Va.: University Press of Virginia, 1989.

Tuck, Richard. *Philosophy and Government, 1572-1651*. Cambridge: Cambridge University Press, 1993.

Twigg, John. *The University of Cambridge and the English Revolution, 1625-1688*. Cambridge: Boydell Press, 1990.

Tyacke, Nicholas. "Anglican Attitudes: Some Recent Writings on English Religious History, from the Reformation to the Civil War." *Journal of British Studies* 35, no. 2 (April 1996): 139–67.

———. *Anti-Calvinists: The Rise of English Arminianism, c. 1590-1640*. New York: Oxford University Press, 1987.

———. "Archbishop Laud." In *The Early Stuart Church, 1603-1642*, edited by Kenneth Fincham, 51–70. London: Macmillan, 1993.

———. *The Fortunes of English Puritanism, 1603-1640*. London: Dr. William's Library, 1990.

———. "Puritanism, Arminianism and Counter-Revolution." In *The Origins of the English Civil War*, edited by Conrad Russell, 119–43. New York: Barnes and Noble, 1973.

———. "The 'Rise of Puritanism' and the Legalizing of Dissent, 1571–1719." In *From Persecution to Toleration: The Glorious Revolution and Religion in England*, edited by Ole Peter Grell, Jonathan I. Israel, and Nicholas Tyacke, 17–50. Oxford: Clarendon Press, 1991.

Tyler, Richard. "The Children of Disobedience: The Social Composition of Emmanuel College, Cambridge, 1596–1645." D. Phil. Thesis, University of California, Berkeley, 1976.

The Tyranny of Tyrannies. N.p., 1648.

Underdown, David. "The Parliamentary Diary of John Boys," *Bulletin of the Institute of Historical Research* 39 (1966): 155–57.

———. *Pride's Purge: Politics in the Puritan Revolution*. Oxford: Clarendon Press, 1971.

———. *Revel, Riot, and Rebellion: Popular Politics and Culture in England, 1603-1660*. Oxford: Clarendon Press, 1985.

Ussher, James. *The Whole Works of the Most Rev. James Ussher*. 16 vols. Dublin: Hodges and Smith, 1843.

Valensi, Lucette. *The Birth of the Despot: Venice and the Sublime Porte*. Translated by Arthur Denner. Ithaca, N.Y.: Cornell University Press, 1993.

Van Lonkhuyzen, Harold W. "A Reappraisal of Praying Indians: Acculturation, Conversion, and Identity at Natick, Massachusetts, 1646–1730." *New England Quarterly* 63 (1990): 396–428.

Vaughan, Alden T. *The Puritan Tradition in America, 1620-1730*. Rev. ed. Hanover, N.H.: University Press of New England, 1997.

Vaughan, Alden T., and Edward W. Clark. "Cups of Common Calamity: Puritan Captivity Narratives as Literature and History." In *Puritans among the Indians: Accounts of Captivity and Redemption, 1676-1724*, edited by Alden T. Vaughan and Edward W. Clark, 1–28. Cambridge: Harvard University Press, 1981.

Vaughan, Robert. "The Act of Uniformity: Its Antecedents and Effects." *British Quarterly Review* 35 (April 1862): 320–23.

Venn, J. A., and John Venn, eds. *Alumni Cantabrigienses. Part I: From the Earliest Times to 1751*. 4 vols. Cambridge: Cambridge University Press, 1922–27.

Vitkus, Daniel J. "Early Modern Orientalism: Representations of Islam in Sixteenth- and Seventeenth-Century Europe." In *Western Views of Islam in Medieval and Early Modern Europe: Perception of Other*, edited by David R. Blanks and Michael Frassetto, 207–30. New York: St. Martin's Press, 1999.

————, ed. *Three Turk Plays from Early Modern England: "Selimus," "A Christian Turned Turk," and "The Renegado."* New York: Columbia University Press, 2000.

[Walker, Clement]. *Anarchia Anglicana: The Second Part of the History of Independency.* London, 1649.

Walker, Thomas A. *Peterhouse.* Cambridge: W. Heffer and Sons, 1935.

Walsham, Alexandra. "'A glose of godliness': Philip Stubbes, Elizabethan Grub Street and the Invention of Puritanism." In *Belief and Practice in Reformation England,* edited by Caroline Litzenberger and Susan Wabuda, 177–206. Aldershot: Ashgate, 1998.

Walzer, Michael. *The Revolution of the Saints: A Study in the Origins of Radical Politics.* Cambridge: Harvard University Press, 1965.

Webster. Thomas. *Godly Clergy in Early Stuart England: The Caroline Puritan Movement, c. 1620-1643.* Cambridge: Cambridge University Press, 1997.

Wedgewood, C. V. *The Trial of Charles I.* London: Collins, 1964.

Wendell, Barrett. *Cotton Mather: The Puritan Priest.* Harbinger Book ed. New York: Harcourt, Brace and World, 1963.

Wertenbaker, Thomas J. *The Puritan Oligarchy: The Founding of American Civilization.* New York: Charles Scribner's Sons, 1947.

Wheelwright, John. "A Fast-Day Sermon." In *The Antinomian Controversy, 1631-1638: A Documentary History.* 2d ed. Edited by David D. Hall, 152–72. Durham, N.C.: Duke University Press, 1990.

White, B. R. "The Twilight of Puritanism in the Years before and after 1688." In *From Persecution to Toleration: The Glorious Revolution and Religion in England,* edited by Ole Peter Grell, Jonathan I. Israel, and Nicholas Tyacke. Oxford: Clarendon Press, 1991.

White, Peter. *Predestination, Policy and Polemic: Conflict and Consensus in the English Church from the Reformation to the Civil War.* Cambridge: Cambridge University Press, 1992.

————. "The Rise of Arminianism Reconsidered." *Past and Present* 101 (1983): 34–54.

Whitelocke, Bulstrode. *Memorials of the English Affairs.* London, 1682.

Whitfield, Henry. "The Light Appearing More and More towards the Perfect Day." 1651. Reprinted in Massachusetts Historical Society, *Collections,* 3d ser., 4 (1834): 100–47.

————. *Strength Out of Weakness: or a Glorious Manifestation of the Further Progress of the Gospel among the Indians of New England.* 1652. Reprint, New York: Joseph Saban, 1865.

Whittaker, Jeremiah. *Christ the Settlement of Unsettled Times.* London, 1643.

Wholsome Severity reconciled with Christian Liberty, or The true Resolution of a present Controversie concerning Liberty of Conscience. London, 1644.

Williams, Griffith. *Jura Majestatis: The Rights of Kings Both in Church and State.* Oxford, 1644.

Williams, Roger. *Christenings Make Not Christians.* London, 1645.

————. *A Key into the Language of America.* 5th ed. London: Gregory Dexter, 1643.

Wilson, J. Dover. Introduction to *Culture and Anarchy*, by Matthew Arnold, edited by Dover J. Wilson. Cambridge: Cambridge University Press, 1969.

Winship, Michael. "'The Most Glorious Church in the World': The Unity of the Godly in Boston, Massachusetts in the 1630s." *Journal of British Studies* 39, no. 1 (2000): 71–98.

———. *Seers of God: Puritan Providentialism in the Restoration and Early Enlightenment*. Baltimore: Johns Hopkins University Press, 1996.

Winthrop, John. "A Short Story of the rise, reign, and ruine of the Antinomians, Familists, and Libertines." In *The Antinomian Controversy, 1631-1638: A Documentary History*. 2d ed. Edited by David D. Hall, 199–310. Durham, N.C.: Duke University Press, 1990.

A Winter Dream. N.p., 1648.

Wolffe, Mary. *Gentry Leaders in Peace and War: The Gentry Governors of Devon in the Early Seventeenth Century*. Exeter: University of Exeter Press, 1997.

Wood, William. *New England's Prospect*. Edited by Alden T. Vaughan. 1634. Reprint, Amherst, Mass.: University of Massachusetts Press, 1993.

Woodhead, Charles. "'The Present Terrour of the World'? Contemporary Views of the Ottoman Empire, c. 1600." *History* 72 (February 1987): 20–37.

Woolrych, Austin. "The Cromwellian Protectorate: A Military Dictatorship?" *History* 75 (June 1990): 207–31.

Worden, Blair. "Calvinisms." *London Review of Books*, 23 January to 6 February 1986, 16–17.

———. "Classical Republicanism and the Puritan Revolution." In *History and Imagination: Essays in Honour of H. R. Trevor-Roper*, edited by Hugh Lloyd-Jones, Valerie Pearl, and Blair Worden, 182–200. New York: Holmes and Meier, 1981.

———. "Milton among the Radicals." Review of *Milton and the English Revolution*, by Christopher Hill. *Times Literary Supplement*, 2 December 1977, 1394–95.

———. "Oliver Cromwell and the Sin of Achan." In *History, Society and the Churches: Essays in Honour of Owen Chadwick*, edited by Derek Beales and Geoffrey Best, 125–45. Cambridge: Cambridge University Press, 1983.

———. *The Rump Parliament*. Cambridge: Cambridge University Press, 1974.

Wycherley, William. *Love in a Wood*. In *The Complete Plays of William Wycherley*. Edited by Gerald Weales. Stuart Editions. New York: New York University Press, 1967.

Yapp, M. E. "Europe in the Turkish Mirror." *Past and Present* 137 (November 1992): 134–56.

Yates, John. *Ibis ad Caesarem, or a Submissive Appearance before Caesar*. London, 1626.

Young, Alexander, ed. *Chronicles of the First Planters of the Colony of Massachusetts Bay from 1623 to 1636*. Boston: Little and Brown, 1846.

Youngs, J. William T., Jr. "The Indian Saints of Early New England." *Early American Literature* 16 (1981–82): 241–56.

Contributors

DWIGHT BRAUTIGAM is professor of history and chair of the History Department at Huntington College in Indiana. His Ph.D. is from the University of Rochester and he co-edited and contributed to *Court, Country, and Culture: Essays in Honor of Perez Zagorin* (1992). He has been a participant in the National Endowment for the Humanities Summer Scholar program and the Calvin College Summer Seminars in Christian Scholarship. He also serves as co-editor of the newsletter for the Conference on Faith and History.

TIMOTHY D. HALL (Ph.D. Northwestern University) is associate professor of colonial and revolutionary American history at Central Michigan University. His published works include *Contested Boundaries: Itinerancy and the Reshaping of the Colonial American Religious World* (1994) and, with T. H. Breen, "Structuring Provincial Imagination: The Rhetoric and Experience of Social Change in Eighteenth-Century New England," *American Historical Review* 103 (1998): 1411–39. He is currently completing a textbook with T. H. Breen entitled *Colonial British America in the Atlantic World,* to be published by A. B. Longman. He is also working with Northern Illinois University Press to complete a modern scholarly edition of Thomas Prince, Jr.'s *Christian History,* the first evangelical periodical published in America and a rich source of material on the Great Awakening of the 1740s.

LAURA LUNGER KNOPPERS is professor of English and director of the Institute for the Arts and Humanities at Penn State University. She has published essays and articles on Milton, Shakespeare, Charles I, and Oliver Cromwell. She is the author of *Historicizing Milton: Spectacle, Power, and Poetry in Restoration England* (1994) and *Constructing Cromwell: Ceremony, Portrait, and Print, 1645–1661* (2000). She is currently working on a book on representations of Charles I and Henrietta Maria.

JOHN MORRILL is professor of British and Irish history at the University of Cambridge and fellow and vice president of the British Academy. He has published numerous essays on seventeenth-century history and has written or edited seventeen books, including *The Revolt of the Provinces: Conservatives and Radicals in the English Civil War, 1630–1650* (1976); *Oliver Cromwell and the English Revolution* (1990); and *The Nature of the English Revolution* (1993). He was president of the Cromwell Association from 1989 to 1999 and is currently writing a book on Cromwell and the Bible.

JOHN NETLAND is professor of English at Calvin College, where he teaches British Romanticism and Victorian literature. He has published articles on Romantic and Victorian religious poetics, including studies of Wordsworth, Coleridge, and Clough, as well as on the late Japanese novelist, Shusaku Endo. His current project, which emanates from his work on Matthew Arnold in the Pew Summer Seminar, is to compile an anthology of Victorian religious discourses.

BARBARA OLIVE is professor of English at Concordia College, Moorhead, Minnesota, where she has chaired the English Department, authored a number of collegewide planning and curriculum documents, and, since 1996, co-directed the women's studies program. Her main area of research lies in Restoration and eighteenth-century studies, with a secondary area in Arabic literature. She has published on Alifa Rifaat's short fiction in *International Fiction Review* and has an essay on Mary Chudleigh and Queen Anne in *Studies in English Literature* (Summer 2002).

RICHARD POINTER is professor of history at Westmont College, Santa Barbara, California. In addition to articles and essays on American religious history, he is the author of *Protestant Pluralism and the New York Experience: A Study in Eighteenth-Century Religious Diversity* (1988). He is currently writing a book on how the encounter with Native Americans shaped Euro-American religion.

STEVEN R. POINTER is professor of history and associate academic dean at Trinity International University in Deerfield, Illinois. His Ph.D is from Duke University, and he has published a number of essays and articles on various topics in American and English church history. His book *Joseph Cook: Boston Lecturer and Evangelical Apologist* was published in 1991. His current research interests are in William Perkins and Cambridge Puritanism.

GLENN SANDERS is professor of history at Oklahoma Baptist University. Educated at Baylor University and Brown University, he regularly teaches courses on Western civilization, medieval Europe, early modern Europe, the Middle East, and historiography. His pedagogical interests include the role of reflection in the improvement of teaching, institutional faculty development, and successful Christian liberal arts programs. His research interests focus on British perceptions of Islam and the Ottoman Turks.

MARGO TODD is professor of history at Vanderbilt University. She has published numerous essays and articles on seventeenth-century British history. Her books include *Christian Humanism and the Puritan Social Order* (1987); *Reformation to Revolution: Politics and Religion in Early Modern England* (1995); and *The Culture of Protestantism in Early Modern Scotland* (2002).

STEPHEN WOOLSEY is professor of English at Houghton College in Houghton, New York. Along with Puritan studies, his research interests include modern and contemporary American literature, especially Southern literature, modern and contemporary English literature, and cross-cultural and colonial literatures, especially African and Indian. He has published articles on fugitive poet Donald Davidson, Cornish poet and novelist Jack Clemo, and American poet Samuel Hazo.

Index